C
PROGRAMMER'S
UTILITY
LIBRARY

FRANK WHITSELL

TAB BOOKS Inc.

Blue Ridge Summit, PA 17214

Notices

IBM is a trademark of International Business Machines, Inc.
Unix is a trademark of A. T. & T.
Smartmodem is a trademark of Hayes Microcomputer Products, Inc.
Lattice is a registered trademark of Lattice, Inc.
WordStar is a trademark of Micropro International, Inc.
Microsoft is a trademark of Microsoft, Inc.

FIRST EDITION
FIRST PRINTING

Copyright © 1987 by TAB BOOKS Inc.
Printed in the United States of America

Library of Congress Cataloging in Publication Data

Whitsell, Frank.
C programmer's utility library.

Includes index.
1. C (Computer program language)   2. Utilities
(Computer programs)   3. IBM Personal Computer—
Programming.   I. Title.
QA76.73.C15W47   1987   005.265   86-23108

ISBN 0-8306-0955-5
ISBN 0-8306-2855-X (pbk.)

Contents

Preface

Most programming languages for the IBM PC supply a generous variety of functions that enable you to access and control the display, the keyboard input, and the DOS. The BASIC interpreter provides a good example, because it is found on virtually every PC. The language incorporates features to deal with nearly every aspect of programming for the PC. There are functions to find and set the display cursor position, to set colors and video modes, and even to access some of the DOS functions. Despite this richness of features, many programmers have abandoned BASIC and switched to the C language. The modularity of C, along with its local variables, speed, and efficiency, is making it the programming community's language of preference for software development.

The C language, however, lacks built-in functions for many of these basic necessities. It is up to you as the programmer to provide what is needed. To obtain these functions, you can purchase commercial libraries or write them yourself. In practice, most of the required functions are probably developed on an as-needed basis. Because such functions are basic to most programs, they will end up in a function library.

This haphazard approach to library development usually results in functions that are not general enough to work in most situations, so the functions are rewritten, or worse, new ones are written that are almost identical to existing functions. In the end, a great deal of time is spent developing the library, and because of the many similar functions and the inconsistencies in the interfaces to them, the programs that call these functions are more complicated than necessary.

I know these problems well, because my personal C library has gone through many changes over the past few years. It has gone from puberty to adulthood, and finally,

I believe it has reached a level of some maturity. In this book, I am passing along many of these functions. They have become wiser with age and experience—and they have spawned an interrupt-driven communications library as an offspring. All of these functions have worn well in my own programs; I hope they will serve you as well.

Introduction

Programming in C, as in any computer language, requires basic functions for console input/output and access to the operating system. Functions for communications are also needed, because the demand for programs with communications capabilities is greater than ever before. The functions in this book are designed to supplement the standard library functions in these areas.

Sooner or later, all C programmers writing for IBM PC machines need many of the functions in this book. They should save a beginner a great deal of time, and more advanced programmers will find some of the techniques to be useful, especially those in the area of communications. The last two chapters provide a library of functions for interrupt-driven communications and a terminal program that demonstrates their use. Communications have always been an area of some mystery to many programmers, only because the information has not been widely available.

Chapter 1 explains how most of the functions were developed and provides hints on getting the most out of them. Chapter 2 presents functions for controlling the video display. There are functions for cursor control, color, and display modes. Also, a simple technique that allows programs to use colors chosen by the program user is developed in this chapter.

Chapter 3 provides a variety of functions for keyboard control and for using the built-in speaker in the PC. There is also an input function that takes advantage of some of the special keys, such as Insert and Delete, for data entry. At the end of the chapter there is a useful program that demonstrates display and keyboard control using the functions from Chapters 2 and 3. The program allows the user to select colors for the display using the technique from Chapter 2.

Chapter 4 develops functions for access to many of the capabilities of DOS. These functions allow expansion of ambiguous filenames, like *.*, within your programs. They also allow more flexible programs through the use of PC environment variables like the PATH. Several programs demonstrate these functions and provide some useful utilities at the same time.

Chapter 5 begins the function library for communications, using polled port input and output. Chapter 6 completes the library with interrupt-driven port I/O functions. Terminal programs are presented in each chapter to demonstrate the use of the library functions.

The functions in Chapters 2 through 4 make up a general function library that can be used with many programs. The functions in the last two chapters form a communications library.

The appendices provide code for functions used in the book that might not be available in all compiler libraries. They should help you adapt the book functions for use with your particular C compiler.

Chapter 1

Laying the Foundation

What is a utility library? The Random House dictionary defines *utility* as "the state or quality of being useful." Thus a utility library must be a collection of useful states or qualities. The meaning is more precise to a programmer: a utility library is a collection of useful programs and subroutines—which is what this book is all about. Most program development requires certain basic functions that are not present in the standard C library; yet these functions are needed over and over again in many different programs. These missing functions form a gap between the standard library and the target computer, in this case, the IBM PC class of computers. The functions and programs presented here were developed to help bridge this gap.

My purpose is to save some C programmers the effort of inventing their own wheel. This chapter explains the basic theory that I have attempted to apply to the functions developed in the remaining chapters. If you wish to modify or expand upon these functions, this information can help. So let's begin with a basic question.

1.1 WHY ISN'T THE STANDARD C LIBRARY ENOUGH?

The C library or libraries, included with your compiler are examples of a utility library. They are collections of useful functions. Without them, it would be necessary to create those functions yourself. When you first began to experiment with C, the standard library probably seemed to contain more functions than you could use, but it didn't take long before you realized there were some serious deficiencies.

Perhaps one of your first discoveries was that the standard library doesn't exist. The library functions vary from machine to machine as well as from one brand of compiler to another. Sometimes the calls to similar functions from one library to the next vary in the arrangement of the arguments passed and the values returned. That is a serious blow to the concept of portability.

Then comes the major disappointment. The standard libraries know nothing about video display capabilities. How do you locate the cursor at a specific position on the screen? How do you take advantage of display attributes and colors? There isn't even a function to clear the screen! As you begin to design programs that are more sophisticated and require more user interaction, you find other deficiencies.

There is a good reason why these functions are missing. They would limit the portability of C. There are hundreds of different terminal models, each defining its particular set of commands to control the display. Special keys, like the arrow keys and function keys, transmit codes that vary from terminal to terminal. Each operating system provides unique functions, as well.

If the C library tried to take all these variations into account, the language would lose much of its portable nature, so a different approach has been taken. Add-on libraries, like the **curses** library found on some Unix systems, provide display controls that are independent of the terminal. They accomplish this independence by defining a standard set of terminal capabilities. Cursor control and the setting of display attributes, like reverse video, are examples of these capabilities. The control commands for each terminal attached to a system are stored in a separate database. The **curses** functions simply search this database for the appropriate command when one of its functions is called.

Because of the add-on library approach, the standard library has not required many changes over the years. While hardware has been continually evolving, the C language has not become outdated. C programs written years ago still work on newer machines.

The functions in this book are designed as an add-on library. They are intended to provide the programmer with the tools needed to develop software systems that would not be possible using only the standard library functions. When a program is moved to a machine with a different display type or operating system, only the library functions need to be changed for the program to operate in the new environment.

1.2 HARDWARE, SOFTWARE, AND REFERENCES

The functions and programs presented in this book were developed on an IBM PC running PC-DOS version 2.1. The PC is equipped with a 20 megabyte hard disk and a monochrome monitor. An external Hayes Smartmodem 1200 was used for the development and testing of the communications functions.

All functions have been tested on a variety of PC compatibles. The display functions have been tested on monochrome and color graphics adapters. I have made an effort to design the functions to operate on as many compatibles as possible. Where a function is dependent on a particular design of the hardware, I have attempted to point out this fact. This should allow you to make adjustments for your configuration. If your PC compatible runs most of the popular software, it is likely that no adjustments will be necessary.

The C Compiler

The Lattice C compiler version 2.15 was used to compile the code, and the PC-

DOS LINK program was used to link the programs. These functions were also tested with the latest version of the Lattice compiler as of this writing, version 3.00. You will need version 2.2 or higher of the DOS linker to link programs with this version of the compiler. You should be able to compile the functions with most of the popular C compilers available for the PC. All of the functions that deal with disk files assume that you are using PC-DOS version 2.0 or higher. Therefore, the only requirement of the compiler is that it makes use of the PC-DOS 2.0 function calls for file access.

Many of the functions use the ROM BIOS and DOS function calls. To make a BIOS or DOS function call, you need a function that loads the processor registers and returns the values that the BIOS and DOS calls return in the processor registers. If your compiler does not provide such a function, you may be able to use the BIOS and DOS interface functions in the appendices. This is discussed in more detail in the next two sections.

If you need the functions in the appendices, you will need the IBM or Microsoft Macro Assembler, any version. You will also need the assembler for the interrupt service routine in Chapter 6.

Reference Materials

No special reference materials are necessary to use the functions in this book. They are all documented as presented. If you wish to modify or expand these functions, there are some references that are essential. You will need the PC-DOS manual if you plan to design your own functions that make DOS function calls. The PC technical reference is needed to design BIOS function calls. It is also extremely useful for many other programming tasks. You can learn a great deal about the PC's hardware and the programming required to control it from the technical reference manual. The manual includes the commented source listing of the BIOS function calls, which is necessary when you are designing a function that calls a BIOS routine.

1.3 ACCESSING THE PC HARDWARE

Why would you want access to the PC hardware? And what do I mean by *hardware*, anyway? I'm referring to the video display, keyboard, disk drives, communications ports, and modems. All this equipment can be controlled directly, through the appropriate programming of certain processor ports. The ports are the processor's means for communicating with the outside world. To the processor, which is an Intel 8088 central processing unit (CPU) in most PC's, almost everything in and attached to your PC is "the outside world." This means that most devices attached to the computer are controlled by a program that directs specific data to output ports defined by the system designers. This can all get quite complicated, but computer system design can be visualized as being somewhat like home design. All the components to be built into the system must be coordinated to prevent a collision; for instance, the computer ports assigned to the video display cannot also be used by the modem.

The data that is output to a device port determines what the device will do. It's a lot like turning on the right switches at the right time and making sure that other switches are off. Knowing just what to do and when to do it can be a big headache. And who needs it, anyway? I just want to put a character on the screen in reverse video. I don't care how it gets done; I have more important things to worry about.

Enter the BIOS. The PC designers took the worry out of getting close . . . to the hardware, that is. By using the BIOS calls you can command the PC to do many wonderful things quite simply. Most of these things are not available through the standard C library.

So what are some of these wonderful things? Setting the display border color, changing text colors and attributes, moving the cursor to a known position on the screen, and changing the appearance of the cursor to a block or even making it disappear entirely are just a few of the possibilities.

DOS function calls open similar frontiers. You can make disk directories, change directories or drives, or find the current directory. A pair of DOS function calls makes it easy to write C programs that use wildcards in filenames, like *.*, in the same manner as they are used with DOS commands. For example, have you ever wished that you could TYPE *.C to send all of the C programs in the current directory to the printer? Chapter 4 contains a modified cat program that can. How many times have you wished that WordStar could find its overlay files from another directory on your hard disk? Chapter 4 shows you how to write C programs that can do that. Making your own programs perform these minor miracles is not difficult, and the users of your programs will love you for it. All you need is the DOS connection.

1.4 CONNECTING TO DOS AND BIOS

Both the DOS and BIOS function calls were designed to be called from assembly language. It is not possible to make a direct call from any other language. But a low-level interface function can be written in assembly language that can be called from C. All this low-level function needs to be able to do is to convert the C call and return sequence to the DOS or BIOS call and return requirements. Many compilers now include one or more DOS and BIOS interface functions in their standard library.

Pre-2.0 versions of the Lattice compiler included a very primitive interface function to DOS only. That function was useless for the DOS 2.0 function calls. If you wanted to access the new DOS calls, you had to write your own interface function. Although many C programmers are proficient in assembly language programming, many more are not, and writing C functions in assembly language requires a thorough understanding of the compiler's code-generation technique.

Avoiding Assembly Language

With the newer compiler versions, it is rarely necessary to write an assembly language function. It is still possible if your compiler documents its call and return procedure. The Lattice compiler provides a good explanation of its technique.

The speed and small size of assembly language functions tempt the programmer. Such functions can execute quickly and are usually much smaller than their C versions, but there are good reasons to avoid them. One is that the nature of assembly language makes it prone to programming errors. A better reason is that your C functions will likely be compatible with future versions of your compiler, while the assembly language functions might not. Any change to the compiler's internal code generation can make your assembly language functions obsolete.

Reaching the Lower Levels with C

Lattice compilers from version 2.0 provide five or more functions for accessing

DOS and BIOS routines. The intdos and intdosx functions call DOS routines. The int86 and int86x functions are for calling BIOS routines. The segread function is also called when either the intdosx or the int86x function is used. Version 3 of the compiler adds several functions to this list. Most of these are to ease the translation of C data types, especially pointers, to the form required by the DOS and BIOS functions.

Using these functions requires some knowledge of the 8088 CPU architecture. It also helps to know a little about the compiler's code-generation technique. You can use the functions in this book without any of this knowledge, but you will need it to design your own functions. Otherwise, you might find yourself hunting some very subtle bugs in your programs. A little study of the functions presented should help you to avoid problems.

Many compilers provide functions similar to these; however, they might have different calling conventions. If so, you will need to make some changes to the functions in the book that call the DOS and BIOS function calls. The changes should be relatively minor; probably you will just have to alter the argument and return scheme. An example should clarify this.

The intdos function can be used to call the DOS routine that writes one character to the standard output. The code shown in Fig. 1-1 will do it.

The intdos function requires a pointer to two unions. REGS is declared in dos.h, which must be included in any program that uses the DOS and BIOS function calls. The first argument contains the values required by the DOS function call. The second argument will contain the values, if any, returned by the DOS call. In this case, nothing is returned.

Your compiler's DOS interface function might require arguments in some form other than a pointer to a REGS union. If so, you will need to adjust accordingly. See Appendix B for the union REGS declaration.

If your compiler does not have DOS and BIOS interface functions, you might be able to use those in the appendices. I have included work-alike assembly-language functions that conform to the same call and return procedure as the Lattice functions. You will need the IBM or Microsoft Macro Assembler to assemble these. You will probably also need to make some modifications to them, to bring them into conformance with your compiler's object code requirements. Needless to say, this can be somewhat complex. I have tried to explain as clearly as possible where modifications might be needed. If you have good compiler documentation and a little assembly language experience, your chances of success are good.

```
int  c;              /* storage for a character             */
union REGS u;        /* define union to store cpu registers */
     .
     .               /* some code that gets a character     */
     .
u.h.ah = 2;          /* DOS function call code for char to stdout */
u.h.dl = c;          /* put char in register DL             */
intdos( &u, &u);     /* char to standard output             */
```

Fig. 1-1. The intdos function.

1.5 MACHINE DEPENDENCE

Functions that call DOS and BIOS routines are not portable. It is wise to isolate such functions into a separate library to be searched by the linker. When moving a program to a new machine that is not a PC-compatible, you can then use the linker on your PC to provide you with a list of your nonportable functions that are called by the program. Just link the program on the PC as usual, except do not specify your nonportable library in the link command. Because your nonportable library is not included in the library search, the attempt to link a C program that uses those functions will cause the link to fail and provide you with a list of unresolved externals. This is simply a list of the functions in your nonportable library that are called in your program. These are the functions that will need to be rewritten for the new machine.

Be careful when using this technique. If any of your nonportable functions have the same name as a function in a library that is being searched (such as the standard library), you will not see it named in the list of unresolved externals. It is not usually a good idea to use names that conflict in this way anyway.

If you are writing a function that is intended to replace a standard library function, which is sometimes necessary, it is better to give it a unique name. Then use a #define in your source code to change the standard library name to your function name. That will prevent the accidental inclusion of a function that was not intended. To illustrate this point, assume that the code segment in Fig. 1-1 was rewritten to act as a replacement for the level two **putchar** macro, as shown in Fig. 1-2. You might want to do this if your intention was to avoid including the level two library functions in the linked program.

write_c could have been named **putchar**, because it does the same thing, including the translation of a newline to the carriage return/line feed pair.

One difference is that this is a function, while **putchar** is a macro. If this function had been named **putchar**, however, and was included in the list of object modules for linking, then the **stdio.h** file would not have to be included (assuming that no other level-two functions are used). This would prevent the invocation of the **putchar** macro and the subsequent inclusion of level-two file routines from the standard library. The resulting linked program would be smaller. Incidentally, calling the **exit** function automatically includes level-two library functions. Call **_exit** instead, to prevent their inclusion.

You can accomplish the same thing by leaving the function with the **write_c** name and adding the line

```
#define    putchar    write_c
```

to the beginning of the source code file. Then you do not have a function in your personal library with the same name as a standard library function. This is also better than typing **write_c** throughout the source code, because you only need to change or eliminate the #define to revert back to the level-two calls.

You probably noticed that **write_c** calls itself. Recursion is an economical form of coding that is well-suited to C. Otherwise, two calls to **intdos** would have to be made, which generates more code. The return value has been converted to **int** to prevent the warning that some compilers give about type conversion in the return value.

```
write_c(c)
char c;
{
    union REGS u;

    if(c == '\n')           /* if this is a new-line...    */
        write_c('\r');  /* add a carriage return       */
    u.h.ah = 2;
    u.h.dl = c;
    intdos( &u, &u);
    return((int) c);
}
```

Fig. 1-2. The write__c function.

1.6 MULTIPLE MEMORY MODELS

Many C compilers for the PC require the programmer to choose the amount of memory that will be available to a program. Earlier C compilers, and some compilers for other languages, do not have this requirement. Rather than being a restriction, the fact that a choice must be made represents an advance in compiler design. You might wonder, if my PC has 640K of memory, isn't that the limit? The answer to that question is a simple yes and no. It depends on your compiler. Some compilers restrict a program to a maximum of 64K for code and data. Some ease that restriction by allowing up to 64K for the code and another 64K for data storage. Others limit the program only by the amount of memory in the system. The most desirable design in a compiler is the one that requires you to make the choice. To explain, I'll use the Lattice compiler as an example because it uses an approach that covers most of the possibilities.

Deciding on the amount of memory to make available to a program is a decision referred to by Lattice as selecting a memory model. It has nothing to do with the amount of memory in any given PC. To understand a memory model, you should realize that a program consists of two partitions: one partition is the program code; the other is the program data. Most compilers for any language divide a program into code and data partitions. The amount of memory allocated to each partition when the program is compiled depends on the program. The primary limitation on program (and data) size is the amount of memory in the computer.

There is a further limitation imposed by the architecture of the 8088 CPU used in most PCs. This limitation is arbitrary, however, depending upon the method that the compiler uses to address code and data. The 8088 most easily accesses code and data in segments less than 64K in size. That is because only a single CPU register, equivalent to two bytes, or 16 bits, is needed to access code or data that is less than 64K in total size (for each). The result is that the most efficient code partition will be less than 64K and will have a data partition that is less than 64K; for a total program size of less than 128K.

If either the code or the data partition is greater than 64K, then two 8088 registers are required to access that partition. This also requires a little more ingenuity in compiler design, which explains why many compilers limit a partition to the 64K segment size. At any rate, it might make more sense to equate this concept with a C pointer. A character pointer, for example, requires two bytes of storage under the 64K limitation. Above that, a pointer would require four bytes. That means all data pointers of any type within a program will be four bytes long, not just those that lie beyond the 64K boundary. Having pointers of different lengths within one program would be impossible for the compiler to manage, because it does not know how many modules will ultimately be linked together to form the final program. Incidentally, this also emphasizes the fact that you cannot depend on a pointer to be the same size as an int. Pointer size, as well as int size, varies from machine to machine.

This two-byte versus four-byte scheme simply means twice as many register loads are required (two rather than one) for access to a code or data partition greater than 64K in size. Obviously, the four-byte-pointer program is going to execute more slowly. It will also require more memory to do the same thing. Of course, all this is taken care of by the compiler and is invisible to the C programmer—invisible, that is, until you start using the DOS or BIOS function calls. Then you must know the size of a pointer or how to program around it. Lattice's version 3 gives the programmer some functions that reduce or eliminate the pointer-size problem. We have to be a little trickier with earlier versions, and those techniques will be explained when they are encountered. Incidentally, you have the same responsibility to determine the size of a pointer if you write an assembly language function.

The Lattice compiler gives the programmer the choice of four memory models, which covers all the combinations of code and data partition sizes available. You can choose the S (for small memory) model, which limits the code partition to 64K and the data partition to 64K. You can do a lot of programming in 128K. Lattice says their compiler is compiled under the small memory model. If that does not impress you, then you have never wondered what it's like to write a compiler. Anyway, the small model will produce the fastest and tightest code of the four models.

A second choice is the large program, small data model, which Lattice calls the P model. In this model, the code may be greater than 64K and the data partition must be less than 64K. Note that the code does not have to exceed 64K. If it doesn't, you might as well take advantage of a small code model. This is probably the second most efficient model. Function calls will require two register loads, but data access will require only one, as in the S model. If you would like a brain teaser, consider this. The small data configuration allows only a two-byte pointer. So how does this model handle the four-byte function pointer it requires? If you are interested, you will find the answer in the compiler and run-time implementation section of the Lattice documentation.

The third model available is the D model (small program, large data). As you might guess, the code must be less than 64K, but the data may be greater than 64K. In most cases, this model is probably less efficient than the P model. Data access usually occurs more frequently than function calls.

The last model is the L model (large program, large data). Both the code and the data partitions may exceed 64K. This model is the least efficient of the four. Note that with any of the large-partition models, the theoretical size limit is one megabyte. This is the maximum memory addressable by the 8088 CPU. In practice, this will be something less than 640k, because that is the largest contiguous block of memory in a PC, and part of that is reserved by the system and by DOS.

Which memory model you use is up to you, but you cannot link together object files compiled under different memory models. That explains why Lattice includes four copies of its libraries, one for each memory model. The choice of memory model will depend on program design. Some compilers might not offer all the combinations available with the Lattice compiler. Obviously, the small model is preferred if the particular application does not need more than 64K for either code or data.

Some applications, however, will require one of the large models. Often, a large-model program could be designed to work as a small-model program by keeping part of the program or data on disk and loading portions as needed. A large program can use overlays to keep the resident code within the 64K limit. Large amounts of data can usually be processed in chunks small enough to stay within the limit.

The major disadvantage of this approach is that frequent disk accesses can slow program execution considerably. An advantage is that the program will work on PCs with smaller memory configurations. There is another advantage inherent in the design of the small model. A stray pointer cannot alter memory used by DOS and the system. A null pointer in the small memory model points to the base of the data segment. Altering the data at that location, by inadvertant use of a null pointer, is certain to upset your program, but altering data with a null or uninitialized four-byte pointer can be disastrous. A four-byte pointer can access or alter any location in memory. Your program could write over DOS or reserved system memory, altering such things as the disk parameter table—bye, bye disk.

Programming Considerations

Earlier in this section, I mentioned that you need to take the memory model into account when using the DOS and BIOS functions. This is true when you are working with pointers, which vary in size depending on which memory model you are using. A little background on the architecture of the 8088 CPU and the workings of the compiler is in order here. Only then can it be understood why pointer size affects your programming for those functions.

The 8088 CPU accesses data in memory by storing the address of a particular data item in CPU registers. Two CPU registers are required to fully specify the address. One of these registers is a base register that effectively points to a 64K block of memory. There are four of these registers, called *segment registers*, labeled CS, DS, SS, and ES. Each is 16 bits wide. CS stands for code segment, DS for data segment, SS for stack segment, and ES for extra segment. These registers may all have the same value, thus pointing at the same 64K segment of memory, or they can all have different values. Each register has its own purpose. Program code is in the code segment. The IP, or *instruction pointer*, is a 16-bit register that points to the offset within the code segment where the next program instruction scheduled for execution resides. Therefore it is said that the next instruction to be executed is at address CS:IP in memory. 32 bits, or four bytes, are required to specify the address.

The same methodology is used to address data. For data, the DS register points to a 64K segment of memory, and one of the CPU's general registers contains an offset within the data segment that completes the address of a data item. There are six of these general purpose registers, labeled AX, BX, CX, DX, SI, and DI. These six registers are usually assumed to contain an offset from DS when they are used to address memory, so a data item is said to be at memory address DS:BX or DS:SI, for example. A segment override instruction is available; it allows the general purpose registers to use one of the other segment registers, CS, ES, and SS, as the base segment.

There is one special purpose register, BP, that is important to Lattice C compilers. It contains an offset for addressing, just as the general purpose registers do, but it defaults to SS, the stack segment, as the base segment. It is used by the compiler to address all data on the stack. Function arguments and **auto** data are always stored on the stack, so SS:BP addresses those data items.

The Lattice compiler uses the CPU registers differently for each memory model. The simplest case is the small model. Here the compiler sets up the segment registers at the start of the program and leaves them unchanged during program execution. Thus all data for the program may be accessed with a 16-bit value, or just one general purpose register. This is because all data is in the data and stack segments addressed by DS or SS, which never change. When a pointer is passed as a function argument, only the two-byte offset value is needed, so data pointers are fully specified in two bytes. Two bytes can address at most 64K, so that explains the small model limitation.

The large models assume that data may be stored or accessed anywhere in memory, not only within a single 64K segment. The segment registers must be loaded along with the general purpose registers whenever a data item is accessed, so pointers are stored in four bytes. That means pointers passed as function arguments are four bytes long too.

So how does this hobgoblin affect our DOS and BIOS functions? If you examine **dos.h** in Appendix B, you will see that the structure XREGS and SREGS contain variables with names that correspond to most of the CPU registers. These variables must be loaded with the values required by the DOS or BIOS function call to be made. If the function call requires a pointer, it usually requires the four-byte version. For example, a DOS function might require a pointer to a filename in registers DS:BX. Before calling that function, the variables **ds** and **bx** must be loaded with the address of a buffer containing the filename. The & operator is not sufficient for all memory models, only for the small one. If the function is compiled under a large data model, the pointer to the filename buffer passed as an argument will be four bytes, yet you will notice that the structure variables are declared as **short**. A **short** is only two bytes. Thus the pointer is going to have to be broken into its segment:offset components before it can be stored in **ds** and **bx** in this example. The functions appearing later on illustrate some methods for solving this problem.

1.7 THE QUESTION OF PORTABILITY

As I said earlier, many of the functions in this book are not portable. They will work on most close PC compatibles, but that is not portability. To be portable, a function must work on any machine with a standard C compiler. Whenever you write a program, you should consider the possibility that you might want that program to run on a different machine. Even if you are sure that you will only run the program on a PC, you can be sure that PC's are bound to change.

Yet it is nearly impossible to write a sophisticated, interactive program on the PC without using some nonportable functions. The problem is not quite as difficult when writing portable programs that will be moved from one Unix system to another, because there are many similarities between Unix systems; but there are major differences between a Unix system and a PC. You can certainly write many C programs that can be moved between a PC and a Unix system without modification, but most such programs are not interactive, at least not to a great degree. They usually operate with command-line parameters and data files, taking their input from the standard input device and writing to the standard output.

That approach is often not sufficient for a PC program. PC users are accustomed to fast, flexible programs. Achieving peak performance sometimes requires a closer tie to the PC hardware. The best approach is usually the one that has been used for years by software companies. Isolate the machine-dependent code into subroutines, or functions, so that only that code must be changed when the machine configuration changes.

Which parts of a program are most likely to need changes when hardware changes? The video display has always been a problem. It seems to be the most dependent variable in the equation. The printer is less of a problem, unless your program uses the printer's graphics capabilities or some other special printer function. The operating system will often require some adaptation. Other variables depend on the program application. Communications programs need to be able to operate with a variety of modems.

The programs in this book illustrate how machine-dependent code can be isolated from the main program. All machine-dependent code is in separate functions called by the nondependent functions—at least that was the plan, though you might find some lapses. Many of these programs have been tested in a Unix environment as well as on a PC. In those cases, only a few functions needed modification. For example, the communications program in chapter 6 was derived from one designed to work on PC's and Unix. The major modifications were to the port input and output functions. It is no secret that writing portable programs is a challenge, or that experience is your best teacher, but the C programming language is probably the most dependable for transport to a variety of machines. That the language is one of the fastest and most economical is just a very valuable fringe benefit.

1.8 A WORD OF CAUTION

There are some risks involved when you are programming hardware control, but a little caution should prevent any problems. One of the most powerful features of the C language is the access it provides to the system internals. This power is due in part to the language's high speed, as some events occur too rapidly for high-level languages.

One of the reasons for the higher speed is that C lacks a guiding run-time system. The run-time system is a *front end* program that controls the execution of your program. Compiled BASIC and COBOL programs are usually governed by a run-time system. The run-time system places a protective shell between your program and the operating system. It will trap many program bugs and issue an error message before terminating execution. An out-of-bounds array index is an example of the type of error that a run-time system might catch, and then notify you of the condition.

Such run-time error messages are an aid to the debugging process. You might wish that C had a run-time system for this reason, but you are fortunate that it does not. The protective shell of the run-time system not only slows execution, but also isolates the program from the operating system. In other words, it takes away some of the programmer's control. C is a true programmer's language; it leaves the decisions to you.

In return for this favor, C programmers gladly accept a little more responsibility. Because the language does not limit your access to the system, certain areas of programming require a little caution. The greatest potential for damage is through direct port input and output. Incorrect output to the video display ports can damage the display. That is the reason that most of the functions in this book use DOS and BIOS calls, where system control is necessary. The DOS and BIOS calls have presumably been well-debugged, and therefore are safe to use.

The only direct port I/O done in this book is to the communications ports, and these functions have been thoroughly tested. Besides, you should not be able to damage a modem or the RS-232 interface with incorrect port I/O—not if the manufacturers have done their homework. So forge ahead with the programs in this book without fear. Just exercise some care when you go out on your own, especially if your experiments are on someone else's computer.

Chapter 2

Video Display Functions

This chapter begins our utility library with a collection of functions that control the video display. There are two basic methods available to control the display on a PC, aside from programming the display ports directly. Perhaps the easiest method is to use the PC-DOS ansi.sys device driver.

Before ansi.sys can be used, there must be a file in the root directory of the boot drive called config.sys. The ansi.sys file must be available on the same drive. The config.sys file must have the following line in it:

```
device=ansi.sys
```

When this setup has been completed, the system must be rebooted to activate the ansi.sys device driver. Various display controls can then be implemented simply by writing the appropriate control codes to the standard output. The DOS manual provides the control codes. For example, the following program line would position the cursor to line 5, column 40:

```
printf("\x1b[5;40H");
```

\x1b is the escape character. The rest of the string defines the cursor positioning command to ansi.sys; ansi.sys makes the PC emulate an ANSI terminal, which accepts escape sequences as commands to perform particular functions.

Most of the C functions in this chapter that provide display control can be written using the ANSI escape sequences defined in the DOS manual. They can also be written using the int86 function to call BIOS routines. For the functions in this chapter,

I have chosen the latter approach for several reasons. The most important reason is that the BIOS provides controls not available through ANSI sequences. Another reason is that the BIOS functions execute more quickly. Because DOS ultimately uses them to perform the function requested in the ANSI command, we are simply bypassing some time-consuming processing. One other very good reason is that the BIOS calls ignore the Control-Break key sequence. If you press Control-Break during standard output, you will find yourself staring at the DOS prompt. This can be frustrating to users, as well as dangerous to data files that may not have been closed before the program was terminated. Finally, you can't be sure that another PC will have **ansi.sys** activated. It's just one more thing to put in the program installation instructions.

There are some instances where the ANSI method might be preferable to BIOS calls. Portability, however, is not one of them. You may find that a few not-so-close PC compatibles will be able to run programs that they otherwise could not (if BIOS calls were used instead), but it won't make the program generally portable to other machine types. You cannot depend on any given machine to be equipped with ANSI terminals.

There is, however, a distinct advantage to using **ansi.sys** if you wish to run your program from a different PC over the phone lines with a modem. If you have a communications program on the local PC that uses DOS function calls to write to the display, like the standard output in a C program, you can dial up your computer and run the program as if you were sitting at your own keyboard. The screen updates will work a little more slowly at 1200 baud, but they will work correctly.

Here is how you can prepare your computer for remote operation: boot it as usual before leaving home; set your modem to auto answer mode; and issue the DOS command **ctty com1:**. Use **com2:** in the command if your modem is connected to that communications port. Note that you will not be able to type anything at your keyboard after you issue the **ctty** command, as this command directs DOS to take its input from the communications port. You can get control back in one of two ways. You can reboot the computer, either with ctl-alt-del or by shutting it off, or you can issue the command **ctty** from a remote computer while you are connected. That will cause DOS to revert back to standard operation.

To dial up your computer at home from the remote location, load the communications program on the remote PC and dial your computer's phone number. When the communications program indicates that you are connected, just press Return once or twice, and you should see the DOS prompt from your computer on the display. You can now run programs on your computer. Not all programs will work over a phone line. Those that bypass DOS for display will not, but you can use the compiler, linker, EDLIN, and your own C programs that write to the standard output.

I can make one suggestion regarding the decision whether to use ANSI commands or BIOS calls: keep two libraries for display control, one that uses the BIOS calls, and one that uses **ansi.sys** commands. Then you can easily create two versions of the same program by linking with each library.

2.1 STANDARD OUTPUT CONSIDERATIONS

Before you begin to write a C program, you should give some thought to the display output method you will use. Display controls are not appropriate for every program. Think of the purpose of your program. Do you want to be able to use it as a filter, or to be able to redirect its input or output? Programs to be used as filters follow a common set of standards. One of these is that the display is left alone. Only the program's data will be output. Think of the inconvenience if the sort program cleared the display or provided cursor positioning. Those commands would end up in the file if the sort output was redirected—not very neat. Worse, the display commands might foul up the operation of another program in a pipeline; for example:

```
dir *.c I sort I find "4"
```

will sort the C files in the current directory or drive and then display only those with the number four somewhere in the line. You might be looking for all files last updated in April. If the sort program provided cursor positioning, you might find files for the wrong reason: because the four appeared in a cursor positioning command from sort.

Another requirement of filters is that they take their input either from the standard input or from command-line arguments, or from both, so that input can be redirected or come from a pipe. The filter output should go to the standard output or standard-error output only. If you think about these few requirements for a minute, you will see that they are important. Programs that adhere to them find uses that you might not have thought of at first, because they are so easily combined with other filter programs.

There are many programs, of course, that are not meant to be filters. A word processing program is not usually thought of as a filter, though you can redirect editor commands from a file to EDLIN. EDLIN takes its input from the standard input. Database management programs probably would not be used as filters, though some operations of such a program would be more useful if they could be. A database manager usually has a highly interactive data entry screen that is not used with redirected input. It seems that there is an argument for the use of standard input and output in almost every situation; however, all of these examples have the need for display controls, to present the user with an easy means for data entry and display.

The point is that the BIOS calls bypass the standard input and output provided by DOS. Actually, in this chapter you are only dealing with standard output versus BIOS output, but in the next chapter you will be considering BIOS input from the keyboard versus standard input. If you don't rely on ansi.sys, then a BIOS call must be used for display output if you wish to use video attributes or colors. If you use ansi.sys, your program is at the mercy of a Control-Break keyboard entry.

It comes down to the choice of risking a Control-Break, or losing the benefits of standard input and output. Fortunately, there is usually a satisfactory resolution to this problem. If the program you are designing requires display controls, then one would not normally expect the output of such a program to be redirected. Therefore, the BIOS functions can be used to control the display, and the standard input can be used to get keyboard entries. In this compromise, input can still be redirected, which is probably the only desirable redirection for such a program. Your program is still vulnerable to Control-Break when using the standard input.

If your program cannot stand a Control-Break, there are a couple of solutions. Rather than using the standard input, you can use the BIOS calls in Chapter 3 to get keyboard input. If the BIOS functions in this chapter and the next are used for display and keyboard data, a Control-Break cannot terminate the program while it is displaying or retrieving keyboard data, but there are other times when a Control-Break can still get you. At the least destructive level DOS will act on a Control-Break during printing, and at worst, it will act on a Control-Break during any DOS function call.

The function in Figure 2-1 can be used to prevent termination of your program by DOS when Control-Break is entered. It effectively disables the Control-Break action. There is also a function to re-enable the Control-Break.

Call brk_off to disable Control-Break termination. This function will work for all memory models. To understand how this function operates you need to know how DOS handles a Control-Break entry. When DOS detects a Control-Break keyboard entry, it executes INT 0x23. INT is an assembly language instruction that performs a software interrupt. It differs from a hardware interrupt only in that it is invoked from a program rather than by a device interrupt. There are 256 interrupts, numbered from

```c
#include <dos.h>

static  char    iret = 0xcf;                /* opcode for IRET */
static  short   intsav[2] = {0,0};
/********/
brk_off()       /* disable control-break */
{
        union   REGS    u;
        struct  SREGS   segr;

        /* if already off, ignore the call */
        if(intsav[0] | intsav[1])
                return;

        /* save current vector */
        peek(0, 0x23 * 4, (char *)intsav, 4);

        /* set new interrupt vector */
        segread(&segr);
        u.x.ax = 0x2523;
        u.x.dx = (short) &iret;
        intdosx(&u, &u, &segr);
}
/********/
brk_on()                /* re-enable control-break */
{
        union   REGS    u;
        struct  SREGS   segr;

        /* ignore if already enabled */
        if(!(intsav[0] | intsav[1]))
                return;

        u.x.ax = 0x2523;
        u.x.dx = intsav[0];
        segr.ds = intsav[1];
        intdosx(&u, &u, &segr);
        intsav[0] = intsav[1] = 0;  /* indicate enabled */
```

Fig. 2-1. The brk_off and brk_on functions.

zero (INT 0) to 255 (INT FF hex), available for use as either software or hardware interrupts. DOS has defined INT 0x23 to be the Control-Break exit. The interrupt number, 23 hex in this case, is used by the 8088 CPU to find the address of the interrupt service routine. Each address is a segment:offset, so four bytes are required. The address storage for interrupts starts at 0:0, the first byte of memory. The address of the INT 0 routine is stored at 0:0 through 0:3. The address of INT 1 is from 0:4 through 0:7. The address of the INT 0x23 routine is at 23 hex * 4 in segment 0, or 0:8C hex.

When INT 0x23 is executed, the 8088 picks up the address at 0:8C and jumps to that routine, after first saving the processor status flags and the return address on the stack. When the interrupt routine finishes, it executes IRET, the interrupt return instruction. The return address and flags are retrieved from the stack, and execution then continues at the instruction following the INT instruction. As you can see, an INT is rather like a CALL to a subroutine. The major difference, aside from the addressing method, is that an INT saves the flags on the stack. A CALL does not. That's why different return instructions are used in each case. An IRET automatically restores the flags and adjusts the stack pointer properly.

When DOS loads at boot time, it stores an address to its Control-Break subroutine in the INT 0x23 location. This routine causes an exit to DOS when a program is executing; **brk_off** alters this action by changing the address, or interrupt vector, to point to an IRET instruction. Thus, when an INT 0x23 is invoked, essentially nothing happens.

The **brk_off** function defines a static location, **iret**, that is initialized to **0xcf**, the one-byte 8088 *opcode* (short for operation code, or instruction) for IRET. An array of two short integers is defined and initialized. This array will be used to hold the original INT 0x23 vector so that it can be restored with the **brk_on** function. Remember that an interrupt vector is a segment:offset address four bytes long. A short integer is two bytes. In memory, the two-byte offset precedes the two-byte segment, so **intsav[0]** will contain the offset, and **intsav[1]** the segment after the call to the **peek** function. Before **peek** is called, however, a check is made to make sure that **brk_off** has not already been called without a subsequent call to **brk_on**. If the check was not made, two successive calls to **brk_off** would result in the address for the IRET instruction being placed in **intsav**. That is not what is wanted.

If the test fails, the **peek** is called to get the current INT 0x23 vector. Because **peek** expects a character pointer, a cast is used to convert the **short intsav** array. The 25 hex DOS function call will be used to set the interrupt vector to point at **iret**. This function call expects the vector in registers DS:DX. That is, the segment of the new vector must be in DS and the offset in DX. The **iret** is in the static data area, and the Lattice compiler guarantees that, for all memory models, DS contains the segment of the static data area. Thus **segread** is called to get DS. Register AH must contain the DOS function call code of 25 hex, and AL must contain the interrupt number 23 hex, which is to be set to the address in registers DS and DX. These values are loaded simultaneously as 0x2523.

Next DX must be loaded with the offset of **iret**. It is cast to a short for two reasons. One is that **x.dx** is declared as a short, but **&iret** is a character pointer. The other is to ensure that only the offset of **iret** is obtained if **&iret** is a four-byte pointer. Finally, **intdosx** is called to place the interrupt vector.

After return from the call to brk__off, Control-Break will not terminate your program. If you wish to re-enable the control-break action, call brk__on. It works like brk__off, except that DS and DX are loaded with the vector that was saved by brk__off. brk__on checks to make sure that it does not load the vector with a null address. Before returning, brk__on resets intsav to nulls, so that another call to brk__off can be made.

It is not necessary to call brk__on if you do not need to re-enable Control-Break within your program. DOS will set it back to its default when your program exits. Unfortunately, brk__off alone is not enough to prevent DOS from messing up a screen display. The break action will not occur, but DOS will display ^C, followed by a carriage return and line feed, if you are using standard input or output calls. To prevent that, you will still need to use the BIOS functions for console input/output.

Try the program in Fig. 2-2 to test brk__off. It prompts you to type a 1 to disable Control-Break, and a 2 to re-enable it. It will continue to display the menu until you type Control-Z followed by a Return, which is the DOS EOF (end-of-file) character, or until you type Control-Break or Control-C with break enabled.

Unfortunately, the intdosx function cannot be used for all DOS function calls. That is why I had to use peek in brk__off. If you are familiar with DOS function calls, you know that function call 0x35 will return the contents of an interrupt vector in ES:BX. The Lattice intdosx function does not return segment registers, so it was necessary to peek the vector. If you use the intdosx function in Appendix D, you can use the DOS function call. The pointer to the SREGS structure passed to this intdosx is used to transfer the segment registers returned by the DOS call into the SREGS structure. You should be aware of this difference, because the values in the structure may be changed after an intdosx call.

Version 3 of the Lattice compiler has eliminated both of the problems we have just been dealing with. If you have that version of the compiler, you can use the onbreak function to disable the break key. You can even call other functions to perform some processing when using the Lattice function. The onbreak function is an assembly language function, so it can handle the necessary interrupt tasks that C functions cannot.

```
main()
{
        char inbuf[81], *gets();

        while(1) {
                printf("\n1. Break off.\n2. Break on.\n");
                if(gets(inbuf) == NULL)
                        break;
                if(inbuf[0] == '1')
                        brk_off();
                else if(inbuf[0] == '2')
                        brk_on();
                else
                        printf("\tPlease enter 1 or 2\n");
        }
}
```

Fig. 2-2. A program that allows you to test brk__off.

Also, the new compiler has a new function for calling DOS functions that will return the contents of segment registers ES and DS. That function is **intdoss** and is to be preferred over the **peek** method. Version 2 users, however, will have to be content with the method shown in Fig. 2-1, unless they wish to code their own assembly language functions.

2.2 DETERMINING THE TYPE OF DISPLAY

Determining the type of display is one of the most perplexing problems to PC programmers. Things were simpler when the only types of displays were monochrome and color. A call to the BIOS equipment-check interrupt was all that was necessary to determine which display adapter was attached. Now that there are several other choices, it is quite difficult to determine what the display capabilities might be in any particular PC compatible. There are monochrome graphics adapters that are compatible with the color adapter, except for color; there are proprietary monochrome graphics adapters that are not compatible with the color adapter; and there are computers with dual display circuitry, capable of emulating both monochrome and color adapters. There are also the new enhanced graphics adapters with new capabilities.

Although it is impossible to determine exactly what display capabilities a particular computer might have, there are some ways to obtain limited information. Depending on the particular application you are programming, this might be enough. The question you need to ask yourself is, "What display capabilities do I want to utilize in this program?" If you are developing an interactive data entry screen, you will probably want text display with a few attributes. You can limit the program to the use of high intensity and reverse video. That combination looks good on the monochrome screen. With the proper selection of display attributes, it will look good on a color monitor too. You will probably also want to set the border color on a color monitor.

If you want to use colors, you might want to take the approach that is used by many programs: let the user choose. You will still need to setup the program with some defaults. Later, I'll make some suggestions for those. Now let's see how to determine some facts about the display type, for different purposes.

The **equipchk** function provides information about the devices available on a system:

```
#include <dos.h>

equipchk()
{
    union REGS u;

    int86(0x11, &u, &u);
    return(u.x.ax);
}
```

This function calls BIOS INT 0x11. Upon return from the BIOS call, register **AX** has bits set according to the devices available. These bit settings are returned by **equipchk**. The technical reference manual describes all the bit settings. Figure 2-3 shows some of them.

The video mode equals 0x0030 if a monochrome card is attached. This is not particularly reliable anymore, as some monochrome graphics adapters return this value.

```
            if(equipchk() & 0xc000)
                there is a printer attached.


            if(equipchk() & 0x0e00)
                there is an RS-232 communications port.


            initial video mode = equipchk() & 0x0030
```

Fig. 2-3. The bit settings returned by equipchk.

If the return value is anything else, you can probably assume that color is available.

The next function will tell you whether a system has monochrome only or graphics capability, in most cases. It will not be able to detect graphics capability on a Compaq computer with the dual display mode set to monochrome. It also does not indicate color capability.

```
get_crt()
{
    union REGS u;

    u.h.ah = 15;
    int86(0x10, &u, &u);
    return((int)u.h.al);
}
```

The get_crt function calls BIOS INT 0x10 with function code 15 to get the current display mode. The return value is cast to int, but only the lower eight bits are significant. Don't forget to include dos.h if you compile this function alone. The following is a list of the most likely return values:

3 = 80 × 25 text mode (graphics adapter)
4 = 320 × 200 low-resolution graphics
6 = 640 × 200 high-resolution graphics
7 = monochrome card

If you are not using graphics, you might want to use the following logic in your program to make certain that the display is in text mode:

```
if(get_crt() != 7)
    set_crt(3);
```

This says that if the machine is not in monochrome mode, set it into 80 × 25 text mode. This works with both the color adapter and the enhanced graphics adapter. Here is the set_crt function:

```
set_crt(mode)
char mode;
{
    union REGS u;
```

```
    u.h.ah = 0;
    u.h.al = mode;
    int86(0x10, &u, &u);
}
```

Nothing is returned by this function.

Note the use of int86 in the last three functions. There is an int86x that allows us to pass segment registers if the BIOS call requires them. The int86 functions are similar to the intdos functions, except that int86 requires the interrupt number as the first argument. The remaining arguments are the same.

I have used hexadecimal constants frequently in the functions that make DOS and BIOS calls. That is because the DOS manual and the technical reference manual refer to the DOS function call numbers and interrupt numbers in hex. Leaving them in hex within the functions makes it easier to refer back and forth between the programs and the manuals.

There are three more functions that are useful in cases in which you might want to access display memory directly. The function in Fig. 2-4 returns the memory segment of the display adapter. The first character of the display is always at offset zero. This function is useful if you want to save a screen in a C array and then put it back on the screen later. Use the following function to move a screen into an array:

```
getscrn(buf)
char *buf;
{
    peek(scr_seg(), 0, buf, 4000);
}
```

Note that buf must be large enough to hold 4000 bytes. This will not work if the display is in a graphics mode. It will work for a monochrome adapter or a graphics adapter in 80 × 25 text mode.

The putscrn function will move an array to the screen:

```
putscrn(buf)
char *buf;
{
    poke(scr_seg(), 0, buf, 4000);
}
```

Be sure that a screen has first been saved in buf before calling putscrn. This function is useful for fast screen changes that are already stored in memory. Both peek and poke use an 8088 block-move instruction that moves 4000 bytes in a flash. A technique

```
scr_seg()
{
    char byte;

    peek(0x40, 0x63, &byte, 1);
    return(byte & 0x40 ? 0xb800 : 0xb000);
}
```

Fig. 2-4. The scr__seg function.

for fast screen updates using **putscrn** is shown in Section 2.9. Note that you cannot **printf(buf)**; **buf** contains the display attribute or color of each character, as well as the characters.

2.3 SETTING THE CURSOR

The appearance of the cursor can be controlled with a BIOS call. That is, it can be changed from an underline to a block, or made to disappear completely. The blinking action is controlled by the hardware, so we can't affect that.

Why would you want to control the appearance of the cursor? You might want to change it to a block to indicate to the user that some special mode in your program has been entered. Or you might want to make it disappear at times when it can be distracting. The **getline** function in Chapter 3 uses a block cursor to indicate that the user has entered the insert mode, as opposed to the type-over mode. The cursor is also turned off when the line is redrawn, to avoid the flash of the cursor as it moves rapidly across the screen drawing a blank line.

BIOS INT 0x10, function one, lets you specify the size of the cursor:

```
#include <dos.h>
static    int   start_line, end_line;

cursize(start, end)
int   start, end;
{
    union REGS u;

    u.h.ah = 1;
    u.h.ch = start_line = start;
    u.h.cl = end_line = end;
    int86(0x10, &u, &u);
}
```

cursize is called with the starting and ending horizontal scan line for the cursor. For a monochrome monitor, the system defaults to a start line of 11 and an end line of 12. These are six and seven, respectively, for the color graphics adapter. Before your program manipulates the cursor size with this function, it must know which monitor adapter is installed.

Why are they different? The monochrome monitor has 350 horizontal scan lines. Divide this by 25 display lines on the screen and you get 14 scan lines per display line. Twelve scan lines are used to display a character. The two remaining scan lines separate the display lines on the screen. The color adapter has 200 scan lines. The same arithmetic shows that there are eight scan lines per display line. Seven are used for character display and one for separation. Thus, the last scan line available for the cursor is either 13 or 7. You can see that if you set the scan lines for the cursor on a color graphics adapter to the settings used for the monochrome, you would be out of range. The cursor would simply disappear.

To make your programs that manipulate cursor size more general, the **curnorm** function can be used to initialize the cursor to the system defaults:

```
curnorm()
{
    if(get_crt() == 7)
```

```
          cursize(11,  12);
     else
          cursize( 6,   7);
)
```

Rather than calling **cursize** directly, you can call **curnorm**. It uses **get_crt** from the previous section to see if a monochrome adapter is installed. If not, it assumes the color card is installed. Before calling this function, your program should make sure that a color card has been set into text mode, as discussed in the previous section. Also, before calling any of the three functions, described in the following paragraphs, you must call either **curnorm** or **cursize**. They initialize the static data.

Notice that **cursize** saves the start and end line arguments in a static area. That makes it possible to write three more functions to manipulate the cursor without having to call **cursize**. They depend on the static data setup accomplished by a call to **curnorm** or **cursize**. Use **curnorm** for general cases, and **cursize** if you know which display adapter is installed. The first function is **curblock**:

```
curblock()
{
     cursize(4, end_line);
}
```

All of the functions that refer to the static data will have to be compiled as one source module, of course. The **curblock** and **curnorm** functions can be used to set the cursor to a block and back to normal, without having to concern yourself with the values to use for **start** and **end**; **cursize** remembers previous settings in **start_line** and **end_line**.

Now you can use **curoff** to turn the cursor off, without losing its current size settings.

```
curoff()
{
     cursize(start_line | 0x20, end_line);
}
```

curoff or **start_line** to set bit five and then calls **cursize** to set the new cursor size. This does not change the current size; it only makes the cursor disappear.

Then you can call **curon** to restore the cursor to its current setting:

```
curon()
{
     cursize(start_line & 0x1f, end_line);
}
```

Bit five is turned off, leaving the start line and end line unchanged. **cursize** turns the cursor back on again. Of course, you can modify the start and end lines in any of these functions if you prefer a different configuration. The program in Fig. 2-5 can be used to test these functions. It lets you test each of the functions that manipulate the cursor size. When entering the start line and end line for program selection one, separate them with a space. This selection allows you to experiment with cursor size directly. That way, you can determine whether you want to change the constants used in the functions for start and end lines. You will see that it is not necessary to call **curon** to turn the cursor back on if you call one of the other functions that sets the cursor size (ex-

```
#include <stdio.h>

main()
{
        int     start, end;
        char    buf[81], *gets();

        if(get_crt() != 7)
                set_crt(3);
        curnorm();
        while(1) {
                printf("\n1. Set cursor size\n2. Normal cursor\n");
                printf("3. Block cursor\n4. Cursor on\n5. Cursor off\n\n");
                if(gets(buf) == NULL)
                        break;
                switch(buf[0]) {
                case '1':
                        printf("Enter start-line end-line, eg: 5 7\n");
                        scanf("%d %d %*c", &start, &end);
                        cursize(start, end);
                        break;
                case '2':
                        curnorm();
                        break;
                case '3':
                        curblock();
                        break;
                case '4':
                        curon();
                        break;
                case '5':
                        curoff();
                        break;
                default:
                        printf("\n\tPlease enter a number between 1 and 5\n");
                        break;
                }
        }
}
```

Fig. 2-5. The program that tests the functions that manipulate the cursor size.

cept curoff, of course). Use curon to turn the cursor back on without changing its size. Note that the first thing the program does is to set the display into text mode, if it thinks that the display is not a monochrome. It then calls curnorm to initialize the start and end lines. To exit the program, type a Control-Z and a Return while the program is waiting for a menu selection.

2.4 ADDRESSING THE CURSOR

It probably comes as a surprise to many new C programmers that the standard library lacks a basic cursor positioning function. This is a necessity in most programs that have interactive data entry screens. As shown in Fig. 2-6 a BIOS call allows such a function to be implemented quite easily. PC BASIC programmers will recognize the name of the function. It is the same as the BASIC statement that performs cursor positioning. I have chosen the first position on the screen to be line one, column one. If you feel more at home with the first position being 0,0, you can change the function accordingly. **locate** checks the line and column values to make sure they are within the valid ranges. If they are not, **locate** returns without doing anything. Otherwise, the union is setup to make the BIOS function call number two of INT 0x10. **bh** is set to zero to indicate that the cursor positioning is desired for video page zero. The line and column must be decremented, because the BIOS call expects the line range between 0 and 24, and the column between 0 and 79. This function can be used with standard output functions.

The lines

```
locate(10, 40);
printf("hello");
```

do just what you think they would do: *hello* is printed on line 10 starting at column 40.

A function that returns the current position is also very helpful, though not absolutely necessary. Your program can be written in such a way that it always keeps track of the current location. That can be a bother, though—especially if it is not necessary. BIOS INT 0x10, function number three, will return the current cursor position:

```
curpos(line, col)
int  *line, *col;
{
    union REGS u;

    u.h.ah = 3;
    u.h.bh = 0;
    int86(0x10, &u, &u);
    *line = u.h.dh + 1;
    *col  = u.h.dl + 1;
}
```

Notice that the **line** and **col** arguments are pointers to integers. The function call must be **curpos(&line, &col)**, unless **line** and **col** are integer pointers themselves that have already been initialized to point at some integer. **line** and **col** must be defined elsewhere in your program.

```
locate(line, col)
int  line, col;
{
    union REGS u;

    if(line < 1 || line > 25 || col < 1 || col > 80)
        return;

    u.h.ah = 2;
    u.h.bh = 0;
    u.h.dh = --line;
    u.h.dl = --col;
    int86(0x10, &u, &u);
}
```

Fig. 2-6. The locate function.

curpos is not the most useful form of a function in all cases. Because it returns nothing, it cannot be used to pass a value to another function. For example, if you want to backspace the cursor, it would be necessary to do something like this:

```
curpos(&line, &col);
/* line and col were defined elsewhere
locate(line, col - 1);
/* backspace cursor one position */
```

It is simpler to do such things if the following two functions are added:

```
curlin()
{
      int   line, col;

      curpos(&line, &col);
      return(line);
}
```

returns the current line. The next function returns the current column.

```
curcol()
{
      int   line, col;

      curpos(&line, &col);
      return(col);
}
```

Now it is possible to backspace the cursor just by writing **locate(curlin( ), curcol( )** − 1). Other cursor manipulations are easier this way too. This also illustrates one of the reasons that **locate** was written to check the validity of the line and column arguments. There is no need to check the value returned by **curcol** in such cases. The cursor will simply stick at the left margin if this **locate** call is made with the cursor in column one.

2.5 SETTING VIDEO ATTRIBUTES AND COLORS

The IBM PC supports two types of video display: monochrome and color. Both of these displays provide a variety of text display characteristics, known as attributes. High intensity and reverse video text display are examples of attributes. The color display, of course, adds color capability. What is an attribute on a monochrome monitor is a color on a color monitor; that is, this is true when the color graphics adapter is in text mode. The monochrome adapter and the color graphics adapter in text mode both contain an attribute byte for each display character. The bit settings of the attribute byte determine the "color" of its associated character.

Programmers know that it is necessary to take advantage of attributes and colors if they want their product to have a professional appearance. Even more important, prudent use of colors or high intensity and reverse video can make a program easier to use. Regardless of the programming language used, a program's screens should be visually pleasing, and well-planned programs reserve certain colors or attributes for specific uses. For example, reverse video might be used for the display of error messages. Consistency is to the benefit of the user, and anything that benefits the user is ultimately beneficial to the programmer.

It follows, then, that control of video attributes is essential. The standard C library provides no functions, however, for setting video attributes and colors. This section and the next few provide a solution to this problem.

The purpose of this section is to begin the development of C functions that provide the programmer with the capability of displaying text attributes and colors as needed. This development will consist of three major parts. The first part is the subject of this section, and will consist of a function that is similar to the BASIC **color** statement. The next two sections present functions that depend on the **color** function.

This first step, the function similar to the BASIC **color** statement, is the simplest. That is because, basically, it does very little. The functions presented in the next section actually do the work, and are more complex. But the **color** function is essential to our objective. The **color** function is shown in Fig. 2-7. Note that this function returns nothing. Its purpose is to convert its arguments into a form required by the ROM BIOS call that will be used to display a character with the specified attribute or color. The foreground and background arguments are identical to those used by the BASIC **color** statement. For example, **color(15, 0)** causes subsequent text to be displayed in high intensity; **color(0, 7)** causes reverse video display; and **color(7, 0)** restores the display to normal, or low intensity. On a color display, **color(4, 1)** causes red text to be displayed on a blue background. See your BASIC reference manual's **color** statement for other combinations.

An example of the use of the color function might be

```
color(0, 7);
/* switch to reverse text display        */
puts( "This is reverse video." );
color(7, 0);
/* switch back to normal display         */
```

except that this won't work! Why? Because the C standard output functions know nothing of character attributes, or our **cattrib** variable. This means that we must provide our own **puts** type of function that makes use of our **cattrib**. That is the subject of the next sections. Before we leave this section, however, there is one more item that may be of interest.

Commonly used attributes and colors can be defined as functions or macros using the **color** function, so that you don't have to remember the numbers. For example, if

```
    /* fore is the foreground color or attribute,        */
    /* back is the background color or attribute.        */

    int   cattrib;     /* stores character attribute      */

    color(fore, back)
    int   fore, back;
    (
        cattrib = (( back << 4 ) ! ( fore & 0x0f )) & 0xff;
    )
```

Fig. 2-7. The color function.

reverse video is used frequently you might use one of the following:

```
/*****/
/* reverse video function                                         */
/*****/

reverse()
{
     color(0, 7);
}

/*****/
/* reverse video macro                                            */
/*****/

#define reverse()   color(0, 7)
```

This can make life a little simpler, since there is less chance for silly mistakes. Now that we have a method for setting the display attribute, we need a way to make it take effect. The next section does just that.

Before moving on, though, there is one more function that is useful with the color graphics adapter. border will set the border color when the adapter is in text mode.

```
border(color)
int  color;     /* 0 - 15 are valid */
{
     union REGS u;

     u.h.ah = 11;
     u.h.bh = 0;
     u.h.bl = color;
     int86(0x10, &u, &u);
}
```

The border is irrelevant in graphics modes, so this function call will have a different effect. The effect varies depending on whether the graphics adapter is in medium or high resolution mode. I will leave it to you to experiment with colors in the graphics modes.

2.6 CLEARING THE SCREEN

The functions in this section depend on the character attribute variable cattrib that was introduced with the color function in the previous section. Why would functions that clear the screen be dependent on the attribute, or color? They are dependent because clearing the screen really means filling it with blanks. A blank is a character, just like any other. It has an attribute associated with it. So the same attribute is used to write a blank to the screen as is used to write any other character.

The BIOS has two function calls that are used to scroll data on the screen. One function scrolls up, the other down. These functions can also be used to clear the screen to blanks. First, the BIOS call that lets us scroll a screen will be shown:

```
#include <dos.h>

scr_wndw(dir, n, r1, c1, r2, c2, att)
```

```
int  dir, n, r1, c1, r2, c2, att;
{
    union REGS u;

    u.h.ah = dir;
    u.h.al = n;
    u.h.ch = --r1;
    u.h.cl = --c1;
    u.h.dh = --r2;
    u.h.dl = --c2;
    u.h.bh = att;
    int86(0x10, &u, &u);
}
```

scr__wndw is referred to in the technical reference manual as the window scrolling functions. dir is the direction of the scroll desired; set dir to six for a scroll up, and to seven for a scroll down. These are the function call codes for BIOS INT 0x10 that provide scrolling. n is the number of lines to scroll. r1 and c1 are the row (or line) and column of the upper left corner of the display portion that is to be scrolled. r2 and c2 are the lower right corner. att is the attribute to be used with the blanks that fill the vacated line or lines. To scroll the screen up one line, as usually happens when a line is printed on the 25th display line, call scr__wndw as follows:

```
scr_wndw(6, 1, 1, 1, 25, 80, cattrib);
```

As you can see, the first two arguments request a scroll up of one line. The window to be scrolled has 1,1 as the upper left corner and 25,80 as the lower right corner; that is, the entire display is to be scrolled. cattrib is passed as the fill attribute, so that the color function can be used to set the desired attribute. Note that cattrib must be declared as an extern int if it is in a different source module. The row and column values have been decremented before passing them to the BIOS call for the same reason as in locate. Because locate assumes that 1,1 is the display home position, scr__wndw was written to conform with the same assumption. If you modified locate to use 0,0 as the home position, you will want to remove the decrements from scr__wndw to remain consistent.

It is apparent from the arguments to scr__wndw that it is quite flexible. It can be used to control a partial area of the display too. Does that give you ideas for "pop-ups?" There is another capability. If the n argument equals zero, the specified window is cleared rather than scrolled. That is the basis for the cls function, which clears the entire screen:

```
extern int cattrib;

cls()
{
    scr_wndw(6, 0, 1, 1, 25, 80, cattrib);
    locate(1, 1);
}
```

cls uses cattrib for convenience. It also homes the cursor, as you would expect a clear-screen function to do. Note that scr__wndw does not change the cursor position.

There are a couple more functions that you might wish to include in this module.

It can be handy to have a function that clears the screen only from the current cursor position to the end of the current line. Figure 2-8 shows such a function. You would probably first call **locate** to position the cursor before calling **cleol**. Some folks prefer to have **cleol** do the cursor positioning for them. Then **cleol** can be called with the line and column as arguments: **cleol(10, 40);**. If you like this method better, just add a call to **locate** within **cleol** in place of the call to **curlin**. In either case, the cursor is left at the **locate** position, ready for the next printing operation on the cleared line.

In conjunction with **cleol**, you often see a **cleop** function—that is, a clear-to-end-of-page function, as shown in Fig. 2-9. **locate** the cursor anywhere on the display and call **cleop**. The remainder of the current line is cleared, as well as all lines below it. **cleop** calls **cleol** to clear the current line. It then adds one to the current line and checks to make sure there are more lines following that need to be cleared before calling **scr_wndw** to do that. As with **cleol**, the cursor is left at the current position. This function can also be modified to work as **cleop(line, col)**, like **cleol** was, if you prefer.

2.7 CHARACTER DISPLAY

Now that the basics are out of the way, we can get to the character display functions that make use of **color**. I would, however, like to back up for just a minute to make sure that I have sufficiently emphasized the importance of the clear-screen functions, particularly **cls**. **cls** does more than clear the display screen. It also sets the attribute, or color, of the entire screen. With no text on the screen, all that is seen after a call to **cls** is the background color. **cls** is an easy way to set the entire background to a uniform color. This may not seem so significant on a monochrome monitor, but it becomes more important if you want your programs to take advantage of a color monitor. You can develop a logic pattern for all of your programs that will setup a monochrome or color monitor. The basic startup logic would go something like this:

```
if(get_crt() < 7) {
    set_crt(3);
    border(b_color);
}
```

This logic says that if this is not a monochrome monitor, then set the display to text mode. It also sets a border color. The usual choice for the border color is the background color that you want for the entire screen. Then the screen background will have the same color from edge to edge. The next step would be to call **color** and **cls** to set

```
cleol()
{
    int line;

    line = curlin();
    scr_wndw(6, 0, line, curcol(), line, 80, cattrib);
}
```

Fig. 2-8. The cleol function.

```
cleop()
{
        int line;

        cleol();
        if((line = curlin() + 1) < 26)
                scr_wndw(6, 0, line, 1, 25, 80, cattrib);
}
```

Fig. 2-9. The cleop function.

the background:

```
color(f_color, b_color);
cls();
```

These steps will ensure that your program starts out with a display screen of uniform appearance, whether it is running on a monochrome or color monitor. Note that **b__color** was used in the call to **border** and the call to **color**. This sets the border and background to the same color. At this point, **f__color** does not show up, as it will not be seen until characters are displayed.

Now on with the character display methods: as I explained earlier, the only way to display attributes in the absence of **ansi.sys** is to make BIOS calls. What is needed, then, is the equivalent of **putchar**. The character should be displayed in the attribute or color that we desire. Because the **color** function sets an external variable, **cattrib**, to the desired foreground and background attributes, a function can be written to use that variable just as the clear-screen functions do:

```
#include <dos.h>
extern  int cattrib;

bwrite(c)
char    c;
{
        union   REGS u;

        u.h.ah = 9;
        u.h.al = c;
        u.h.bh = u.h.ch = 0;
        u.h.cl = 1;
        u.h.bl = cattrib;
        int86(0x10, &u, &u);
}
```

bwrite calls BIOS INT 0x10 function 9 to write a character and attribute at the current cursor location. Register CX must contain the number of times to write the character. This is set to one, for a single character. This BIOS function does not advance the cursor. Repeated calls to this function will cause each character to be written over the top of the previous character. That is, the current cursor location is not changed by a call to this function. Obviously, this function alone is not enough. In fact, you will probably never call this function directly. Another function is needed to make this function perform like a call to **putchar**. Actually, two more functions are needed:

```
btty(c)
char    c;
{
        union   REGS    u;

        u.h.ah = 14;
        u.h.al = c;
        u.x.bx = 0x0001;
        int86(0x10, &u, &u);
}
```

btty is a function that makes another BIOS INT 0x10 call, this time to function 14. It does advance the cursor position like **putchar**. Unfortunately, it does not allow the use of colors and attributes. We are going to use it, though, because it will handle some of the control characters for us.

Figure 2-10 shows the function that will work almost like **putchar**. The cursor is advanced as might be expected, and color can be used. As you can see, this function is somewhat more complex than the two previous ones, but neither of those alone or in combination will do what is needed. **bwrite** handles the color/attribute problem, and **btty** handles the cursor problem. You could solve the problem by calling **btty** with a character, after each call to **bwrite** with that character. That is a shotgun approach, however, that is neither very elegant or efficient in terms of speed. **bputcr** in Fig. 2-10 is a far better approach. It would be needed anyway, as it does some things that **btty** does not.

btty is used for its handling of some of the control characters. Let's see how **bputcr** takes advantage of this. When **bputcr** is called, its first action is to see if the character is one of a few of the possible control characters. If the character is a BELL, backspace, linefeed, or carriage return, then **btty** is called to handle the character. In addition, if the character is a backspace, **bwrite** is called to write a blank over the new cursor position established by the backspace action. This is done because the BIOS tty function causes a nondestructive backspace. Normally, you would prefer the destructive backspace, so **bputcr** takes care of that.

btty does nothing for a tab control character, ASCII 9. **bputcr** will expand a tab character to the next eight-column tab stop by replacing it with the appropriate number of blanks. Otherwise, you would see a funny character instead of the nicely aligned columns that you expect. You probably noticed that **bputcr** calls itself to do this. Finally, if the character is none of those control characters, then it is treated as a regular display character. That is the **default** action of the **switch** in this function. **bwrite** is called to display the character with the attribute last set by a call to **color**.

Even though **btty** is used to handle carriage returns and line feeds, which also results in scrolling if a line feed occurs on the last line of the display, **bputcr** must take care of cursor positioning in all other cases. Thus after the character has been displayed with **bwrite**, the current position is obtained. The current column position is incremented and checked for overflow beyond the right margin. **bputcr** also handles line wrap. This occurs when a character is displayed in the last column, column 80. Some terminals and printers do not attempt to handle line wrap. That is, any characters beyond the right margin simply disappear. I prefer that the characters wrap around to the next

```
/********/

bputcr(c)
char    c;
{
        int     row, col;

        switch(c) {
        case 7:
        case 8:
        case 10:
        case 13:
                btty(c);
                if(c == 8)
                        bwrite(' ');
                break;
        case 9:
                bputcr(' ');
                while((curcol() - 1) & 7)
                        bputcr(' ');
                break;
        default:
                bwrite(c);
                curpos(&row, &col);
                if(++col > 80) {
                        col = 1;
                        if(++row > 25) {
                                row = 25;
                                scr_wndw(6,1,1,1,25,80,cattrib);
                        }
                }
                locate(row, col);
                break;
        }
}
```

Fig. 2-10. The bputcr function.

display line. That is the way **putchar** and DOS work too.

If the column is beyond the right margin, then the column is reset to one and the current line is incremented. If the new line is not beyond the bottom of the display, then the cursor is located to the new position with a call to **locate,** and the function is done. If the new line is greater than 25, however, the screen must be scrolled. The current line is reset to the bottom line, and **scr_wndw** is called to perform the scroll. Then the call to **locate** positions the cursor for the next character display on the bottom line.

Looking at all the logic a character goes through before it finally finds its way to the screen probably makes you think that this function is going to update the screen very slowly. Actually, it is much faster than the C library functions, and even faster than DOS. That is because they too must go through the same logic and are concerned with other things, as well. With **bputcr** you will be able to create displays not only with greater speed but also with color. This function is not interrupted by a Control-Break.

You might be wondering why **bputcr** was so named. The **putc** part, of course, comes straight from C. I used the **b** to indicate that this function depends on BIOS calls to display the character. This is to emphasize that the output cannot be redirected, because standard output is bypassed. The r added to the end of the name stands for *raw*. It means that this is a raw output function, in that a new line is not translated into a carriage-return line-feed sequence as is done by the standard output functions. Sometimes translation is not desired. bputcr can be called directly to avoid this translation. To maintain compatibility with the C output functions, however, you might want to call bputc.

```
bputc(c)
char c;
{
      if(c == '\n')
            bputcr('\r');
      bputcr(c);
}
```

bputc can be called whenever you need the translation operation. It just adds a carriage return whenever it sees a newline character. I have found that my programs usually call bputc, resorting to bputcr only for special situations. One of those special situations is when writing communications programs. You will see bputcr used in those programs in Chapters 5 and 6.

Finally, an equivalent to puts is needed to display entire strings using color.

```
bputs(s)
char *s;
{
      while(*s)
            bputc(*s++);
}
```

Obviously, this function displays an entire string at the current color setting. Notice that it calls bputc rather than bputcr. I have not found a need in my own programming for untranslated string output, so I have not created such a function. If you need one, just change the call to bputc to bputcr. You might want to name that function bputsr for consistency.

2.8 VIDEO ATTRIBUTES AND COLORS REVISITED

The purpose of this section is to integrate the functions for video control. The setcolor program presented later in this section uses many of the functions developed in this chapter. It illustrates the basic technique you would follow in using these functions. The setcolor program allows a user to select the colors or attributes for a program.

If you have not already done so, now would be a good time to combine the functions from this chapter into a link library. Many of the programs presented from here on use many of these functions, as well as those developed later on. The new functions can be added to the library as they appear. Keeping the functions in a library will ease the link process.

There is one more set of functions that will be used in the setcolor program. These functions will be called to set the actual display attributes or colors. You might want to compile all of the functions in Fig. 2-11 in a module called colorsub.c and then add this module to the link library.

```
int      sub_clrs[][2] = (
(0 , 1),
(15, 1),
(0,  7));

lolite()
{
        color(sub_clrs[0][0], sub_clrs[0][1]);
}

hilite()
{
        color(sub_clrs[1][0], sub_clrs[1][1]);
}

reverse()
{
        color(sub_clrs[2][0], sub_clrs[2][1]);
}

set_bord()
{
        if(get_crt() == 3)
                border(sub_clrs[0][1]);
}
/********/
```

Fig. 2-11. The module that allows your programs to interface conveniently with the setcolor program's output.

The purpose of the module in Fig. 2-11 is to allow your programs to interface conveniently with the **setcolor** program's output. It works this way. A user executes the **setcolor** program to set the colors desired. These colors, which are arguments to the color function, are saved in a disk file. Any program that calls the functions in Fig. 2-11 can then use the colors selected by the user. A small function in the **setcolor** program is used to read the file containing the color arguments selected by the user. This function can easily be incorporated into your programs. Your program would simply call this function to read the color file, if it exists. Otherwise, default colors are used. **setcolor** demonstrates this concept.

Notice that the first thing that is done in Fig. 2-11 is that an array is initialized with six digits. These correspond to the foreground and background attributes for three different color combinations. The first two digits, that is sub__clrs[0][0] and sub__clrs[0][1], were selected for use by the lolite function as the foreground and background attributes, respectively. lolite was so named because the values chosen will produce low intensity characters on the monochrome display. On a color card, these values produce black text on a blue background. Note that set__bord will set a border to the same color as the lolite background, if it finds that the display is in 80-column color text mode.

The hilite function uses the next two values, which produce high intensity characters on the monochrome display and white characters on the same blue background on the color display. **reverse** produces reverse video on the monochrome display and black text on a gray background on the color display with the last two values.

These functions are meant to represent a technique. You may add to them for other color combinations that your particular application might require. Of course, you will need to add more elements to the sub_clrs array for storage of the new color combinations. The array was made externally available so that another function can access the array directly. setcolor, for example, loads this array with the user-selected colors that are stored in the colors file. Your application would do the same thing. The point is, if your program calls the functions in Fig. 2-11 rather than making direct calls to the color function, then your program does not need to be changed in order to change the colors displayed, nor is the user "stuck" with your choice of colors. Instead, the user can select whatever colors he might desire (with setcolor), and your program can easily use those selections. These functions also make it a little easier to use display attributes and colors in a consistent fashion throughout your program.

The setcolor Program

The setcolor program in Fig. 2-12 uses most of the video functions that have appeared so far in this chapter. The program has one screen, as shown in Fig. 2-13. Selections one through three in the top half of the screen correspond to the color settings that will be used by the lolite, hilite, and reverse functions in the colorsub.c module presented earlier in this section. All three functions and the set_bord function will be used to display this screen. The entire screen will be redrawn whenever the color is changed, so that the user can see the effect of the color selection immediately.

The primary indicators of the current color selection are the first three menu selections. That is, menu selection one will be displayed with lolite, two with hilite, and three with reverse. If you are running setcolor on a monochrome display, you may need to adjust the contrast control on the display to see the difference between lolite and hilite. The rest of the screen is drawn in lolite, except for the title and the two input prompts, which are drawn with hilite. The background and the border colors are set to the lolite background, if setcolor thinks this is a color display.

To change a color setting, the user types a one, two, or three and Return. Then foreground and background colors are selected from the bottom half of the screen. The two numbers corresponding to the desired foreground and background colors are typed with a space separating them. As soon as the user presses Return, the screen is redrawn with the new colors.

When all colors have been set as desired, the user selects menu item four to save the current color settings and exit the program. The color values, as used by the color function, are written in an ASCII file called color.cfg. When setcolor starts up, it checks for the existence of this file. If found, the program sets its colors to those in the file. The setcolor function get_colors does the checking and loading. This function illustrates how your own application can use the colors saved by setcolor.

setcolor makes some assumptions about the way a program will be using color or attributes like bold and reverse video. If these assumptions do not correspond to your particular application, you might need to modify setcolor to use colors in a manner consistent with the application. Of course, you can create a different version of setcolor for each application program. To avoid confusion in such cases, be sure to have each setcolor version write a color.cfg file with a unique filename. Alternatively, if your

```
/**
* NAME
*       setcolor - set / save display attributes or colors
*
* DESCRIPTION
*       Displays color settings found in "color.cfg", if any. Otherwise,
* default colors are used. Color changes are displayed and saved, if desired,
* into "color.cfg".
*
*       Applications wishing to use the setup in color.cfg may do so by
* using a function like get_colors, below, and the functions in colorsub.c
* within the application.
**/

#include <stdio.h>

/* remove these four #defines to use window.c functions                 */
#define wcls    cls
#define wputs   bputs
#define wlocate locate
#define refresh()
/********/

struct  menu    {
        int     row;
        int     col;
        int     (*set_clr)();
        char    *txt;
        };

extern  int     lolite(), hilite(), reverse();

static  char    clr_num[3][6];

static  struct  menu    menu1[] = {
{ 4,37, lolite, clr_num[0]},
{ 5,37, hilite, clr_num[1]},
{ 6,37, reverse,clr_num[2]},
{ 1,35, hilite, "COLOR SETUP"},
{ 2, 1, lolite,
"================================================================================"
},
{ 4, 9, lolite, "1. Low intensity  (lolite)"},
{ 4,49, lolite, "4. Save and exit"},
{ 5, 9, hilite, "2. High intensity (hilite)"},
{ 5,49, lolite, "5. Quit, do NOT save setup"},
{ 6, 9, reverse,"3. Attention!     (reverse)"},
{ 8,17, hilite, "Enter a number: "},
{ 9, 9, hilite, "Enter foreground background numbers (eg. 4 0): "},
{11, 1, lolite,
"============================ COLOR SELECTIONS ==============================="
},
{12,17, hilite, "Foreground"},
{12,49, lolite, "||"},
{12,56, hilite, "Background"},
{13,49, lolite, "||"},
{14, 1, lolite,
```

Fig. 2-12. The setcolor program.

```
"    O - black              8 - dark gray          ||      O - black"},
{15, 1, lolite,
"    1 - blue               9 - light blue         ||      1 - blue"},
{16, 1, lolite.
"    2 - green             10 - light green        ||      2 - green"),
{17, 1, lolite,
"    3 - cyan              11 - light cyan         ||      3 - cyan"),
{18, 1, lolite,
"    4 - red               12 - light red          ||      4 - red"),
{19, 1, lolite,
"    5 - magenta                   13 - light magenta    ||      5 - magenta"),
{20, 1, lolite,
"    6 - brown             14 - yellow             ||      6 - brown"),
{21, 1, lolite,
"    7 - light gray        15 - white              ||      7 - light gray"),
{22, 1, lolite,
"=================================================================================="
},
{ 0, 0, (int (*)()) 0, NULL}};

static   int      prmpt[][2] = {8,33,9,56};
static   char     clrfile[] = "color.cfg";
/********/

main()
{
        int     i, fore, back, c;
        char    buf[80];
        FILE    *fp;
        extern  int      sub_clrs[][2];

        if(get_crt() < 7)
                set_crt(3);
        get_colors();

        while(1) {
                set_bord();
                lolite();
                wcls();
                for(i = 0; i < 3; i++)
                        sprintf(clr_num[i],"%2d %2d",
                                sub_clrs[i][0],sub_clrs[i][1]);

                do_menu(menu1);
                get_prmpt(prmpt[0][0], prmpt[0][1], buf);
                for(i = 0; (c = buf[i]) == ' '; i++);
                switch(c) {
                case '1':
                case '2':
                case '3':
                        get_prmpt(prmpt[1][0], prmpt[1][1], buf);
                        if(sscanf(buf,"%d %d", &fore, &back) > 1) {
                                if(fore >= 0 && fore <= 15)
                                        sub_clrs[c - '1'][0] = fore;
                                if(back >= 0 && back <= 7)
                                        sub_clrs[c - '1'][1] = back;
                        }
                        break;
                case '4':
                        locate(25,5);
                        if((fp = fopen(clrfile, "w")) == NULL) {
                                reverse();
                                bputs(" Cannot write ");
```

```
                                        bputs(clrfile);
                        } else {
                                for(i = 0; i < 3; i++)
                                        fprintf(fp,"%d %d ",
                                                sub_clrs[i][0],sub_clrs[i][1]);
                                fprintf(fp,"\n");
                                bputs(" Color setup saved.");
                        }
                case '5':
                        locate(25,1);
                        lolite();
                        exit(0);
                        break;
                }
        }
}
/********/

get_colors()
{
        extern  int     sub_clrs[][2];
        FILE    *fp;
        int     c[3][2], i;

        if((fp = fopen(clrfile, "r")) != NULL) {
                if(fscanf(fp,"%d %d %d %d %d %d", &c[0][0], &c[0][1],
                        &c[1][0], &c[1][1], &c[2][0], &c[2][1]) == 6)
                        for(i = 0; i < 3; i++) {
                                sub_clrs[i][0] = c[i][0];
                                sub_clrs[i][1] = c[i][1];
                        }
                fclose(fp);
        }
}
/********/

get_prmpt(row, col, s)
int     row, col;
char    *s;
{
        char    *ps = s;
        int     c;

        locate(row, col);
        hilite();
        while((c = getch()) != '\r')
                switch(c) {
                case 8:
                        if(ps > s) {
                                bputc(c);
                                ps--;
                        }
                        break;
                case ' ':
                        *ps++ = c;
                        bputc(c);
                        break;
                default:
                        if(c >= '0' && c <= '9') {
                                *ps++ = c;
                                bputc(c);
                        }
```

```
                        break;
            }

        *ps = '\0';
}
/********/

do_menu(pm)
struct menu *pm;
{
        for(; pm->row; pm++) {
                wlocate(pm->row, pm->col);
                (*pm->set_clr)();
                wputs(pm->txt);
        }
        refresh();
}
/********/
```

program already uses a configuration file, you can modify **setcolor** to use your present configuration file.

The assumptions that **setcolor** follows are fairly simple. First, it assumes that **lolite** will be the primary color setting used by an application. That is, most of the screen will be drawn in **lolite**. That is why the entire background and the border are set to the **lolite** background color before any text is displayed. To conform to this assumption, your application should do the same when it starts. Incidentally, you will probably want to change the wording of the **setcolor** menu selections to something more meaningful in the version of **setcolor** that you provide to the users of your programs.

Secondly, **setcolor** assumes that **hilite** will be used selectively in limited situations to provide emphasis, such as in titles and input prompts, for example. **reverse** might be used for error messages and warnings. Of course, there is no reason why you cannot use **reverse** or **hilite** for any reason you desire. That would represent no change in the philosophy of **setcolor**. As written, **setcolor** really presents few limitations to an application's use of color or attributes. After all, the user is free to change things around with **setcolor** anyway. The point is that **setcolor** illustrates one possible technique for developing consistency in the use of colors throughout an application, as well as allowing the user some choice in the matter.

I would like to make a few comments about the **setcolor** programming. It illustrates one way in which your application can be written to make use of the colors saved by setcolor. In Fig. 2-12, the first thing you will see is some #define statements. They redefine some functions used in the program that will be developed in the next section. They are not needed at this point, though, so they are changed to existing functions. The new functions are added to speed the screen display; otherwise, the program is not changed. If the program is entered as it appears in Fig. 2-12, it will be necessary to remove only the #define statements to create a version of **setcolor** that uses the functions developed in the next section. The next part of the code begins the development of the screen display.

While the **setcolor** screen in Fig. 2-13 is not complicated, there is a lot of information packed into it. Because some parts of the screen had to be displayed in specific color attributes, it was not possible to simply display a line at a time. This problem exists with most interactive program screens. To create the original screen appearance, I used an editor to enter the screen just as I wanted it to appear, without colors of course. After printing the screen to hardcopy, it was easy to use a data processing ruler, with one-tenth inch markings, to determine the column of individual display items. The screen did not need to be retyped into the program. It was just edited into it.

To control the individual display items, **struct menu** is declared to contain certain information about each one. The structure contains four items of information: the row and column placement, a pointer to a function, and a pointer to the text itself. The function pointer will be initialized to point to the particular function needed to set the color for the corresponding display text. The **lolite**, **hilite**, and **reverse** functions are declared so the compiler can create the appropriate information for the linker to initialize the pointers. Jumping ahead into the **main** function for just a moment, another external declaration is made. This time it is to the **sub_clrs** array. Normal applications will not need such a declaration, because they will not be altering the information in the array. **setcolor** will, and will also be displaying its contents.

Continuing in the data definitions, a three by six character array called **clr_num** is defined to hold the text contents of the **sub_clrs** array for display on the screen. Then an array of **menu** structures is defined and initialized with the data for the entire display screen. This array has been named **menu1**. If there were more screens, they could be defined in other similar arrays with names like **menu2**, and so on. Notice that the **txt** pointers of the first three **menu1** array elements are initialized to point to the **clr_num** array. The order of appearance of display items in the **menu1** array is immaterial. These items could just as easily have been defined in any position within the **menu1** array. They were placed at the beginning here only to emphasize their role as variable display fields. The remaining display fields are constants. The last element of the **menu1** array contains null values for all variables in the structure, to indicate the end of the array. **int (*)( )** casts the zero to a null function pointer.

```
                           COLOR SETUP
===============================================================================

      1. Low intensity  (lolite)   O  1      4. Save and exit
      2. High intensity (hilite)  15  1      5. Quit, do NOT save setup
      3. Attention!     (reverse)  O  7

           Enter a number:
      Enter foreground background numbers (eg. 4 O):


=========================== COLOR SELECTIONS ==================================
         Foreground                      ||      Background
                                         ||
      O - black        8 - dark gray     ||      O - black
      1 - blue         9 - light blue    ||      1 - blue
      2 - green       10 - light green   ||      2 - green
      3 - cyan        11 - light cyan    ||      3 - cyan
      4 - red         12 - light red     ||      4 - red
      5 - magenta     13 - light magenta ||      5 - magenta
      6 - brown       14 - yellow        ||      6 - brown
      7 - light gray  15 - white         ||      7 - light gray
===============================================================================
```

Fig. 2-13. The screen from the setcolor program.

Any screen defined as a **struct menu** array can be displayed with the **do__menu** function in the program. This function is passed a pointer to a **struct menu** array with nulls in the last element assumed for the end; in this case, the call is **do__menu(menu1)**. **do__menu** loops through the array until **pm – >row** equals zero. Of course, any null variable in the array can be used for the termination test. Each loop iteration positions the cursor, calls the color-set function, and displays the text. Remember that the previous #**define** statements changed the function names that appear in **do__menu** as **wlocate** and **wputs**.

To end the static data definitions, a two by two **int** array named **prmpt** is defined to contain the screen location for the user input, and the name of the file that will contain the saved colors is defined.

The data represents the largest part of the program, in a way. The logic is fairly simple. At startup, **setcolor** checks the display mode with a call to **get__crt**. If it appears that there is a color card, it is set to the 80-column text mode. **get__colors** is called to load any user-defined colors into the **sub__clrs** array. Notice that **setcolor** does not care what happens in **get__colors**. If the **color.cfg** file is not found, the default values in **sub__clrs** will be used. A nice addition to this program would be to add a return value to the **get__colors** function so that the calling routine could tell if the file has been located. If not, the program could display a message stating that it was using default colors.

The main program loop then begins at **while(1)** and stays within this loop until the user selects an exit from the menu. When this loop is entered, **set__bord** is called. It will set a border only if the current display mode was set to three above. Then a uniform background is set with the calls to **lolite** and the clear-screen function. **wcls** is one of the redefined functions that will be developed in the next section. Recall that the clear-screen function fills the screen with the attribute currently set, and the attribute was set with the call to **lolite**. The contents of **sub__clrs** is converted to ASCII and stored in the **menu1** array for display with a call to **sprintf**. Finally, the screen is displayed with **do__menu**.

Now that the screen has been displayed with the current colors, all that is left to do is to get the user's selections and repeat the loop. The **get__prmpt** function positions the cursor after the input prompt and gets a string of digits from the keyboard. **get__prmpt** recognizes only digits, backspace, and Return as input. The **getch** function is a Lattice and Microsoft compiler library function for direct console input. It returns a character each time a key is pressed. **getchar** will not work here because it buffers input until return is pressed. In addition, **getch** does not translate a return to a newline, as the standard library functions do, so the test is for \r rather than \n. **get__prmpt** is called to get both the menu choice and the color selections. After color selections are returned, **sub__clrs** is set to the new selections according to the menu choice. The loop is then repeated to set the screen and border to the new colors.

The user can choose to save the current colors, in which case the contents of **sub__clrs** is written to the file. This menu selection drops through to the next menu choice, which is an exit, without saving the colors. The next section adds a few functions to replace some of the screen display functions used in **setcolor**. Even though the screen updating is pretty fast with the BIOS functions, the new ones will make the update appear instantaneously.

2.9   CREATING FAST SCREENS

As we have seen earlier in this chapter, screens can be updated quickly by writing directly to the screen memory. A screen such as the one in **setcolor** can be created within program memory, and then placed in display memory at once. This gives the appearance that the screen pops into place, rather than being written a character at a time.

The functions in Fig. 2-14 provide a way to build a screen image in program memory and then to move that image to the physical display screen. The name of this module is **window.c.** It includes functions that are counterparts to the BIOS functions developed earlier in the chapter. That is, there are functions for cursor manipulation and text display. The difference between the **window** functions and the BIOS functions is that all **screen** manipulations occur in a memory buffer rather than on the display screen. When you are ready for the image to appear on the display, your program calls the **refresh** function.

There are two reasons why the **window** functions create screens so much more quickly than the functions that make BIOS calls. One reason has already been discussed the entire display is moved at once with the **poke** function. Because the **poke** function moves memory with the 8088 block-move instruction, there is no faster way to put data on the screen. The second reason is because of the fact that no BIOS calls are made. BIOS calls to the video interrupt take time. Many of those calls must program the video display circuitry. Probably the slowest call is the one that displays a character. This call enters two delay loops that wait for a horizontal retrace. Displaying a character between retrace intervals prevents snow from appearing on the color display. If horizontal retrace is ignored when data is moved to the display memory, snow is barely noticeable if there is a second or more between writes to display memory. Most menu displays are spaced much more than a second apart, so the snow is negligible. If, however, each character were displayed in rapid succession without waiting for retrace—that is, by calling **refresh** in a loop for each character—the snow would be very visible. Therefore, functions like **refresh** work fine for entire menu displays that generally stay on the screen for at least a few seconds. I have used the **refresh** function on color displays with little or no snow appearance. This problem does not occur with the monochrome display.

Because no BIOS calls are made to position the cursor or move a character to the memory screen, updates occur quickly. I think you will be pleased with the speed at which **setcolor** rebuilds its screen using the window functions. The screen change after each color selection is instantaneous. All you need to do to add the window functions to **setcolor** is to remove the **#define** statements at the beginning of the **setcolor** program. Then compile and link with the **window** module.

You will notice that there is a **window.c** function corresponding to most of the BIOS cursor control and display functions. Each function name in **window.c** is the same as its BIOS function counterpart, except that a **w** has been added at the beginning of each name. The existing character attribute set by **color** is used by the window functions, as you can see by the external declaration of **cattrib.**

When you are using the window functions, it is important to call **wcls** before any of the others. **wcls** sets the cursor to the home position and fills the memory screen in the WINDOW structure with blanks. Note that the cursor I am talking about here

```
/**
* NAME
*       window.c -- module for window functions
*
* DESCRIPTION
*       Provides several functions for manipulating a memory buffer
* as if it was the display screen.
**/
extern  int     cattrib;          /* pull in color() function          */


struct  swindow {
        int     row;
        int     col;
        char    scrn[25][160];
};
#define WINDOW  struct swindow


static  WINDOW  wndw;
static  WINDOW  *pw = &wndw;


/*********/
wlocate(line, col)
int     line,col;
{
        if(line < 1 || line > 25 || col < 1 || col > 80)
                return;
        pw->row = line;
        pw->col = col;
}
/*********/
wcurlin()
```

Fig. 2-14. The window module.

```
{
        return(pw->row);
}
/********/
wcurcol()
{
        return(pw->col);
}
/********/
wcls()
{
        short   blank;

        blank = (cattrib << 8) | 32;
        repmem(pw->scrn[0], (char *) &blank, 2, 2000);
        pw->row = pw->col = 1;
}
/********/
wputs(s)
char    *s;
{
        while(*s)
                wputc(*s++);
}
/********/
refresh()
{
        poke(scr_seg(), 0, pw->scrn[0], 4000);
}
/********/
wscroll()
{
```

```
          short     space;


          movmem(pw->scrn[1], pw->scrn[0], 4000 - 160);

          space = (cattrib << 8) | 32;

          repmem(pw->scrn[24], (char *)&space, 2, 80);

}

/*********/

wputcr(c)

char      c;

{

          switch(c) {

          case 8:

                    if(pw->col > 1) {

                              pw->col--;

                              wputcr(' ');

                              pw->col--;

                    }

                    break;

          case '\r':

                    pw->col = 1;

                    break;

          case '\n':

                    pw->row++;

                    break;

          case '\t':

                    wputcr(' ');

                    while((pw->col - 1) & 7)

                              wputcr(' ');

                    break;

          default:

                    pw->scrn[pw->row - 1][pw->col * 2 - 2] = c;

                    pw->scrn[pw->row - 1][pw->col * 2 - 1] = cattrib;
```

```
                    pw->col++;

                    break;
        }


        if(pw->col > 80) {

                    pw->col = 1;

                    pw->row++;

        }


        if(pw->row > 25) {

                    pw->row = 25;

                    wscroll();

        }
}
/*********/
wputc(c)
char    c;
{
        if(c == '\n')

                    wputcr('\r');

        wputcr(c);
}
/********/
wcleol()
{
        short   blanks, space;

        blanks = 81 - pw->col;

        space = (cattrib << 8) | 32;

        repmem(&pw->scrn[pw->row - 1][pw->col - 1],(char *)&space, 2, blanks);
}
/*********/
```

```
wcleop()

{

        short blanks, space;


        wcleol();
        if(pw->row < 25) {
                blanks = (25 - pw->row) * 80;
                space = (cattrib << 8) | 32;
                repmem(pw->scrn[pw->row],(char *)&space, 2, blanks);
        }

}
/********/
```

is simply a WINDOW position stored in the structure, not the display screen cursor. Because these functions do not manipulate the real cursor, the display cursor is at an unknown position when the WINDOW is moved to the display screen with a call to **refresh**. A subsequent call to **locate** is needed to position the real cursor. You can see that **setcolor** takes care of this. The screen is created in WINDOW by the **do_menu** function, if the #define statements have been removed. Then **do_menu** calls **refresh** to move the WINDOW to the display screen, upon return from **do_menu**, **get_prmpt** is called; it calls **locate** to position the cursor for user input.

As demonstrated by **setcolor**, you will want to set **color**, as with a call to **lolite**, before calling **wcls**. It fills the WINDOW with the current attribute just as **cls** fills the display screen with the current attribute. **setcolor** mixes calls to the window functions with calls to the BIOS functions; they combine conveniently.

The functions in **window.c** perform similarly to their BIOS counterparts, but there are some differences worth noting. Most importantly, the window functions are not portable. In the interest of speed, I took advantage of the knowledge that the 8088 stores a **short int** in two bytes, and that the bytes are stored in least significant, most significant order. That is why the character-attribute combination may appear to be backwards when they are combined into the **short** (see **wcls**). If you prefer portability over speed, you can change the **scrn[25][160]** to an array of structures. For example, a structure can be created for the character and attribute:

```
typedef   struct    (
    char c;
    /* stores the character */
    char a;
    /* stores the attribute */
    ) CHARACTER;
```

and **struct swindow** would be changed to:

```
struct      swindow {
    int  row;
    int  col;
    CHARACTER scrn[25][80];
    } wndw;
```

A character and attribute can then be stored into the WINDOW structure with the following, assuming the **c** contains a **char:**

```
pw->scrn[0][0].c = c;
pw->scrn[0][0].a = cattrib;
```

These lines would put a character and attribute into the first character position. Don't forget to subtract one from the **row** and **col** when using them as array indexes; the above index would be [pw – >row – 1][pw – >col – 1] if you are following the assumption that the home position is at **1,1**, as these functions currently assume.

What we are doing here is defining a 25 by 80 array of CHARACTER structures. Filling an area with blanks, as would be necessary in **wcls**, would be done with a looping mechanism. This reduces, but does not eliminate, the portability problem. The functions will still be quite fast, but remember that assuming this type of display still limits portability from a hardware standpoint. We have, however, eliminated the dependence upon the way that the 8088 stores a data type, for now **wcls** could be written:

```
wcls()
{
    int  r, c;

    for(r = 0; r < 25; r++)
        for(c = 0; c < 80; c++) {
            pw->scrn[r][c].c = c;
            pw->scrn[r][c].a = cattrib;
        }
}
```

Some of the other functions will have to be modified to account for this new WINDOW structure; in particular, those functions that refer to the **scrn** array. I don't want to take all the fun out of it, though, so I will leave that up to you.

Chapter 3

The Keyboard

Working with the IBM PC keyboard is simpler than working with the video display. There is not the variety of keyboard types to deal with that there is with display types. There are, however, a few different ways available to retrieve keyboard input. This choice brings up the question of how keyboard input should be handled for a particular program. If you have ever tried to write an interactive program using **getchar**, you know that there are problems. As I mentioned in Chapter 2, **getchar** buffers input until return is pressed. Therefore, it is impossible to write a program with a **live** keyboard. That is, the program cannot examine each character as it is received from the keyboard. This prevents such things as single-character action commands.

You have seen some programs that take advantage of the PC's special keys—the function keys, and the Insert and Delete keys, and so on. To do this, those programs must be using a function other than **getchar** for their keyboard input. The two most common solutions to this problem are to make a direct call to the DOS or to the BIOS functions.

3.1 STANDARD INPUT CONSIDERATIONS

As with the standard output, you must consider whether your program needs the capability to redirect input. This ability is a must for filter programs. Even when input is not redirected, filter programs usually do not require much interaction with the user. Often, the command line is the only input required. In these cases, the standard input functions like **getchar** and **gets** are the best, if not the only, choice.

Many compilers provide a console input function that does return a character as it is received; that is, it returns a character without buffering. The **getch** function of the Lattice library does this by making direct calls to DOS. Because **getch** calls a DOS function, input can be redirected to programs that use this function (in DOS versions 2.0 and up). The results are not entirely satisfactory, though. If a file being redirected as input does not contain the DOS end-of-file character, Control-Z, the program hangs waiting for more input. The only way to regain control of the computer is to press control-break or reboot. Those solutions are, of course, unacceptable. Either causes immediate termination of the program, and if you have disabled control-break with the functions in Chapter 2, only a reboot will get you out.

getch can be modified to call a different DOS function so that it will recognize the end of a file whether the marker is present or not. Calling DOS function 0x3f with the **intdosx** function to return a single character will signal end-of-file in any case. This function can be very useful. Input can be redirected, but is not buffered the way it is with **getchar**. Using function 0x3f, you can create programs that do not link in the standard input routines from the library, reducing the size of an EXE file by as much as 10,000 bytes. You will probably also need a function for standard output that bypasses the library routines. DOS function 0x40 is the answer. It can be used to replace the **putch** function, and has the advantage that it returns an error compatible with **putchar**.

These modified **getch** and **putch** functions are not the perfect solution, unfortunately. DOS function 0x3f echoes each input character, which is not supposed to occur according to the definition of **getch**. The best solution would be to use the original version of **getch** when standard input is connected to the keyboard, and to use 0x3f when input is redirected. Obviously, the program is going to have to determine whether or not input is coming from the keyboard "on the fly." Then the program could call the appropriate **getch** function. How does the program find where the standard input is coming from? The DOS IOCTL function 0x44 can provide that information.

Determining the Source of the Standard Input

The **get_dev** function in Figure 3-1 accepts a file handle as an argument. It returns device information about that file handle as a series of bit settings. These bit settings are described in Figure 3-2, in the **ioctl.h** header file. To find out if the standard input is connected to the console, we only need to #include <ioctl.h> and use the following program line:

```
int  stat;

if((stat = get_dev(0)) != -1)
    if((stat & ISCIN) == ISCIN)
    ...standard input is the console.
```

The zero argument to **get_dev** is the file handle for standard input. ISCIN is a bit mask to test for the console as input device. This function is used in the modified **getch** function. Alternatively, to see if the standard output, file-handle number one, is to the console, you can use the following:

```
#include <ioctl.h>
int  stat;

if((stat = get_dev(1)) ! = -1)
```

```
/**
* NAME
*         get_dev -- return device information
*
* SYNOPSIS
*         dev = get_dev(handle)
*
*         int     dev;                 device info bits, as defined in ioctl.h
*         int     handle;              file handle for request
*
* DESCRIPTION
*         Returns information about the specified file handle. This function
* can be used to see if standard input or output has been redirected. See
* ioctl.h for the format of the return information.
*
* RETURN
*         File information bit flags as defined in ioctl.h.
*         -1 if error.
**/

#include <dos.h>

#define CARRY    1         /* carry flag mask                                */

/********/

get_dev(handle)
int     handle;
{
        union   REGS    u;

        u.h.ah = 0x44;
        u.h.al = 0;
        u.x.bx = handle;
        if(intdos(&u, &u) & CARRY)
                u.x.dx = -1;                    /* error return             */
        return(u.x.dx);
}
/********/
```

Fig. 3-1. The get_dev function.

```
if((stat & ISCOT) == ISCOT)
...standard output is the console.
```

You probably noticed that something different has been done with the intdos function call in get_dev. The intdos and int86 function calls return a value that has been ignored in previous functions. The value returned is that of the CPU status flags. Some of the DOS and BIOS functions return with the 8088 flags set to indicate something that occurred in the function. In the case of the 0x44 DOS function, the carry flag is set if an error occurred. Many of the DOS functions new with version 2.0 use the carry flag as an error indicator. The flags register is a 16-bit register, and the carry flag is represented by bit zero. Therefore, a logical AND with one will produce a nonzero value if the carry bit is set, and a zero value if it is not set. CARRY has been defined as one. If the AND operation produces a nonzero result, we know that the carry flag was set by the DOS function call; that is, that an error has occurred. Usually, a number is returned in register AX indicating the type of error. These numbers are defined in the DOS manual. **get_dev** ignores this error number, but you could examine **u.x.ax** after return from this function to get the error number if the carry flag is set. The most likely reason for an error return from this DOS function is that an invalid or unopened file handle was supplied to it. Therefore, **get_dev** returns only a −1 as an error indicator.

If you are at all familiar with assembly language programming, you know that there are several bits in the flags register that are used to flag various results of the execution of an assembly language instruction. You also know that some of the bits are not used for anything. The most often used flags for DOS and BIOS returns are the carry and zero flags. These defines will take care of the and mask needed to check those two flags:

```
#define CARRY 1
/* carry flag, mask bit 0 */
#define ZERO   0x40
/* zero flag,  mask bit 6 */
```

Then

```
if(int86(intnumber, &u, &u) & ZERO)
```

is true, the zero flag is set. Before testing for any of the status flags, you must be certain that the DOS or BIOS function you are calling defines a flag. The flags will always be returned by the **intdos** and **int86** functions, but they are meaningful only if the particular DOS or BIOS function being called uses the flags to indicate something upon return from the call. The documentation for each DOS and BIOS function call will tell you if it is setting a flag for examination by the caller. In the case of DOS, if a function says that it will return an error number in AX, then you must check the carry flag before assuming that a value in AX is an error number.

If you are using Lattice Version 3, you can use their **getfc** function call in place of **get_dev**. You can still use **ioctl.h** to decode the bit settings, but the program logic

```
/**
 * NAME
 *        ioctl.h -- header file for get_dev function
 **/

#define ISEOF    0x40                    /* zero if end-of-file on input */
                                         /* rest are non-zero if true    */
#define ISDEV    0x80                    /* true if device (else a file) */
#define ISCIN    (ISDEV | 1)             /* true if console input dev    */
#define ISCOT    (ISDEV | 2)             /* true if console output dev   */
#define ISNUL    (ISDEV | 4)             /* true if null device          */
#define ISCLK    (ISDEV | 8)             /* true if clock device         */
#define ISBIN    (ISDEV | 0x20)          /* true if binary, else ASCII   */
#define ISCTRL   (ISDEV | 0x4000)        /* true if ctrl strings accepted*/
/*********/
```

Fig. 3-2. The header file for the get_dev function.

will be a little different;

```
#include <ioctl.h>
int    stat;

if(getfc(0, &stat) != -1)
if((stat & ISCIN) == ISCIN)
...standard input is the console.
```

Here, a pointer to an int is passed to **getfc** to contain the status bits. The error return is the same as for **get_dev**.

Improved Console Input/Output

The Lattice library provides the source code for **getch** and **putch** in a module called **conio.c**. The entire module with all modifications is reproduced in Fig. 3-3. Most of the functions in the module have been modified to behave more as the standard library functions do. This makes it easier to substitute these functions with the library functions, because fewer code changes should be necessary. For example, **getch** and **putch** now produce a return value of −1 to indicate EOF and error, respectively. This is the same as the return values provided by **getchar** and **putchar**. All of the functions that were modified have also been renamed. Because the replacements work differently, it could cause problems to leave them with the same names.

The **getch** function has been named **dgetcr** to indicate that it is a DOS input function and that the input is untranslated (as **getch** input is). **dgetc** has been added to provide translated input; that is, carriage returns are translated to newlines on input. **dgetcre** is the replacement for **getche**; it produces untranslated input with echo. The only change made here was to have **dgetcre** return minus one on EOF.

The **putch** function has been named **dputcr**, the untranslated DOS output function. **dputc** is the translated function. **undgetc** allows a single character to be pushed back onto the input from any of the three input functions.

On the first call to **dgetcr**, which is also called by **dgetc**, the value of a static function pointer is null. Finding this, **dgetcr** calls **get_dev** to see if standard input is connected to the console. **dgetcr** uses the results of this call to initialize the **get_ch** function pointer to either **getch1** or **getch2**. **getch1** is similar to the original version of **getch** in **conio.c**, except that it returns a −1 as an EOF indicator if a Control-Z character is received. Because **getch1** is called only when input is from the console, the Control-Z must be typed from the keyboard to indicate EOF. **getch2**, on the other hand, is called if input is not from the keyboard. This function calls DOS function 0x3f, which terminates either on Control-Z or the physical end-of-file. When the end of input is sensed, by checking the returned byte count from DOS, a −1 is returned. To check the operation of the new functions, use a simple program like:

```
#include <extkeys.h>
/* special key translation */
_main()
{
int  c;

while((c = dgetc()) != -1)
     if(c < K_BASE)        /* display if not a special key */
{
          dputc(c);
```

```
/**
 * DESCRIPTION
 *
 * Modifications to Lattice CONIO.C module:
 *
 * dgetcr -- uses DOS ioctl function to select input function.
 *           Untranslated input. Returns -1 as EOF.
 *
 * dgetc  -- Calls "dgetcr" for input and translates \r to \n.

 * getch1 -- called by dgetcr if std input NOT redirected.
 * getch2 -- calls DOS function 0x3f. Called by dgetcr if input is redirected.
 *
 * dgetcre -- returns -1 as EOF.
 *
 * dputcr -- uses DOS call 0x40 for output. Untranslated. Returns -1 on error.
 * dputc  -- translated output, calls "dputcr" and translates \n to \r\n.
 *
 * pushback -- modified to store -1 when empty. Allows pushback of PC special
 *       keys as defined in "extkeys.h"
 **/

/**
 *
 * This module defines the various console I/O functions.
 *
 **/
#include <dos.h>          /* for intdos calls */
#include <ioctl.h>        /* for get_dev call */
#include <extkeys.h>      /* to translate PC special extended key codes */

#define BDOS_IN   8       /* input function for "dgetcr" */
#define BDOS_INE  1       /* input function for "dgetcre" */
#define BDOS_OUT  6       /* output function for "putch" (not used)*/
#define BDOS_CKS  11      /* check keyboard status for "kbhit" */

static int  pushback = -1;       /* character save for "undgetc" */
/**/
/**
 *
 * name          dgetcr -- get character from console, untranslated
 *               dgetcre - get character from console and echo it, untranslated
 *
 * synopsis      c = dgetcr();
 *               int c;           input character
 *                                must be int for -1 return on EOF
 *
 * description   These functions obtain the next character typed at
 *               the console or, if one was pushed back via "undgetc",
 *               returns the previously pushed back character. PC extended
 *               keys are returned in a single call as an "int" defined
 *               in "extkeys.h".
 *
 **/

static  int      (*get_ch)() = (int (*)()) 0; /* pointer to input function */


dgetcr()                          /* Returns EOF of -1 */
{
```

Fig. 3-3. The conio.c module with modifications.

```c
        int     c, getch1(), getch2();

/* if ptr not initialized, set according to ioctl */
        if(!get_ch)
                get_ch = (get_dev(0) & ISCIN) == ISCIN ? &getch1 : &getch2;

        if(pushback != -1) {
                c = pushback;
                pushback = -1;
                return(c);
        }

        if((c = (*get_ch)()) == 0)
                c = (*get_ch)() + K_BASE;
        return(c);
}
/********/
static int      getch1()            /* input without echo, returns -1 on ^Z */
{
        int     c;

        if((c = bdos(BDOS_IN)) == 26)
                c = -1;                     /* EOF */
        return(c);
}
/********/
static int      getch2()            /* input with echo, for redirect only   */
{
        char    buf;
        union   REGS r;
        struct  SREGS seg;

        segread(&seg);
        seg.ds = seg.ss;            /* ds has segment of buf             */

        r.x.ax = 0x3f00;            /* read from file or device func. call */
        r.x.bx = 0;                 /* use stdin                         */
        r.x.cx = 1;                 /* read 1 char.                      */
        r.x.dx = (short) &buf;      /* ds:dx => buf                      */
        intdosx(&r, &r, &seg);
        if(r.x.ax == 0) return( -1);    /* EOF                          */
        return((int)buf);
}
/********/

dgetc()             /* translated input, \r translated to \n            */
{
        int     c;

/* translate \r to \n and ignore any \n */
        if((c = dgetcr()) == '\n')
                c = dgetc();
        if(c == '\r')
                c = '\n';

        return(c);
}
/********/

dgetcre()           /* input with echo; no translate; returns -1 on ^Z  */
{
        int c;
```

```
        if(pushback != -1) {
                c = pushback;
                pushback = -1;
                return(c);
        }
        if((c = bdos(BDOS_INE)) == 26)
                c = -1;              /* EOF on ^Z */

        return(c);
}
/********/
/**
 *
 * name          dputcr -- send character directly to console
 *
 * synopsis      dputcr(c);
 *               char c;          character to be sent
 *
 * description   This function sends the specified character directly
 *               to the user's console.
 *
 **/

dputcr(c)        /* returns -1 on error */
char c;
{
        union REGS r;
        struct SREGS seg;

        segread(&seg);
        seg.ds = seg.ss;

        r.x.ax = 0x4000;        /* write to file or device func call  */
        r.x.bx = 1;             /* write to stdout                    */
        r.x.cx = 1;             /* write one byte                     */
        r.x.dx = (short) &c;    /* char to write                     */
        intdosx(&r, &r, &seg);
        if(r.x.ax != 1)
                return( -1);    /* error return, such as disk full.   */
        return((int)c);
}
/********/

dputc(c)                /* translated output, \n translated to \r\n   */
char    c;
{
        if(c == '\n')           /* translate \n to \r\n */
                dputcr('\r');

        return(dputcr(c));
}
/********/
/**
 *
 * name          undgetc -- push character back to console
 *
 * synopsis      r = undgetc(c);
 *               int r;          return code
 *               char c;          character to be pushed back
 *
 * description   This function pushes the indicated character back
 *               on the console.  Only a single level of pushback is
```

```
*                       allowed.  The effect is to cause "dgetc" or "dgetcr"
*                       to return the pushed-back character the next time
*                       one of them is called.
*
* returns               r = -1 if character already pushed back
*                         = c otherwise
*
**/
undgetc(c)
int c;
{

        if (pushback != -1) return(-1);
        pushback = c;
        return(c);
}
/********/
/**
*
* name                  kbhit -- check if character has been typed at console
*
* synopsis              status = kbhit();
*                       int status;                1 if character typed, else 0
*
* description           This function checks to see if a character has been
*                       typed at the user's console since the completion of
*                       the last read operation.  The character typed can
*                       be obtained by a "getch" call.
*
* returns               0 if no character has been typed
*                       1 if a character is waiting to be read
*
**/
kbhit()
{
        return(bdos(BDOS_CKS) != 0);
}
/********/
```

The header file **extkeys.h** is shown in the next section. It is used to translate the PC's special keys so that only a single call is needed to retrieve them. All of the special keys are returned as their scan code plus K_BASE. This header file defines K_BASE equal to 256; thus an integer is needed to store the return value from **dgetc**, which is necessary also to receive the −1 EOF indicator. Here, the special keys are being ignored. By examining **dgetcr**, you can see that the translation of the special keys occurs in the program line:

```
if((c = (*get_ch)()) == 0)
    c = (*get_ch)() + K_BASE;
```

By using this approach, calling programs do not need to make two calls to the **dgetc** functions whenever a special key is received. This is explained in more detail in the next section, where this technique is also used for the BIOS keyboard input functions. These DOS functions and the BIOS functions in the next section for keyboard input were written to behave exactly the same way. That allows programs that call either or both input functions with the same logic to be written.

Notice that the main function is __main, with a leading underscore. This prevents the library __main module from being linked into the program, which prevents the file routines from being included. Yet input and output can still be redirected. When writing routines that don't need the file functions, you can create much smaller programs this way. Of course, no command line arguments are provided. If you need those, but not the file functions, you can use the Lattice __main.obj module. It passes **argc** and **argv** to **main** but does not include the file functions. Note that the entry to __main.obj is __main, so you must name your function **main** in this case.

I would like to call your attention to **getch2** again. This function calls **segread** to get the CPU segment register contents. The Lattice library contains **segread**. Appendix E also contains a **segread** if your compiler does not have a similar function. The SREGS structure is declared in **dos.h**. DOS function 0x3f requires a buffer to hold the input data. The buffer is defined by the caller, and DOS expects a pointer to this buffer in registers DS:DX. Thus, before calling the DOS function, we must be sure that DS and DX are properly initialized to the segment:offset of a buffer. In **getch2**, a one-byte buffer has been defined as **char buf** to hold the input character. We need to break the address of **buf** into its segment and offset portions. **buf** is **auto** data, meaning that it must be on the stack, which is referenced by the stack segment (SS) register. **segread** gives us the current SS contents, which are stored into DS by way of **seg.ds** when **intdosx** is called. A few lines down, r.x.dx is assigned the offset of **buf** by casting its address to a **short**. This method of acquiring a C variable address guarantees that the C function will work for all memory models. If **seg.ss** was not assigned to **seg.ds**, you would find that the **getch2** function would fail in a large data model.

There is a more efficient way to do this with the Lattice compiler. When a large data model is specified to the compiler, it defines the label LPTR. **getch2** could take advantage of this by not calling **segread** and assigning **seg.ds** unless LPTR is defined:

```
#ifdef LPTR
     segread(&seg);
     seg.ds = seg.ss;
     intdosx(&r, &r, &seg);
#else
     intdos(&r, &r);
#endif
```

In the small data models, DS and SS are equal, so the version for those models can use **intdos** rather than **intdosx**. The resulting code will be smaller and faster. If your compiler is not Lattice, but provides small and large data models, you might check the documentation to see if it defines an LPTR type of symbol.

There is an easier way to break a pointer into its segment:offset portions with version 3 of the Lattice compiler:

```
makedv(&buf, &r.x.dx, &seg.ds);
```

This function is all that is needed for all memory models. **segread** is not necessary, and there is no need to check for LPTR. **makedv** breaks the address of **buf** into its segment:offset portions regardless of the pointer size.

These modified functions can be very useful when you need character-by-character control of keyboard input and display output, and still need redirection and pipe capability. They will not work with the color output functions in Chapter 2, unless you use the ansi.sys codes in place of the BIOS calls to display a character. Also, there are some functions in the Lattice library that use the functions in conio.c—specifically cgets, cputs, cscanf, and cprintf. They will not work properly with the modified functions because they are not expecting the EOF return code or the newline translation. One of the reasons that the modified functions were given different names was to keep the library functions from trying to use them. You can bypass cscanf by using sscanf, and cprintf by using sprintf. But, if you need a cgets and cputs that work with the modified getch and putch, you will need to add your own. Later, in Section 3.4, I present a replacement function for cgets that can use getch, but it is really designed for interactive programs. Therefore, it may be a bit overkill where a simple gets type of function will do.

I will leave it as an exercise for you to design a cgets that calls the modified getch, that is, dgetc or dgetcr, for its input. cgets should allow backspacing and recognize both EOF and newline. For compatibility with gets, cgets should replace the newline with a null byte, and it should return a pointer to the string argument passed to it. That pointer should be null when EOF is received, but the null pointer must not be returned until the next call to cgets if there are any characters in its buffer. You can create cgets in such a way that it will ignore other control characters, or you can get fancy and echo them the way DOS does. For example, Control-A is echoed by DOS as ^A. Then you can decide whether to echo ^G or sound the bell, and whether to echo a tab character as ^I, expand it, or ignore it. cgets is not so simple. Before you get discouraged, let me give you a hint. DOS function 0x3f, used by getch, will accept more than one character in a request. This solution, too, is not as easy as it first appears, but it does take care of some of the details. It also takes over control of the keyboard, which means your program will not have the same options as it would if you designed your own string input with dgetc and dputc. You will have to decide which is better for your application. Where a great deal of control is needed, the getline function in Section 3.4 might be just what you are looking for. Before tackling cgets, you might want to try cputs; it is a great deal simpler. Because the modified functions have different names, there is no reason why you cannot use cgets or cputs for line input/output while using the modified functions for character input/output.

3.2 BIOS CONTROL OF KEYBOARD INPUT

Whether you use the standard library functions or the direct console functions for standard input and output, the data is ultimately passed through DOS. This is a necessity for redirection capability. Some programs, however, have no need for input redirection, or they might need it in one place, but not in another. Where redirection is not needed, there might be good reasons for greater control over keyboard input. The BIOS keyboard input function can provide better control.

The functions in Fig. 3-4 rely on BIOS INT 0x16 for keyboard input. Accordingly, they have been named with the letter b as the first character of the function name. As with the BIOS video display functions, this is to emphasize that these functions are direct BIOS calls; therefore, their input cannot be redirected. These functions also differ in the way that they treat the PC extended key functions.

```
/**
 * NAME
 *      bscancr -- untranslated BIOS scan for character from keyboard
 *      bscanc  -- translated scan for character
 *      bgetcr  -- wait for a character from keyboard, untranslated
 *      bgetc   -- wait for a character, translated
 *      unbgetc -- push character back onto input
 *
 * SYNOPSIS
 *      c = bscancr();
 *      c = bscanc();
 *      c = bgetcr();
 *      c = bgetc();
 *      stat = unbgetc(c);
 *
 *      int     c;              returned character
 *      int     stat;           -1 if character already pushed, else c
 *
 * DESCRIPTION
 *      bscancr and bscanc check to see if a character is ready for input
 * from the keyboard by calling BIOS INT 0x16. If no character is waiting,
 * -1 is returned. If a character is ready, it is retrieved from the keyboard
 * buffer and returned to the caller. If the character is one of the two
 * character special keys, such as a function key, the scan code plus 256
 * is returned. EXTKEYS.H may be included in programs using these functions
 * to test for the special keys. bscancr returns carriage return characters,
 * while bscanc translates a carriage return to a newline.
 *
 *      bgetcr and bgetc wait for a key to be typed. The return is the same
 * as above, except that -1 is not returned. They call the scan function
 * until a key is received. bgetcr is the untranslated function, while bgetc
 * translates a carriage return to a newline.
 *
 *      unbgetc will store one pushed back character that was returned by
 * any of the above input functions.
 *
 * RETURNS
 *      bscancr and bscanc return -1 if no character is ready. Otherwise,
 * all functions return the character. 256 is added to the scan code of a
 * special key, so that two calls are not necessary to get a special extended
 * key code. unbgetc returns -1 if a character had already been pushed back,
 * otherwise the character is returned.
 *      bgetc and bgetcr return -1 upon receipt of ^Z, as an EOF indicator.
 *
 * CAUTIONS
 *      The calling program must examine the return character for EOF (-1).
 * The input cannot be redirected, because these are direct BIOS calls.
 **/
#include <dos.h>
#include <extkeys.h>

#define ZERO    0x40            /* zero flag */

static  int     pushback = -1;  /* holds pushed back character from unbgetc */
bscancr()                       /* untranslated */
{
        int     c;
        union   REGS    u;
```

Fig. 3-4. The keyboard input functions.

```
        if(pushback != -1) {
                c = pushback;
                pushback = -1;
                return(c);
        }
        u.h.ah = 1;
        if(int86(0x16, &u, &u) & ZERO)
                c = -1;                 /* no character ready */
        else {
                u.h.ah = 0;
                int86(0x16, &u, &u);
                if((c = u.h.al) == 0)
                        c = u.h.ah + K_BASE;
        }
        return(c);
}
/********/

bscanc()                                /* translated */
{
        int     c;

        return((c = bscancr()) == '\r' ? '\n' : c);
}
/********/

bgetcr()                                /* wait for char, untranslated */
{
        int     c;

        while((c = bscancr()) == -1) ;
        if(c == 26)                     /* return -1 for EOF if ^Z */
                c = -1;
        return(c);
}
/********/

bgetc()                                 /* wait for char, translated */
{
        int     c;

        while((c = bscanc()) == -1) ;
        if(c == 26)
                c = -1;                 /* return -1 for EOF if ^Z */
        return(c);
}
/********/

unbgetc(c)                              /* push character back on input */
int     c;
{
        if(pushback == -1)
                pushback = c;
        else
                c = -1;
        return(c);
}
/********/
```

The extended key functions are those keyboard keys that return a zero as a character, in conjunction with a one-byte scan code. The numbered function keys F1 through F10 and the arrow keys are examples. The zero is returned to indicate that the scan code must be examined to determine which key was pressed. DOS and the C library functions handle this by first returning the zero character to the caller. The calling program must examine the returned character to see if it is a zero. If so, another call must be made to retrieve the scan code. The following program will produce strange results when one of the special extended keys is pressed.

```
while((c = getch()) != -1)
    putch(c);
```

This example copies the standard input to the standard output. When a special key is pressed, **getch** returns a zero that is output by **putch**. This usually produces a blank on the display. On the following call to **getch**, the scan code of the special key is returned and output by **putch**. What is displayed then depends on which special key was pressed. The scan code often corresponds to a standard ASCII character. For example, if the F1 key had been pressed, you would see a blank followed by a semicolon (;). It so happens that the scan code of the F1 key is the ASCII code for the semicolon. Because the program above did not first check for the zero code, it incorrectly attempted to display a key that is considered a nondisplay key. This next example shows the correct procedure.

```
while((c = getch()) != -1)
    if(c == 0)
        getch();
    else
        putch(c);
```

In this example, the return character is checked to see if a special key was pressed. If so, **getch** is called again to remove the scan code from the input. Here, the special keys are simply being ignored. If the character is nonzero, then it is displayed.

As you see in the above example, this kind of coding gets a little messy in a program where keyboard input is called for from many different places in the program. The functions in Fig. 3-4 were designed to simplify the coding for keyboard input. They do not require two calls to retrieve a special key code. Instead, these functions add 256 to the scan code of a special key and return that value. This means that any variable storing a return value from these functions must be an **int**, as a **char** cannot receive a value larger than 255. This is not new, however, as the C library input functions require the variable to be an int also. An **int** is necessary to store the −1 returned by those functions as an end-of-file indicator.

Programs that call the functions in Fig. 3-4 can use the header file in Fig. 3-5 to decode special key codes. The **extkeys.h** header file is only a partial listing of all the possible codes, but it needs to contain only those codes that your program will actually use. After testing a return value for all the special keys used by your program, it can just ignore any value that does not meet one of the tests. Something like the logic shown in Fig. 3-6 will work fine.

```
/**
 * NAME
 *         extkeys.h -- header file for bscanc, bgetc functions
 *
 * DESCRIPTION
 *         The BIOS keyboard input functions add K_BASE to the scan code
 * of the PC's extended key functions. This header file defines labels for
 * some of the special keys.
 **/

#define K_BASE    256                    /* offset added to scan code       */

#define K_F1      (59+K_BASE)            /* scan code, func. keys 1 - 10    */
#define K_F2      (60+K_BASE)
#define K_F3      (61+K_BASE)
#define K_F4      (62+K_BASE)
#define K_F5      (63+K_BASE)
#define K_F6      (64+K_BASE)
#define K_F7      (65+K_BASE)
#define K_F8      (66+K_BASE)
#define K_F9      (67+K_BASE)
#define K_F10     (68+K_BASE)
#define K_HOME    (71+K_BASE)
#define K_END     (79+K_BASE)
#define K_UP      (72+K_BASE)            /* up-arrow                        */
#define K_DN      (80+K_BASE)            /* down-arrow                      */
#define K_LEFT    (75+K_BASE)            /* left-arrow                      */
#define K_RIGHT   (77+K_BASE)            /* right-arrow                     */
#define K_PGUP    (73+K_BASE)            /* PgUp key                        */
#define K_PGDN    (81+K_BASE)            /* PgDn key                        */
#define K_INS     (82+K_BASE)            /* Ins key                         */
#define K_DEL     (83+K_BASE)            /* Del key                         */

/*********/
```

Fig. 3-5. The header file for the keyboard input functions.

In this example, bgetc is called to get a character from the keyboard. If the return value is greater than or equal to K_BASE, defined as 256 in extkeys.h, then a special key was pressed. The only two special keys used in the example are F1 and F2. If the return value is neither of those, then the key is ignored.

As you know, the PC recognizes many special keys not included in extkeys.h. For example, a unique scan code is generated for each function key in combination with one of the shift, alternate, and control keys. This gives a possible 40 different function keys. There is a scan code for each of the alpha keys when used in combination with the alternate key. If you want to supplement extkeys.h with some of the other scan codes, a little program like the one shown in Fig. 3-7 will help. This program prints the ASCII value of any key except the Escape key, one per line. If the key is a special key, a zero is printed followed by the scan code on the same line. If you run this program and press A, B, F1, and the C keys, you will see the following:

```
65   A
66   B
 0   59
67   C
```

```
#include <extkeys.h>
#define ESCAPE 27                          /* escape key ASCII code  */

while((c = bgetc()) != ESCAPE) {    /* escape key ends input */
     if(c >= K_BASE)                 /* then its a special key */
          switch(c) {
          case K_F1:
               ... function key one processing...
               break;
          case K_F2:
               ... function key two processing...
               break;

          default:
               continue;              /* ignore and get next char */
          }
     ... processing for standard characters...
}
```

Fig. 3-6. A program that tests your special return values.

Looking at Fig. 3-4, you will see that there are four functions that return keyboard input. Only one of them, **bscancr**, makes the BIOS call to get a character. The other three ultimately depend on this function. **bscancr** is the input counterpart to Chapter 2's **bputcr**. **bputcr** is the raw, or untranslated, output function. **bscancr** is the raw input function, and it is a keyboard scanning function. It does not wait for a key to be pressed if one is not ready. The BIOS INT 0x16 function number one is used to determine if a character is waiting in the keyboard buffer. Here we must test the processor status flags again. This interrupt call sets the zero flag (bit 6 of the return value) if no character is waiting. If no character is available, **bscancr** returns a −1. If there is a character in the buffer, INT 0x16 function number zero is called to retrieve the character from the buffer. Further, the character is checked to see if it is a special key. The BIOS call returns a character in register AL. If the value in AL, which is transferred to **u.h.al** by the **int86** function, is zero, then the scan code is obtained from **u.h.ah**; 256 is added to this value before the character is returned to the caller of **bscancr**.

You will notice that **bscancr** checks to see if a character has been pushed back onto the input by **unbgetc**. **unbgetc** works the same as the library function **ungetc**.

```
main()
{
     int  c;

     printf("Press any key. Escape to exit.\n");
     while((c = bgetc()) != ESCAPE)        /* terminate on escape key */
          if(c < K_BASE)
               printf("%3d %c\n", c, c);
          else
               printf("  O %d\n", c - K_BASE);
}
```

Fig. 3-7. A program that prints the ASCII value of any key except the escape key.

It is valid to call **unbgetc** with a character received from any of the input functions in Fig. 3-4.

The **bscanc** function works like **bscancr**, except that it adds translation of carriage return to newline. **bgetcr** and **bgetc** are the untranslated and translated functions, respectively, that wait for a character to be typed before returning. While there can be no input redirection with the BIOS input functions, **bgetc** and **bgetcr** have been written to return – 1 as an EOF indicator, for compatibility with **getch** and **getchar**. **bgetc** and **bgetcr** return – 1 when a Control-Z is received. Note that **bscanc** and **bscancr** return – 1 to indicate that there are no keystrokes waiting in the keyboard buffer. They do not return – 1 upon receipt of a Control-Z. With the BIOS input functions, your program will have to allow some character to indicate when a user is finished with input, if your program receives its input in an otherwise infinite loop. That's because Control-Break will not work. For example, the only way out of the following piece of code is to reboot the computer.

```
while(c = bgetc())
    if(c < K_BASE)
        bputc(c);
```

The BIOS keyboard functions in Fig. 3-4 will never return a zero value, so the above loop test is never false. Technically, the Control-@ key combination is the null character, with value zero. This is not the same as the digit zero, which has a value of 48. The BIOS will return a zero value upon receipt of a Control-@, but the **bscancr** logic will interpret this as a special key and return the key scan code plus K__BASE. The scan code is three, so the calling program receives three plus K__BASE, or 259. This does not interfere with any of the special key codes, however, because the scan code is unique.

One special key combination is Control-Break. It returns a zero character like the other special keys. It also returns a zero scan code. Thus, the value returned by **bscancr** for Control-Break is K__BASE. Although Control-Break has no effect on the BIOS console functions, you will see an effect when the program exits to DOS. Upon return to DOS, you will see the DOS representation of a Control-Break, ∧C, on the screen. Even worse, your program can have a delayed reaction to the Control-Break entry. This happens because DOS sets a flag when the Control-Break interrupt (INT 0x1B) occurs. The next DOS function call that checks this flag will cause DOS to perform its usual Control-Break routine. The best defense against this is to use the **brk__off** function from Chapter 2. Of course, if your program makes no DOS function calls, it is not necessary to turn **brk__off**.

While we are on the subject of Control-Break again, there is something else I would like to discuss. You have probably realized that the Control-Break action can be totally disabled by modifying **brk__off** to replace INT 0x1B rather than INT 0x23. There is nothing wrong with this approach, but a couple of cautions apply if you want to do this. First, your program MUST call **brk__on** before exiting. DOS will not automatically replace the INT 0x1B vector as it does with the INT 0x23 vector when a program exits. If your program fails to restore the original INT 0x1B vector, sooner or later (probably sooner) the computer will go out to lunch. Once your program has exited, the IRET instruction will be overwritten by another program load. The next time an unsuspecting user presses Control-Break, the now invalid INT 0x1B vector will send the computer off to do who-knows-what. I am sure that I don't need to tell you that THAT is not good.

Another problem to this approach is that DOS treats a Control-C the same as Control-Break. Replacing the INT 0x1B vector will not prevent DOS from acting on Control-C. DOS executes INT 0x23 upon receipt of either Control-Break or Control-C. Therefore, what is really needed is a replacement of both the INT 0x1B and INT 0x23 vectors. In most cases, the **brk_off** function should be sufficient as it stands. The BIOS functions for console input and output can be used where the ∧C echo from DOS would interfere, and the DOS functions can be used where the ∧C echo is not so critical. The **brk_off** function will prevent DOS from terminating program execution.

3.3   BEEP: A DIGRESSION ON A SOUND IDEA

Before we continue with the development of the keyboard functions, let's take a short side trip. In many interactive programs, it can be useful to create sound from the PC's built-in speaker. For example, a short beep can alert the user that he is about to make some error.

In the next section, we are going to make a short beep on the speaker when the user tries to type more data into an input field than the program allows. At first thought, that may seem unnecessary. After all, the user can see when his typing reaches the end of an input field, can't he? Remember that touch typists don't always watch the screen very closely when typing in large amounts of data, so they would appreciate it if the program would let them know when the address they're typing into the mailing label program is too long to fit on the line. It can be aggravating when the computer just sits there silently ignoring our key strokes, while we merrily type away. We might not find out until much later that half the address is missing. A little beep from the speaker can be much like the bell on a typewriter. It lets us know when we have run out of space.

Again, however, the standard C library doesn't give us a function for creating sound on the PC speaker, but it does provide us with the tools we need to do the job ourselves. Creating sound on the PC requires port input/output. We can use the **inp** and **outp** functions provided in the Lattice library to perform port input and output. Most C compiler libraries have these two functions. If yours doesn't, see Appendix F. You may be able to adapt those functions to work with your compiler.

The **sound** function in Figure 3-8 allows quite a bit of flexibility in creating sound from the PC's speaker. It can create sound over a range extending from a very high pitch to very low. The duration of the sound can be varied from as little as one-tenth second to as much as 25 seconds in one-tenth second increments. You can easily modify the duration length and increment it if you need greater flexibility there.

Note that the value used for **freq** and the pitch of the sound are an inverse relationship. Calling **sound(100, 5)** will produce a very high pitched sound for one-half second. Values less than 100 are usually inaudible. Calling **sound(32767, 5)** will produce a half-second tone so low that you may not be able to hear it. Values in the middle ranges usually produce the best results.

If your PC is a compatible that has a different (probably faster) clock speed, you'll need to adjust the number #defined as TENTH. You can arrive at an approximate value

```
/**
 * name: sound.c
 * synopsis
 *        sound(freq, dur);
 *
 *        int      freq;    frequency, range 100 - 32767; high val = low pitch
 *        int      dur;     duration of sound in 1/10 second units,
 *                          range 1 - 255 gives .1 to 25.5 second duration
 *        Nothing returned.
 **/

#define TENTH    1460L    /* number of loops for 1/10 second delay      */
                          /* for IBM PC clock speed of 4.77 mhz         */

sound(freq, dur)
int      freq, dur;
{
        int old;
        long delay;

        dur &= 0xff;                        /* limit to max. of 255       */
        outp(0x43, 0xb6);                   /* select timer               */
        outp(0x42, freq & 0xff);            /* least sig. byte of freq    */
        outp(0x42, (freq >> 8) & 0x7f);     /* most sig. byte             */
        old = inp(0x61);                    /* save current port value    */
        outp(0x61, old | 3);                /* turn speaker on            */
        for(delay = dur * TENTH; delay > 0L; delay--);  /* delay          */
        outp(0x61, old);                    /* turn speaker off           */
}
/********/

beep()           /* call sound to beep the speaker                        */
{
        sound(1500,4);
}
/********/
```

Fig. 3-8. The sound function.

by dividing the clock speed of your computer by 4.77 and multiplying the result by 1460. That result should be placed in the code as the #define. Thus, if your machine has a 6.0 megahertz clock speed, 6.0 / 4.77 * 1460 = 1836. Don't forget to type it into the code as 1836L, since this is a long value. Also, the compiler you are using can affect the speed. The value used in this code was derived using the Lattice compiler. Different code generation techniques of other compilers can create loops that execute at a different speed.

Now that we have the basic sound generation function, we can add a short function to our library that is convenient when all we want is a short beep. The beep function in Fig. 3-8 will sound a pleasant beep for four-tenths of a second. Unless you are writing music, you might use this function call more than you'll use direct calls to sound.

Before leaving this section, I'd like to offer a word of caution. Direct port output on the PC can be dangerous if you make a mistake. Although unlikely, it is possible to damage your computer. I say this only because it should be understood that output to the PC's ports should not be done with wild abandon. If you are careful when typing in the port numbers and data in this program, you have nothing to fear.

3.4 A LINE INPUT FUNCTION FOR INTERACTIVE PROGRAMS

The standard library **gets** function takes a line from the standard input. The input is terminated, and the line is returned to the caller when a newline is received. Because **gets** reads from the standard input, the input can be redirected. **gets**, however, is usually not adequate for highly interactive programs. Interactive programs often have structured screen layouts, where the program must be able to keep a tight reign on the cursor position. You don't want the user typing over input prompts and other screen information.

There are other reasons why **gets** is inadequate for data entry screens. The program cannot test and act on individual keystrokes. That means that your program will not be able to respond to special keys like the function keys and the arrow keys, nor can the program limit the amount of input to a specific field size. Because **gets** does its own echoing to the display, your program cannot make use of display color attributes. Obviously, a word processing program could be nothing more than a line editor if it relied solely on **gets** for its input. There could be no fancy insert or delete modes, or any of those other things that make word processors so handy to use.

We now have enough tools at hand to create our own line input function that can be used for highly structured input needs. It's not quite a word processor, but this input function incorporates many of the features that users have come to expect from quality PC programs. The **dgetline** function in Figure 3-9 can form the basis of a complex data entry screen. It calls **dgetc**, from section 3.1, for its input; this is why it is called **dgetline**. The beginning **d** indicates that it depends on a DOS function for its keyboard input. This allows input redirection. Where the BIOS input is needed, this function requires only one minor change to call **bgetc** for its input. I keep two versions of this **getline** function in my library: this one, and one called **bgetline**, which calls **bgetc** for its input.

When writing a program that uses one of the **getline** functions, I usually put a line at the beginning of the program like the following:

```
#define    getline    dgetline
```

Then I call **getline** in the program itself. If I decide to change the program later to use the other version, I only need to change the #define. Because **dgetline** and **bgetline** work identically, except for the input call, I will be referring to both of these functions as **getline**. When it is necessary to distinguish, I will refer explicitly to either **dgetline** or **bgetline**.

From a user's point of view, the **getline** function allows a variety of input editing capabilities. First, a default value can be displayed when calling **getline**. If this is the response the user desires, it is only necessary to press Return (assuming that the Return key is allowed as one of the **getline** exit keys (more about exit keys later). Otherwise, the input can be edited.

Four of the PC's special keys are used by **getline**. These are the Delete, Insert, Left arrow, and Right arrow keys. In addition, the backspace key is treated in a special way. The user can use the PC Delete key to delete the character at the current cursor position. All characters to the right of the cursor are moved left one position to fill in the vacated space. To clear the entire input line, the user can simply hold the

```
/**
 * NAME
 *       dgetline -- get line from std input using DOS function
 *
 * SYNOPSIS
 *       c = dgetline(in_str,lgth,brkval);
 *
 *       int      c;       exit-char
 *       char     *in_str;          string to store input
 *       int      lgth;    max. number of char's to accept; in-str must be
 *                         at least lgth + 1 char's long for '\0' at end.
 *       int      brkval[]; array of integers to use as break values. These
 *                         define the input characters that cause dgetline
 *                         to terminate and return to caller.
 *                         NOTE: last value in brkval list must be zero.
 *
 * DESCRIPTION
 *       dgetline accepts one line of input from the standard input. It will
 * return to the caller when one of the brkval characters is received, or
 * upon receipt of EOF (-1).
 *       All input can be forced to uppercase by setting uc_on to 1 in the
 * caller's code:
 *       extern int uc_on;
 *       ...
 *       uc_on = 1;         force dgetline input to uppercase
 *
 * RETURNS
 *       brkval character or -1 if EOF.
 *
 * CAUTIONS
 *       dgetline returns the PC extended keycodes as the scan code plus
 * K_BASE, defined in extkeys.h. If one of the extended keys is included
 * in the brkval list, it must be in the form specified in extkeys.h.
 *       Do not forget to terminate the brkval list with a zero integer.
 **/
#include <ctype.h>
#include <extkeys.h>

#define TRUE   1
#define FALSE  0

#define BKSP 8   /* backspace key */

/* Define ext'd ASCII codes, all defined in extkeys.h               */
#define BAK K_LEFT       /* left arrow */
#define FWD K_RIGHT      /* right arrow */
#define INS K_INS        /* Insert key */
#define DEL K_DEL        /* Delete key */

/* set_cur will choose a block cursor if in Insert mode             */

extern   int     curblock(), curnorm();
static   int     (*cur_type[])() = {curnorm, curblock};
#define set_cur(flg) (*cur_type[flg])()

int      uc_on = FALSE; /* set to TRUE before call, to enable u/c conv'n */
static   int     in_line,in_col,cur_line,cur_col;
static   int     ins_on;
```

Fig. 3-9. The dgetline function.

```c
dgetline(in_str,lgth, brkval)
char    in_str[];
int     lgth, *brkval;
{
        char    *ptmp,*ps=in_str;
        int     c,i;

        ins_on=FALSE;                           /* start with Insert off      */
        set_cur(FALSE);                         /* and a normal cursor        */
        bputc('[');                             /* bracket the input field    */
        in_line = cur_line = curlin();
        in_col = cur_col = curcol();
        locate(in_line,in_col+lgth);
        bputc(']');                             /* bracket at end of input field*/
/* pad in_str with trailing blanks to 'lgth' */
        for(i=strlen(in_str);i<lgth;i++)
                in_str[i] = ' ';
        in_str[lgth] = '\0';

/* display current contents of in_str                                         */
        sho_def(in_str);

/* get input *******************/

        while(TRUE) {
                if(isbrkc((c = dgetc()), brkval) || c == -1)
                        break;  /* exit if break character or EOF     */

                switch(c) {
                case BKSP:      /* destructive backspace              */
                        if(ps > in_str) {
                                ptmp = --ps;
                                while(*++ptmp)
                                        *(ptmp - 1) = *ptmp;
                                *--ptmp = ' ';
                                cur_col--;
                                sho_def(in_str);
                        } else
                                beep();
                        break;

                case DEL:
                        if(ps < (in_str + lgth)) {
                                ptmp = ps;
                                while(*++ptmp)
                                        *(ptmp - 1) = *ptmp;
                                *--ptmp = ' ';
                                sho_def(in_str);
                        }
                        break;

                case INS:
                        ins_on ^= TRUE;
                        set_cur(ins_on);
                        break;

                case BAK:
                        if(ps > in_str) {
                                ps--;
                                locate(cur_line,--cur_col);
                        }
                        break;
```

```
                case FWD:
                        if(ps < (in_str + lgth)) {
                                ps++;
                                locate(cur_line,++cur_col);
                        }
                        break;
                default:
/* ignore ctl char's & all other special keys                          */
                        if(c < 32 || c >= K_BASE)
                                break;
                        if(ps < (in_str + lgth)) {
                                if(uc_on)
                                        c = toupper(c);
                                if(ins_on) {
                                        if(isspace(in_str[lgth-1])) {
                                                ptmp = in_str + lgth - 1;
                                                while(ptmp > ps) {
                                                        *ptmp = *(ptmp - 1);
                                                        ptmp--;
                                                }
                                                sho_def(in_str);
                                        } else {
                                                beep();
                                                break;
                                        }
                                }
                                *ps++ = c;
                                cur_col++;
                                bputc(c);
                                break;
                        } else {
                                beep();
                                break;
                        }
                }               /* end outer switch */
        }               /* end while(TRUE)  */
/* clean-up before exit */
        set_cur(FALSE);                         /* restore cursor to normal   */
        locate(in_line,in_col-1);               /* remove []'s around field   */
        bputc(' ');
        locate(in_line,in_col+lgth);
        bputc(' ');


/* remove trailing blanks */
        ptmp = in_str + lgth - 1;
        while(isspace(*ptmp) && ptmp >= in_str)
                ptmp--;
        *++ptmp = '\0';

        return(c);          /* return break character                      */
}


/********/
static  sho_def(s)          /* display input line                          */
char    *s;
{
        curoff();                               /* turn cursor off            */
        locate(in_line,in_col);
        bputs(s);
```

```
        locate(cur_line,cur_col);        /* restore cursor position      */
        curon();                         /* turn cursor on               */
}
/********/
/* isbrkc(), tests to see if brk char                                    */

static isbrkc(c, ip)
int     c, *ip;
{
        for(;*ip != 0; ip++)
                if(c == *ip)
                        return(TRUE);

        return(FALSE);
}
/********/
```

Delete key down until all characters have been deleted.

Upon entry into **getline**, the default mode is strikeover. That is, any character the user types replaces any character already in the current cursor position. When the user attempts to type beyond the input field, the speaker beeps to inform the user that the field is full. Alternately, the user can select insert mode by pressing the Insert key. This transforms the cursor into a block to indicate that the user has entered insert mode. Pressing the Insert key again returns **getline** to the strikeover mode, and the cursor is returned to normal. In insert mode, a typed character is placed at the current cursor position, and the cursor is advanced one position. Any characters to the right of the inserted character are moved right one position. If the input field cannot accept any more characters, the speaker beeps.

The user can use the left and right arrows on the keypad to move the cursor one character position at a time toward the beginning or the end of the input field. No change is made to the field contents by the arrow key usage. The backspace key, however, has been implemented as a destructive backspace. Regardless of the cursor position within the input field, the backspace key will delete the character to the left of the cursor position. Any characters to the right are moved left to fill the vacated space, and the cursor is moved left one position.

It is difficult to visualize how all this works. Nevertheless, I believe you will find that the **getline** operation is quite intuitive in operation. In fact, you will probably find that it works in a manner similar to editors you have used. I would also like to point out that **getline** is more than a line input function. It was designed to input entire screens full of data. Just how that is accomplished will be better understood when you see the programming details of **getline** and a program that illustrates its usage.

getline Programming Details

With **getline**, you can use any special keys that you need to implement full-screen input, help screens, and so forth. For example, the up-arrow key can be used to move to the previous input field, and the down-arrow to move to the next one. A function key can be used to call up a help screen or perform some other activity. The way that this is done using **getline** is embedded in its implementation.

You can see in Fig. 3-9 that **getline** is called with three arguments. The first argument is the input buffer that will receive the user's input. Any information in this buffer will be displayed upon entry into getline; that's how default information can be displayed. This input buffer is a normal C string. It is terminated with a \0 byte. If the first character of the input buffer is \0, a blank field is displayed by getline.

The second argument is the maximum length of the input to be accepted. The input buffer must be at least this length plus one to allow for a \0 to be placed at the end of the input. getline uses square brackets ([]) to bracket the current input field. These brackets are removed when getline returns to the caller. This serves to highlight the current input field. When there are many input fields on a screen, it is easier for the user to see where input is expected with these brackets displayed. The maximum input field length that getline can handle is 78 characters. The edit processing in getline is not designed to work over multiple lines, and the brackets take up two spaces on an 80-column line. If multiple lines are needed for one input field, they must be treated by your program as separate fields for input purposes. The screen position of the input field is determined by the calling program. That is, the input prompt and any locate (cursor positioning) needed is done by the calling program. Then getline displays any input default and the brackets starting at the current cursor position. getline does not set any color attributes. If you want the input data to appear as hilite or reverse, your program would have to call the appropriate color setting function before the call to getline.

The calling program usually performs the following steps when using getline:

1. Locate the cursor to the screen position for the input prompt.
2. Set the desired color attribute for the input prompt.
3. Display the input prompt.
4. Locate the cursor to the desired input position.
5. Set the color for the input data.
6. Call getline.
7. Check the return value from getline to determine what to do next.

The return value from getline is an int that is either EOF (– 1), or one of the "break" values. Because dgetline input can be redirected, the calling program must check for EOF. When input is not redirected, both versions of getline return EOF if Control-Z is typed.

The break value returned by getline is determined by the third argument to getline. Notice that brkval is an array of type int, not char. The last value in the array must be zero. If the only element of this array is zero, then getline will return only upon receipt of EOF. That is not usually a desirable situation. You would probably want to at least include the newline as a break character:

```
static int brkval[] = { '\n', 0 };
```

This defines a two-element int array. getline is called with a pointer to this array, and will return to the caller only upon receipt of a newline or EOF. The zero terminator in the array lets getline know when it has reached the end of the array, because the array is of an arbitrary length. Because a pointer to the array is passed to getline, your program can define as many different break-value arrays as it needs to fit varying situations.

The reason the break values are defined as int is so that the special key codes defined in **extkeys.h** can be included as break values. Then, for example, your program could define an array like this:

```
static int brkval[] = {'\n', K_UP, K_DN, K_F1, 0};
```

This array tells **getline** to return to the caller upon receipt of any of the following values: newline, up arrow, down arrow, or function key one. If the value returned by **getline** is not EOF, then it is one of these values. It is up to the calling program, of course, to examine the return value and decide what to do. In this case, it might decide to interpret the up arrow as a user request to return to the previous input field. The newline and down arrow might both be interpreted to mean that the user has finished input in the current field and wishes to advance to the next. The F1 key could indicate a request for a help screen.

The break values are checked before **getline** does any other processing. Therefore, if the array contains one of the **getline** command keys, then that command key is effectively disabled. That is, **getline** will return to the caller rather than acting on that key. Thus, if a break array contains the delete key, that key will not be processed by **getline**, but rather will be returned to the caller.

In some situations, it is convenient to force user input to be either all upper- or all lowercase letters. **getline** has one externally available int, which is called **uc_on**. The default action of **getline** is to allow input in both upper- and lowercase when alpha characters are entered. A calling program can declare **uc_on** as an **extern** and set the value to one (TRUE). Then all alpha input will be forced to uppercase. Setting **uc_on** back to zero (FALSE) disables the action.

To create the BIOS input version of **getline**, simply add a #define to the code in Fig. 3-9:

```
#define   dgetc    bgetc
/* use BIOS input function */
```

You will also want to change the name of the function, perhaps to **bgetline**, to differentiate between the two **getline** functions. Note that **bgetc** does its own translation of special keys to the **extkeys.h** format, just as **dgetc** does. It also returns EOF (−1) if Control-Z is typed.

The input string is returned with any user input modifications and terminated with a ∖0 character. Any trailing whitespace is removed from the input string; therefore, a blank string will have a ∖0 as its first character. Remember that the input buffer passed to **getline** must be at least one byte longer than the lgth argument to allow for the ∖0. **getline** will accept up to lgth characters and add the null byte.

3.5 LABELS: A DATA ENTRY PROGRAM USING GETLINE

The labels program in Fig. 3-10 illustrates the usage of **getline** to retrieve a screen of data. The program also makes use of many of the functions introduced in this and

```
/**
* NAME
*        labels -- print any number of a mailing label (3-1/2 x 15/16)
*
* SYNOPSIS
*        labels [colorfile]
*
* DESCRIPTION
*        The labels command prints a standard mailing label from the standard
* input. It will print a sample label for printer alignment tests.
*        The optional colorfile is the pathname to a file such as that
* produced by the setcolor program. If no colorfile is specified, labels
* will search the current drive/directory for a file named "color.cfg".
*        This program assumes 1-up labels.
**/

#include <stdio.h>
#include <extkeys.h>

#define getline dgetline
#define TRUE     1
#define FALSE    0

#define LBLLTH   36                      /* max. label line + 1             */
static   char    label[6][LBLLTH];
static   char    iobuf[81];
static   char    sample[2] = "Y";
static   char    qty[5] = "1";

struct   fld_def          {
         int      row;
         int      col;
         char     *name;
         char     *buff;
         };

struct   fld_def fld[] = {
         {10,10,"Line 1: ",label[0]},
         {12,10,"Line 2: ",label[1]},
         {14,10,"Line 3: ",label[2]},
         {16,10,"Line 4: ",label[3]},
         {18,10,"Line 5: ",label[4]}
         };

static   char    def_clr[] = "color.cfg";          /* default color file   */
static   char    *cfile = def_clr;
static   int     brkval1[] = {'\n',K_DN, 0};
static   int     brkval2[] = {'\n', K_UP, K_DN, 0};
static   char    *clr_msg[] = {" No color file loaded. Using default colors. ",
                               " Color file loaded. "};
extern   int     uc_on;                        /* to control getline

/********/
main(argc, argv)
int      argc;
char     *argv[];
{
         int      i, c, edit, cur_lin, num, count, clr_flag;
         char     *string();
```

Fig. 3-10. The labels program.

```
FILE    *prnfp;

if(argc == 2)
        cfile = *++argv;
else if(argc > 2) {
        fprintf(stderr, "usage: labels [colorfile]\n");
        exit(1);
}

if(get_crt() < 7)
        set_crt(3);

clr_flag = get_colors(cfile);
set_bord();
lolite();
cls();
locate(1,37);
hilite();
bputs(" LABELS \n");
lolite();
bputs(string(79,'_'));

if((prnfp = fopen("prn:","w")) == NULL) {
        bputs("\nCan't open printer device\n");
        exit(1);
}

locate(24,10);
reverse();
bputs(clr_msg[clr_flag]);

label[5][0] = '\0';

while(TRUE) {
        locate(6,10);
        lolite();
        bputs("Type ^Z to exit.");

        locate(7,10);
        bputs("Do you want to print a sample label (Y/N) ? ");
        uc_on = TRUE;
        hilite();
        if(getline(sample,1,brkval1) == EOF)
                eof_exit();

lolite();
locate(24,1);
cleol();
if(sample[0] == 'Y') {
        locate(8,10);
        bputs("Press ENTER when printer is ready...");
        while((c = dgetc()) != '\n' && c != K_UP && c != EOF);
        locate(8,10);
        cleol();
        if(c == EOF)
                eof_exit();
        else if(c == K_UP)
                continue;
        for(i = 0;i < 5;i++)
                strcpy(label[i],string(34,'H'));

        prnlbl(label[0],prnfp);
```

```
            for(i = 0;i < 6;i++)
                    label[i][0] = '\0';

            continue;
    }

    locate(7,10);
    cleol();
    for(i = 0;i < 5;i++) {
            locate(fld[i].row,fld[i].col);
            bputs(fld[i].name);
    }

    edit = TRUE;
    cur_lin = 0;
    uc_on = FALSE;
    while(edit) {
            lolite();
            locate(fld[cur_lin].row,fld[cur_lin].col);
            bputs(fld[cur_lin].name);
            hilite();
            c = getline(fld[cur_lin].buff,34,brkval2);
            switch(c) {
            case EOF:
                    eof_exit();
                    break;
            case K_UP:
                    if(--cur_lin < 0)
                            edit = FALSE;
                    break;
            default:
                    if(++cur_lin > 4)
                            edit = FALSE;
                    break;
            }
    }

    if(c == K_UP)
            continue;

                    locate(20,10);
                    lolite();
                    bputs("No. of labels ? ");
                    hilite();
                    if((c = getline(qty, 3, brkval2)) == K_UP)
                            continue;
                    else if(c == EOF)
                            eof_exit();

                    locate(20,40);
                    lolite();
                    bputs("Press ENTER when printer is ready...");
                    while((c = dgetc()) != '\n'&& c != EOF && c != K_UP) ;
                    locate(20,40);
                    cleol();
                    if(c == K_UP)
                            continue;
                    else if(c == EOF)
                            eof_exit();

                    if(sscanf(qty,"%d",&num) < 1 || num < 1)
                            continue;
```

```
                        locate(20,40);
                        hilite();
                        bputs("Escape key will abort printing . . .");
                        for(count = 0; count < num; count++) {
/* allow escape key to stop print                                               */
                                if(bscanc() == 27)
                                        break;

                                locate(22,20);
                                lolite();
                                bputs("Labels printed:   ");
                                sprintf(iobuf,"%d.   \n",count+1);
                                hilite();
                                bputs(iobuf);
                                prnlbl(label[0],prnfp);
                        }
                        locate(20,40);
                        lolite();
                        cleol();
                }
}
/****************************/

prnlbl(line,fp)
char    line[][LBLLTH];
FILE    *fp;
{
        int     i;

        for(i = 0; i < 6; i++)
                fprintf(fp,"%-34.34s\n",line[i]);
}

/********/

get_colors(cf)                  /* returns TRUE if file loaded, else FALSE      */
char    *cf;
{
        extern  int     sub_clrs[][2];
        int     c[3][2], i, load;
        FILE    *fp;

        load = FALSE;
        if((fp = fopen(cf, "r")) != NULL) {
                if(fscanf(fp,"%d %d %d %d %d %d", &c[0][0], &c[0][1],
                        &c[1][0], &c[1][1], &c[2][0], &c[2][1]) == 6) {
                        load = TRUE;
                        for(i = 0; i < 3; i++) {
                                sub_clrs[i][0] = c[i][0];
                                sub_clrs[i][1] = c[i][1];
                        }
                }
                fclose(fp);
        }
        return(load);
}
/********/

static  char    str_buf[81];

static  char    *string(n, c)
int     n;
```

```
char      c;
{
        if(n > 80)
                n = 80;
        setmem(str_buf, n, c);
        str_buf[n] = '\0';
        return(str_buf);
}
/********/

eof_exit()
{
        locate(24,1);
        lolite();
        cleol();
        bputs("Bye.\n");
        exit(0);
}
/********/
```

earlier chapters. The purpose of the **labels** program is to provide a simple way to produce standard mailing labels. It is not a mailing list program. That is, it does not build
a database of entries to print on mailing labels. What it does do is print one or more
labels that have been entered into the screen by the user. I use the program to print
labels with my own address and the addresses of people or businesses with whom I
have regular correspondence. It saves a lot of time addressing envelopes and packages. Once every few weeks, I load my printer with labels and run this program to
rebuild a supply of address labels.

While it is a fairly simple task to create a program that prints mailing labels from
user-supplied input data, it is somewhat more complex to incorporate some of the features found in **labels**. This program has been designed around the **getline** function of
the previous section to provide an extremely flexible user interface. In addition, the
screen color attributes can be configured by a user who also has the **setcolor** program
in Chapter 2. In this program, the user never gets locked into a situation. No matter
where the user is on the data entry screen, it is a simple matter to back up to make
a correction, or to quit the program. The program can be used interactively, or input
can be redirected from a file of label entries.

The **labels** program can accept one optional command-line argument. This is the
filename (or pathname) of the **color.cfg** file produced by **setcolor**. If the **color.cfg** file
is on the current drive/directory, it is not necessary to enter the filename. It will be
loaded automatically. Then the color attributes selected by the user will be used by
labels. If **labels** does not find the color file, it uses the default colors established by
the **colorsub.c** module of Chapter 2.

When **labels** is first executed, it asks if you wish to print a sample label. If you
do, you can accept the default response of YES by pressing the Return key. Then five
lines of the letter H are printed, to allow label alignment. This procedure may be
repeated until you are satisfied with the alignment. It can also be done again at any
time while the program is running.

After the alignment, answering N to the question produces the five-line label area
on the screen. When the user has filled in any of the five lines as desired and pressed

80

Return or the down arrow on the fifth line, the program asks for a count. This is the number of these labels that will be printed. The progress of the printing process is displayed on the screen. Then the whole process is repeated, from the sample query to entering another label. Previously entered information is retained for all prompts. That way, only the information that has changed needs to be retyped.

All of the **getline** editing features are available wherever user input is required, except of course when the program prompts for the pressing of the Return key. At any time before printing begins, the user can press the up-arrow key to back up. If he is in the label area, the input area moves up to the previous line. If the user has advanced as far as the count field or the "Press ENTER when the printer is ready..." prompt, the program will return to the sample query. Then the Return key or the down-arrow key can be used to move to the desired input field. At any prompt, a Control-Z can be typed to exit the program. While printing is in progress, the Escape key can be used to stop the printer, even if the input has been redirected from a file. This is possible because the BIOS input function **bscanc** is used to check the keyboard during printing.

The redirection capability can be convenient for those labels that you reprint regularly. For example, the following text file can be created with any ASCII editor to permit the printing of labels without the need to retype the information every time **labels** is run.

```
n
Okeefenokee Mortgage Company
Installment Loans Dept.
1234 Bayshore Drive, Suite 12
Miami
Florida 33103
5
<blank line>
n
Aunt Mary Jacobs
Route 7, Box 103
Hogeye, AR 72602
<blank line>
<blank line>
2
<blank line>
<end of file>, this is not actually typed into the file.
```

Two labels for printing have been specified, and the responses necessary for all input prompts have been included. The n on the first line is the response to the query for a sample label print. You will need to run **labels** interactively to allow label alignment, because the program will not wait for you to check the alignment if input has been redirected.

There is a line for every **labels** prompt for each label in this sample input file. There must be a blank line following the label count to get past the prompt that wants you to press the Return key when the printer is ready. Also, all label lines in this file that follow the first label must have enough trailing blanks to overtype data left in the line from the previous label. In the above example, the first label line of the second label is shorter than that line of the first label. That would cause some of the data from the first label's line one to appear in the output of the second label, unless the second label has enough blanks at the end of each line. This happens because the program does not clear lines for the next entry, but retains the information instead. In interactive use, this feature is often helpful. When redirecting from a file, however, there is less need to retain previous data.

It is possible to modify **labels** to work both ways; that is, you can have the program retain previous label data when it is being used interactively, as it does now, and also have the program clear label lines before starting a new label when input has been redirected. You can do it with three program lines using the **get_dev** function in Section 3.1. Remember that **getline** assumes a blank input line when passed an input buffer where the first byte is \0. If you would like **labels** to work this way, I will leave the modification to you. You might want to refer to the **get_dev** usage in the modified **getch** function of section 3.1 and the code that prints a sample label in **labels**.

There are only a couple of other things in the **labels** program that I would like to mention. First, the primary design consideration in the program was that it would be used interactively most of the time. That is why so much of the effort went into the screen design and user interface. This type of program also lends itself quite well to input redirection, because of the repetitive nature of its input information. You are likely to reprint the same labels over and over. It is convenient to store these labels in their own file and redirect input from that file rather than rekey the information each time. Because the end-of-file can be reached at any time, if the redirected file is not properly constructed, it is necessary to check at every input request. **labels** will terminate whenever an end-of-file is encountered. This prevents the program from hanging, waiting for more input from a redirected file, and locking the user out of the program.

Secondly, **labels** uses a slightly modified version of the **get_colors** function from the **setcolor** program. In this version, **get_colors** accepts a filename argument and returns a value. The filename argument is what allows the program to accept a filename on the command line as an alternate color file. The return value is simply TRUE or FALSE (one or zero) to indicate whether the passed filename argument resulted in a successful load. **labels** uses the return value to determine which of two messages to display.

If you are using Lattice C Version 3, there are a couple of minor changes you should make to **labels**. These relate to the opening of the printer device. There are a couple of ways this can be handled in Version 3. One way is this: due to a difference in the handling of devices in Version 3, device names like CON, PRN, and LPT1 cannot include the terminating colon. Therefore, in the program line that opens prn:, you should delete the colon. In addition, you should call **setnbf(prnfp)** after the open, as now the output will be buffered to 512 bytes unless the file is set to nonbuffered. Previously, devices were automatically opened in a nonbuffered mode.

There is an easier method with this version of the compiler. First, there is no longer any need to open the print device. With Version 3, Lattice now defines a *standard print* device in **stdio.h** just like the standard output, called **stdprn**. To use this method, delete the program lines that open the printer. In the calls to **prnlabel**, or in **prnlabel** itself, call **fprintf** with **stdprn** as the FILE pointer argument.

Chapter 4

Tapping The
Power Of DOS

The PC-DOS manual describes a number of service routines available to assembly language programs. We have already seen some of these in previous chapters. C programs can access these routines, or DOS function calls, through the intdos library functions.

The only DOS function calls used in previous chapters dealt with console input/output, and disabling the Control-Break key sequence. These barely scratch the surface of the DOS function calls. There are the usual file handling calls found in any disk operating system. The C library provides that interface through its own file manipulation functions, but there are many other DOS functions that the C library ignores. C programs can be much more powerful by using some of those function calls. (Note that many of these "ignored" functions are now included in Lattice Version 3, along with some other very useful functions for sorting data and for dealing with PC networks that are compatible with DOS 3.1.)

4.1 TAKE ADVANTAGE OF DOS FUNCTION CALLS

Some DOS function calls are so useful that you will wonder how you ever lived without them. This chapter provides C functions that get or set the system date and time. There is a set of functions to expand ambiguous filenames, like *.*, that make your C programs run like DOS commands. There is another group of functions that allow your programs to examine and use *environment* variables; for example, your program can examine the PATH to find its data files. Then they don't have to be in the current drive/directory.

The C Connection

The C programmer's key to the use of DOS function calls is a pair of library functions called intdos and intdosx. They are very similar in operation to the int86 and int86x functions. The only difference is that the intdos functions always call the same software interrupt, INT 0x21. This interrupt is reserved for access to DOS function calls. Because the intdos functions always call INT 0x21, there is no interrupt-number argument passed to them. The desired DOS function is selected by passing a function number in register AH.

The other arguments to intdos are the same as those to int86, so we can use the REGS union. intdosx accepts segment registers in the SREGS structure, like int86x. These declarations appear in dos.h. They are reproduced in Appendix B. If your compiler does not include the intdos functions, you may be able to use those in Appendix D. These are C language functions that rely on the assembly language int86x function in Appendix C.

Lattice Version 3 adds the intdoss and int86s to access DOS and BIOS functions. These eliminate the problem of not being able to obtain segment registers returned by these calls. A different data structure defined as **union REGSS** in **dos.h** now includes storage for the DS and ES segment registers. These are the registers most often used by DOS for returning data.

4.2 TERMINOLOGY

The concept of *tree-structured directories* was brought to the PC with the introduction of DOS 2.0. This extremely useful system of disk file management allows a floppy or hard disk to be subdivided into an arbitrary number of logical partitions, called *subdirectories*. The partitions are named by the user, and may be added, altered, or removed from the system at will. Hard disk owners find this type of directory system indispensable for grouping and tracking large numbers of programs and data files. We have the Unix operating system developers to thank for this convenience and many of the other features found in PC-DOS. It is to the credit of Microsoft that, of all the computer operating systems out there, they chose Unix as the one to emulate in their operating system for the PC. Now, Microsoft, how about giving us more features of that very powerful system? We could use redirection of the standard error output and event trapping. Most of all, why not add a shell script language to replace those inept .BAT files?

With the powerful new features in post-2.0 PC-DOS versions came a new terminology—new to PC users, that is. Before getting any deeper into this chapter, I would like to make sure that we understand each other with regard to some of this terminology. Specifically, there is sometimes a little confusion about exactly what is meant by *filename* and *pathname*. For the purposes of this book, let's agree on some basic definitions.

The PC-DOS manual defines these concepts, and those are the definitions that will be used here. I would like to add, though, that in actual use, filename and pathname are often used interchangeably. Where any of the programs in this book refer to a filename as a command-line argument, for example, a full pathname is also acceptable. In other words, filename and pathname refer to a disk file. That may seem obvious, but there is some confusion when a pathname does not end with a filename. In this case, what we really have is a directory name. (Let's forget for a moment that a directory, itself, is just a file. The usual PC application does not consider a directory a file, but rather a location.)

It is often convenient to refer to the individual components that make up a pathname. For this purpose, a directory name refers to a pathname that terminates with a directory, not a file. For example, the root designator, a backslash, (\), is a directory name. Many users create a directory called DOS to contain the DOS programs. In this case, \DOS is a directory name, and \DOS\CHKDSK.COM is a pathname. CHKDSK.COM is the *basename* of this pathname. It is also a filename. Thus, a path is made up of a directory name and a basename. The directory name may be prepended with a drive designator, like A:. Of course, a directory name may consist of several directory names. If a directory called UTIL is created from the DOS directory, then \DOS\UTIL is also a directory name; it refers to a location on the disk.

These definitions are not complete, but they will serve our purposes for this book. Where the terms filename, pathname, directory name, and basename are used, you can assume they conform to the above examples. Now that any existing confusion has been compounded, we can continue.

4.3 THE SYSTEM DATE AND TIME

DOS provides four function calls for finding and setting the system date and time. The ndate function in Fig. 4-1 calls DOS function 0x2a to get the current date. DOS returns the date as three numeric values, one each for the month, the day, and the year. The year is returned as a four-digit value; that is, it will return 1987, not 87. Note that ndate returns these three values in int variables. The caller must pass pointers to the three integers. If the caller passes three integers, rather than their addresses, strange things will happen.

Figure 4-1 includes another function, called sdate that illustrates how ndate is called. The purpose of sdate is to return the current date in string form. A character pointer is passed to this function. The pointer must address a character array with at least 11 bytes available to store a string in the form mm-dd-yyyy plus the \0 terminator. Then sdate returns the pointer that was passed.

ndate is most useful where the numeric value of the date is needed for internal computations, such as finding the number of days between two dates. The sdate function is more useful for display purposes. If your program prompts the user to enter a date, it can use the sdate function in a call to the getline function in Chapter 3 to provide a default value.

```
char newdate[11], *sdate();
   ...
c = getline(sdate(newdate), 10, brkval);
```

This call to getline results in the sdate function being called first to fill newdate with the current date. getline displays the current date upon entry. Note that sdate must be declared char * when the return value is used.

Figure 4-2 contains two similar functions to return the system time. DOS function call 0x2c returns the current time in the same manner as the date—as four numeric

```
/**
* NAME
*       ndate      -- returns system date in integer form
*       sdate      -- return system date as a string
*
* SYNOPSIS
*       ndate(pm, pd, py);
*       ps = sdate(s);
*
*       int      *pm, *pd, *py;          integer pointers for month, day, year
*       char     *ps;                    char ptr returned by sdate
*       char     *s;                     buffer for storage for date
*
* DESCRIPTION
*       ndate - returns the system date as three integers for the month,
*               day, and year. Note that pointers to integers are passed to
*               this function.
*
*       sdate - returns the date as a string in the form m-dd-yyyy, and
*               the string is \0 terminated. sdate must be declared char * if
*               the return value is used.
*
* RETURNS
*       The sdate function returns a pointer to s, the buffer
* passed to store the return info.
*       ndate returns nothing, but the current date is placed where the
* integer pointers direct (hopefully to an integer).
**/

#include <dos.h>

/********/

ndate(m, d, y)
int      *m, *d, *y;      /* NOTE: these are integer pointers !!          */
{
        union    REGS u;

        u.h.ah = 0x2a;
        intdos(&u, &u);
        *y = u.x.cx;
        *m = u.h.dh;
        *d = u.h.dl;
}

/********/

char     *sdate(s)
char     *s;
{
        int      m, d, y;

        ndate(&m, &d, &y);
        sprintf(s, "%2d-%02d-%d", m, d, y);
        return(s);
}
/********/
```

Fig. 4-1. The ndate and sdate functions.

```
/**
* NAME
*       ntime   -- returns system time in integer form
*       stime   -- returns system time as a string
*
* SYNOPSIS
*       ntime(ph, pm, ps);
*       pt = stime(s);
*
*       int     *ph, *pm, *ps;           integer pointers for hour, min, second
*       char    *pt;                     char ptr returned by stime
*       char    *s;                      buffer for storage of time
*
* DESCRIPTION
*       ntime - returns the system time as three integers for the hour,
*               minute, and second. The hour is in the range 0 - 23. Note
*               that pointers to integers are passed to this function.
*
*       stime - returns the time as a string in the form hh:mm:ss, and
*               the string is \0 terminated. stime must be declared char * if
*               the return value is used.
*
* RETURNS
*       The stime function returns a pointer to s, the buffer passed to
* store the return info.
*       ntime returns nothing, but the current time is placed where the
* integer pointers direct (hopefully to an integer).
**/

#include <dos.h>

/********/

ntime(h, m, s)
int     *h, *m, *s;     /* NOTE: these are int pointers !!                */
{
        union   REGS u;

        u.h.ah = 0x2c;
        intdos(&u, &u);
        *h = u.h.ch;
        *m = u.h.cl;
        *s = u.h.dh;    /* note 1/100's seconds are available in DL       */
}                       /* ...but are not returned by ntime               */

/********/

char    *stime(st)
char    *st;
{
        int     h, m, s;

        ntime(&h, &m, &s);
        sprintf(st, "%02d:%02d:%02d", h, m, s);
        return(st);
}
/********/
```

Fig. 4-2. The ntime and stime functions.

values. Note that **ntime** returns only three of these, the hour, the second, and the minute. The fourth value is hundredths of a second. Because I have never needed to know the time to the hundredth of a second, I did not bother to return it. **ntime** expects three **int** pointers as **ndate** does. The **stime** function in Fig. 4-2 calls **ntime** and returns the current time as a string. Because **stime** is defined as **char *** and returns the pointer it was passed, it can be used like **sdate** in the above example.

Lattice now includes the function **getclk** in Version 3 to return the system date and time. Both are returned as six integers with a single call to this function.

The system date can be set with DOS function call 0x2b. The **setndate** function in Fig. 4-3 is the inverse of **ndate**. It sets the date according to the three integers passed. Note that these are not pointers. If the date appears invalid to DOS, **setndate** returns minus one; otherwise zero is returned. These are the values that DOS itself returns in register AL. **setndate** cannot just **return(u.h.al)** because AL is a one-byte register, which contains 0xff if the call was unsuccessful. Some compilers consider this as a positive value of 255 decimal (as the Lattice compiler does in Version 2), while others might consider it minus one (as Lattice Version 3 does). That is, some compilers treat characters as unsigned values, while others treat characters as signed values. Because you cannot rely on a character being either signed or unsigned, **setndate** is implicitly defined as an **int** function (by the lack of a type declaration), and an **int** is explicitly returned.

The **setsdate** function in Fig. 4-3 is the inverse of the **sdate** function. It takes the date as a string argument. The string is decoded into three integers, and **setndate** is called to set the date. The return value is the same. **setsdate** allows some flexibility in the construction of the date string. The description section in Fig. 4-3 explains the variations allowed.

The functions in Fig. 4-4 allow the system time to be set in the same manner as the date is set. The return values are the same. If DOS considers the time to be invalid, minus one is returned. The time can be set with integers or a string argument.

In Version 3, Lattice also includes a function called **setclk** to set the date and time with a single call. Six integers are passed. If either the date or time is invalid, the function indicates so, but you will not know which was incorrect. Version 3 also includes several other time and date functions. Most of these are Unix compatible functions that can be used in place of the **getclk** function if Unix compatibility is of concern to you.

4.4 POINTERS AND MEMORY MODELS

I have already mentioned the problem with C pointers for the different memory models when using the **intdos** or **int86** class of functions. I would like to bring the information together into one place here because the problem becomes more important in this chapter.

Many of the DOS function calls require a four-byte address, which has nothing to do with the C memory model we happen to be using. It is just a requirement of the particular DOS call. DOS always wants the segment portion of the address in a segment register, either DS or ES. While the **intdosx** function allows us to pass segment registers to DOS, it does nothing to help us obtain the segment address of a C variable. The **segread** function is only of limited use in this problem. Specifically, it is only useful when all C data is in the same segment.

```
/**
* NAME
*       setndate -- set system date with integer arguments
*       setsdate -- set system date with string argument
*
* SYNOPSIS
*       stat = setndate(m, d, y);
*       stat = setsdate(s);
*
*       int     m, d, y;                month, day, and year as integers
*       char    *s;                     string containing date
*       int     stat;                   indicates invalid date
*
* DESCRIPTION
*       setndate - sets the system date from three integers for the month, day,
*                and year. If the date is invalid, -1 is returned, else zero.
*
*       setsdate - sets the system date from a string in the form m-d-y or
*                m/d/y. y may be two or four digits. m and d may be one or
*                two digits. The return is the same as for setndate.
*
* RETURNS
*       The date setting functions return zero if successful, otherwise
* -1 is returned.
**/

#include <dos.h>

/********/

setndate(m, d, y)
int     m, d, y;
{
        union   REGS u;

        u.h.ah = 0x2b;
        u.x.cx = y;
        u.h.dh = m;
        u.h.dl = d;
        intdos(&u, &u);
        return(u.h.al ? -1 : 0);
}

/********/

setsdate(s)
char    *s;
{
        int     m, d, y;

        if(sscanf(s, "%2d-%2d-%4d", &m, &d, &y) != 3)
                if(sscanf(s, "%2d/%2d/%4d", &m, &d, &y) != 3)
                        return( -1);

        if(y < 1900)
                y += 1900;

        return(setndate(m, d, y));
}
/********/
```

Fig. 4-3. The setndate and setsdate functions.

```
/**
 * NAME
 *       setntime -- set system time with integer arguments
 *       setstime -- set system time with string argument
 *
 * SYNOPSIS
 *       stat = setntime(h, m, s);
 *       stat = setstime(buf);
 *
 *       int     h, m, s;               hour, min, second as integers
 *       char    *buf;                  buffer containing time to set
 *       int     stat;                  indicates invalid time
 *
 * DESCRIPTION
 *       setntime - sets the system time from three integers for the hour,
 *              minute, and second. The hour must be in the range 0 - 23.
 *              If the time is invalid, -1 is returned, else zero.
 *
 *       setstime - sets the system time from a string in the form h:m:s. Hours
 *              are assumed to be between 0 and 23. h, m, and s may be either
 *              one or two digits. The return is the same as for setntime.
 *
 * RETURNS
 *       The time setting functions return zero if successful, otherwise -1
 * is returned.
 **/

#include <dos.h>

/********/

setntime(h, m, s)
int     h, m, s;
{
        union   REGS u;

        u.h.ah = 0x2d;
        u.h.ch = h;
        u.h.cl = m;
        u.h.dh = s;
        u.h.dl = 0;        /* set 1/100's seconds to zero          */
        intdos(&u, &u);
        return(u.h.al ? -1 : 0);
}

/********/

setstime(st)
char    *st;
{
        int     h, m, s;

        if(sscanf(st, "%2d:%2d:%2d", &h, &m, &s) != 3)
                return( -1);

        return(setntime(h, m, s));
}
/********/
```

Fig. 4-4. The setntime and setstime functions.

The Lattice compiler makes sure that all C data is in the same segment only in the small data models. In large data models, where a data address is four bytes rather than two, the data may be in any segment. There are a few ways, though, that we can find the segment address. Perhaps the easiest way is to purchase the Version 3 upgrade. In this version, functions have been added that solve the problem. makedv is a function in the new library that will load the segment:offset of a C variable into two integers as required by the intdosx or intdoss (Version 3 only) call. The makedv function works for all memory models.

When developing a library of functions to be used by programs that we create later, it is important that the library functions work for any memory model. It is a real pain to keep a different source code version for each memory model. Any change to a library function would require all versions of the function to be updated. What if we are using Version 2 of the compiler? As we have already seen, there are some ways around the problem. It is still possible to create one source code version that will work for all memory models.

One of the ways we can obtain a four-byte pointer is by treating it as two short integers by using a process called *type punning*. This is not a portable way to do things, but intdos functions are not portable anyway, so there is nothing to lose. This method is demonstrated in the functions in the next section. Another way is to make sure the data we are addressing is static data. Lattice says that all static data is accessible via the DS register. We can't be sure that the data is static in all cases. Where this is not known, we can type pun or we can move the data to a known segment before addressing it. Besides moving the data to a static area, we could move it to an auto area. Then the data is in the stack segment, addressed by the SS register. This method has already been demonstrated in the dgetcr function of Chapter 3.

Of the methods available to us, makedv in Version 3 is the most efficient. Type punning is the most efficient in Version 2. Obviously, having to move the data is the least efficient in terms of speed. The data may have to be moved twice: once from the caller's location to our known location, and again back to the caller's location, if the data has changed. Moving the data, however, may be the most reliable method if you don't know how your compiler stores pointers or don't know how to tell at compile time whether a small or large data model is being used. All of these methods will be demonstrated in this chapter. You can choose the method that best fits your situation.

The function in Fig. 4-5 emulates the Lattice Version 3 makedv function. The arguments and returns are the same, and this one will also work for all memory models. If you later upgrade to Version 3 of the Lattice compiler, you will not need this version of makedv, but all your programs that call this function will work without modification.

makedv in Fig. 4-5 depends on the Lattice compiler's LPTR definition. The compiler defines LPTR for either of the large data models; otherwise it is undefined. If you are using a different compiler, you may be able to use this function too. You will need a segread function, or you must be able to adapt the one in Appendix E to your compiler. If your compiler defines some symbol other than LPTR to mean the same thing, just change the symbol in makedv, or you can define it yourself. When you are compiling with a large data model, add the following line to the beginning of makedv:

```
#define   LPTR 1
/* not necessary with Lattice compiler */
```

```
/**
 * NAME
 *      makedv -- return segment:offset (vector) of C data
 *
 * SYNOPSIS
 *      makedv(d, doff, dseg);
 *
 *      char    *d;       C data pointer
 *      short   *doff;    pointer to storage for returned offset
 *      short   *dseg;    pointer to storage for returned segment
 *
 * DESCRIPTION
 *      This function breaks a C data pointer into its segment:offset
 * portions. This function is primarily designed for use with the int86x
 * and intdosx functions.
 *
 * RETURNS
 *      Upon return from this function, the short pointed to by doff will
 * contain the offset portion of the "d" address, and the short pointed to
 * by dseg will contain the segment address of "d".
 *
 * NOTES
 *      "d" is the address of C data.
 *
 * EXAMPLE
 *      The following will return the vector of a character array.
 *
 *      #include <dos.h>
 *      char    filename[] = "anyfile";
 *      union   REGS    r;
 *      struct  SREGS   seg;
 *      ...
 *      makedv(filename, &r.x.dx, &seg.ds);
 **/

#include <dos.h>

makedv(d, doff, dseg)
char    *d;
short   *doff, *dseg;
{
#ifdef  LPTR
        short   *pi;

        pi = (short *) &d;
        *doff = *pi++;
        *dseg = *pi;
#else
        struct  SREGS seg;

        segread(&seg);
        *doff = (short) d;
        *dseg = seg.ds;
#endif
}
/********/
```

Fig. 4-5. The makeder function.

The makedv function in Fig. 4-5 compiles in two completely different ways. If LPTR is defined, type punning is used to obtain the segment and offset of the pointer argument d. Four-byte pointers are stored in offset, segment order in the Lattice compiler. This is the arrangement needed by the assembly language LES instruction. If LPTR is not defined, the pointer is a two-byte offset in the data segment. It is stored in *doff by casting it to a short. Then the DS register contents are obtained with a segread call, and stored into *dseg.

4.5 PROCESSING AMBIGUOUS FILENAMES

DOS provides two function calls that are helpful in expanding ambiguous filenames. An ambiguous filename is any filename that contains a DOS wildcard character. The DOS wildcard characters are ? and *. ? matches any single character, and * matches zero or more characters. Thus, COPY A:*.* B: copies all files from drive A: to drive B:.

Ambiguous filenames can be used with almost any DOS command, but they are rarely available in programs. Even the DOS utilities will not accept wildcards in the filename. Wouldn't it be nice if you could type something like

```
find "func(" *.c
```

to search all C files in the current directory? Using a pair of DOS functions, it is quite simple to incorporate this capability into your own programs. It is really hard to imagine why the DOS utilities didn't.

DOS function 0x4e accepts a full pathname and returns the first matching filename. It doesn't care, if the filename is explicit; that is, it will work with \a\b*.c as well as with \a\b\prog.c. DOS function 0x4f is used to find any subsequent matches. These DOS functions have been incorporated into the two functions fff and fnf, respectively, in the code in Fig. 4-6. As a suggestion, you might name this module DIRSRCH.C. The directory search functions depend on the dirsrch.h header file in Fig. 4-7. It defines a data structure to be used when you are accessing the data returned by these functions.

fff requires two arguments. The first is a pointer to a struct file__dat buffer into which DOS will place information about the file found, if any. The pathname to be used for the search is passed as a character pointer for the second argument. The return value from fff should be checked for zero before assuming the call was successful. If it was successful, the filename and other information will be in filebuf. This same buffer must be passed, unaltered, to fnf if the search is to be continued. The basic logic to be used with these functions is shown in Fig. 4-8. These two functions rely on the makedv function from the previous section to work with all memory models.

DOS returns the file information in an area known as the *Disk Transfer Area* (DTA). This area is normally at offset 0x80 in the Program Segment Prefix, but it may be changed with DOS function 0x1a. So that multiple calls to fff can be made without disturbing the file information needed for fnf, the DTA is set to filebuf by both the fff and the fnf functions. With DOS Version 2.0, the DTA is no longer used for disk file data transfers, so it is probably safe to move the DTA as we need. DOS will reset it when our program exits. Our programs can store as many different filebuf areas as we need.

None of the other DOS functions used in this book rely on the DTA. It would be wise, however, to check the details in the DOS manual when writing your own func-

```
/**
 * NAME
 *       fff, fnf - find first file, find next file
 *
 * SYNOPSIS
 *       err = fff(filebuf, pathname);    find first file
 *
 *       err = fnf(filebuf);              find next file
 *
 *       int     err;                     error return
 *       struct  file_dat *filebuf;       DOS buffer for return data
 *       char    *pathname;               filename to search for
 *
 * DESCRIPTION
 *       fff searches the pathname for the first matching file. fnf returns
 * all subsequent files that match the pathname pattern.  The pathname is
 * supplied only to fff.
 *
 * RETURNS
 *       Error return from both functions is 0 if a match was found, and
 * the file's data is in filebuf.  See dirsrch.h for the file_dat structure.
 * Non-zero error return indicates no match was found.  The errors are
 * defined in dirsrch.h, according to the DOS manual.
 *
 * CAUTIONS
 *       The data placed in filebuf by fff must not be altered if fnf is
 * to be called for the next match.
 *
 *       These functions alter the DOS DTA. To my knowledge, the DTA is not
 * used by PCDOS Vers 2.x except for these DOS calls. If you experience
 * strange behavior when using these functions, you may need to reset the DTA
 * to its previous status before fff and fnf return. Note that I have used
 * these functions in many circumstances with no problems.
 **/

#include <dos.h>
#include <dirsrch.h>

#define CY        1                  /* carry flag mask                     */

int      fattrib = 0;                /* file attribute for searches         */

fff(filebuf, pathname)
struct   file_dat *filebuf;
char     *pathname;
{
        union   REGS    u;
        struct  SREGS   s;

/* set DTA to filebuf                                                       */
        makedv((char *) filebuf, &u.x.dx, &s.ds);    /* get seg:offset */
        u.x.ax = 0x1a00;
        intdosx(&u, &u, &s);

/* find first file                                                          */
        makedv(pathname, &u.x.dx, &s.ds);
        u.x.ax = 0x4e00;
        u.x.cx = fattrib;            /* file mode to search for             */
        return((intdosx(&u, &u, &s) & CY) ? u.x.ax : 0);
}
```

Fig. 4-6. The fff and fnf functions.

94

```
/********
* find next file
********/

fnf(filebuf)
struct   file_dat *filebuf;
{
        union   REGS    u;
        struct  SREGS   s;

/* must be sure DTA is set to filebuf                          */
        makedv((char *) filebuf, &u.x.dx, &s.ds);
        u.x.ax = 0x1a00;
        intdosx(&u, &u, &s);

/* find next file                                              */
        u.x.ax = 0x4f00;
        return((intdosx(&u,&u,&s) & CY) ? u.x.ax : 0);
}
/********/
```

tions that use other DOS calls. Make sure that those DOS functions do not depend on the DTA before incorporating fff and fnf into a program. If any DOS functions do depend on the DTA, you may be able to reset it after it is used in these functions. DOS function 0x2f returns the current DTA in ES:BX. Unfortunately, intdosx cannot be used to retrieve ES, unless you are using the version in Appendix D in this book. Lattice Version 3 can do it, using intdoss, so your problem is solved if you have that version of the compiler.

If you have Version 3 of the Lattice compiler, you might want to check into the dfind and dnext functions. They perform a service similar to fff and fnf. One of the major differences is that they do not actually change the DTA location. Another is that the file attribute that defines which files are to be included in a search is passed as an argument to dfind. fff, on the other hand, makes the attribute available in the external integer fattrib. The fff default attribute of zero includes only normal files in the search; no hidden files or directories will be located. Later programs will show how the attribute can be manipulated to provide different search capabilities. You can also get this information from the DOS manual and from the Lattice Version 3 manual.

Lattice Version 2 users do have an alternative, if they find that they do not want to change the DTA. The startup module, C.ASM, defines the location of the Program Segment Prefix. Thus, fff and fnf can be modified to move data from the DTA to filebuf, rather than changing the DTA. To adopt this method, remove the code from fff and fnf that changes the DTA. Then use peek to move the data from the DTA after the DOS call in fff, as shown in Fig. 4-9. In fnf you need to use poke before the DOS call to move the contents of filebuf to the DTA.

Lattice users can examine the data segment declarations in C.ASM for the definition of __PSP. It is defined as two words. The first word is the offset; the second is the segment. In the peek in Fig. 4-9 __psp[1] is the segment argument, and 0x80 is the offset cast to a character pointer.

If you have other than a Lattice compiler, you might find in the documentation that it too defines the location of the PSP. If so, you can use this method by adapting the variable name to your implementation. Note, however, that there can be a problem

```
/**
* name:   dirsrch.h
*
*        Structure for accessing the information returned by the DOS file-
* search calls, fff and fnf.
*
**/

/***********************
this is the data returned in the caller's buffer
***********************/

struct  file_dat      {
        char    rsrv[21];         /* reserved DOS info for 'next' calls  */
        char    attrib;           /* file attribute                      */
        unsigned time;            /* file's time                         */
        unsigned date;            /* and date, in bit format             */
        long    size;             /* file's size                         */
        char    name[13];         /* filename'\0'                        */
};

/* constants for error-codes returned by 'find-first' & 'find-next' file*/
/* 0 is returned if a match is found                                    */

#define FNF    2       /* file-not-found ('find-first' only)            */
#define NMF    18      /* no-more-files  ('find-first' and '-next')     */

/**************************************************************************/
```

Fig. 4-7. The dirsrch header file.

with this method, because it assumes that the DTA has not been changed from the DOS default. Unless you have an overriding reason to do otherwise, I suggest that you stick with the versions of fff and fnf in Fig. 4-6. Most programs that change the DTA do so before they use it; thus the method in Fig. 4-6 should be safe.

Other File Information

By examining the file_dat structure in Fig. 4-7, you can see that the DOS find-file functions return additional information about a file. Besides the filename, which is

```
#include <dirsrch.h>
struct     file_dat file;
int        fstat;
char       pathname[] = "\a\b\*.c"; /* find all .c files in \a\b */
    ...
if((fstat = fff(&file, pathname)) != 0) { /* look for first match */
    printf("No match for %s\n", pathname);
    exit(1);
}
while(fstat == 0) {
    printf("%s\n", file.name);     /* process each file found */
    fstat = fnf(&file);            /* get next file           */
}
```

Fig. 4-8. The logic to be used with the fff and fnf functions.

```
            extern      short _psp[2];        /* for access to PSP */

                ... after the intdosx call & before returning ...
            if((intdosx(&u, &u, &s) & CY) == 0) {
                u.x.ax = 0;      /* call was successful, setup for return */
                peek( _psp[1], (char *) 0x80, filebuf,
                      sizeof(struct file_dat));
            }
            return(u.x.ax);
```

Fig. 4-9. The peek logic for Lattice Version 2 users.

```
/**
 * NAME
 *      fdate -- return file date as a string
 *      ftime -- return file time as a string
 *
 * SYNOPSIS
 * ps = fdate(s,date);
 * ps = ftime(s,time);
 *
 * char *ps;                    Pointer to "s"
 * char *s;                     String to store date/time into: mm-dd-yyyy
 *                              Time returned in format: hh:mm:ss
 * unsigned date;               Date in packed format as returned by DOS file-
 *                              search function call.
 * unsigned time;               Time in packed format as returned by same.
 *
 * DESCRIPTION
 *      These functions unpack the file date and time as returned by
 * the "fff" and "fnf" functions, and store them in the supplied string area.
 * The string is null terminated, so allow room for the extra byte.
 *
 * RETURN
 *      A pointer to the supplied buffer is returned. If the return value
 * is to be used, be sure to declare these functions "char *".
 **/

/**** date 16-bit format ****/
/* <15 14 13 12 11 10 9> <8 7 6 5> <4 3 2 1 0>                              */
/*          Year         Month    Day                                      */
/* 0-119 (base: 1980)    1-12     1-31                                     */


char    *fdate(s, date)
char    *s;
unsigned date;
{
        int     m,d,y;

        y = (date >> 9) + 1980; /* add base year                          */
        m = date >> 5 & 0x0f;
        d = date & 0x1f;

        sprintf(s,"%2d-%02d-%d",m,d,y);
```

Fig. 4-10. The fdate and ftime functions.

```
        return(s);
}
/*******************************************************************************/
/**** time 16-bit format ****/
/* <15 14 13 12 11> <10 9 8 7 6 5> <4 3 2 1 0>                         */
/*      Hour            Minute       Second, (divided by 2)            */
/*      0-23            0-59         0-29                              */

char    *ftime(st, time)
char    *st;
unsigned time;
{
        int     h,m,s;

        h = time >> 11;
        m = time >> 5 & 0x3f;
        s = (time & 0x1f) * 2;   /* adjust to seconds                 */

        sprintf(st,"%02d:%02d:%02d",h,m,s);
        return(st);
}
/********/
```

returned in the FILENAME.EXT format, the file attribute, time, date, and size are returned. The attribute of the file defines whether the file is a system file, a hidden file, a read-only file, a volume label, or a directory. It also contains the archive bit, used by the DOS backup program. The size of the file is a long integer, easily converted to display format with printf. The time and date are in a special packed format, each contained in 16 bits. The first 21 bytes are reserved by DOS for use with find-next-file calls.

The file date and time can be used in their packed format for simple comparisons with another file's date or time. If you want to display the date or time, or to access the individual components, they must be unpacked. The fdate and ftime functions in Fig. 4-10 unpack the date and time and return them as strings in a buffer supplied by the caller. These functions return a pointer to the supplied buffer, so they can be used in the manner shown in Fig. 4-11.

If you are using Lattice Version 3, you might want to make a change to the file_dat structure for the date and time variables. Lattice now includes several functions for manipulating the file date and time as a long integer. Therefore, you could change the unsigned date; unsigned time; declaration to long datetime;. The Lattice ftunpk function will unpack the date and time into a six character array. Then stpdate and stptime can be used to convert this array to a string.

If you are not using the find-file functions, either those in Fig. 4-6 or the Lattice Version 3 functions, and just want to obtain a file date and time, Lattice provides getft. It returns the file date and time in a long integer that can be used with ftunpk. ftpack and setft provide the opposite services; they pack the file date and time from a character array into a long integer and use it to set a file date and time.

4.6 SORTED FILE LISTS

Whenever ambiguous filenames are specified in a Unix command, the files are

98

```
#include <dirsrch.h>
char dbuf[11], tbuf[9], *fdate(), *ftime();
struct file_dat file;

    ...                  /* code that calls fff or fnf to load struct */
printf("%s %s\n", fdate(dbuf, file.date), ftime(tbuf, file.time));
```

Fig. 4-11. Logic to be used with fdate and ftime.

provided in sorted order. In some situations, this convenience is unimportant. In many others, however, it is essential. For example, the Unix **cat** command sends its filename command-line arguments to the standard output, one after the other. The command

```
cat chap.1 chap.2 chap.3
```

reads the three files in the order on the command line and sends them to the standard output. If these three files were the only files in the current directory that begin with chap, the following command would have the same effect, and requires less typing:

```
cat chap.*
```

This command on a PC would present the files to **cat** in various orders at different times, only occasionally providing them in sorted order. They would be in sorted order only if they were built consecutively in the current directory. If any one of them is later modified, the order in the directory might change, thus changing the order in which these files would be presented. It is apparent from the naming of the files that they have some logical order to their creation. Maybe they are consecutive chapters of a book or of some software documentation. Obviously, a command like **cat chap.*** is not very useful with these files if the files are presented in random order to **cat**.

The PC-DOS find-file functions simply locate files by directory position, but our programs do not have to be satisfied with that order. The filenames can be sorted before processing, and the **sort** function in Fig. 4-12 can be used to perform this chore.

The **sort** function is a very quick in-memory sort. It is a modified Shell-Metzner routine that will sort a thousand lines in less than two seconds (in the small data models, longer in large data models). This routine is also easily adaptable to provide sorting of any data type. In this version, it performs an ascending sort in ASCII sequence. The speed is due, in part, to the fact that it swaps character pointers rather than the character strings themselves.

To adapt **sort** to perform a descending order, only the compare needs to be changed; it should be changed to greater-than-or-equal. To sort numeric data types, the compare and swap routines only need to be changed. Other types of string compares can be done by providing your own compare function. Then you could add dictionary sorting, fold upper and lowercase together, and so on.

Creating the Filename List

In order to use the **sort** function, all the filenames matching an ambiguous specifi-

```
/**
 * NAME
 *      sort -- sort a list of character pointers
 *
 * SYNOPSIS
 *
 *      sort(d, n);
 *
 *      char    *d[];   list of character pointers
 *      int     n;      number of pointers in list
 *
 * DESCRIPTION
 *      "sort" performs an ascending sort in ASCII sequence. The character
 * pointers are sorted based on the comparison of the character strings they
 * point to.
 *
 * RETURN
 *      Nothing is returned, but "d[]" is in sorted order.
 **/

sort(d, n)
char    *d[];
int     n;
{
        int     p, i, j, k;
        char    *ptmp;

        for(p = n/2; p > 0; p /= 2)
                for(k = n - p, j = 0; j < k; j++)
                        for(i = j; i >= 0; i -= p) {
                                if(strcmp(d[i], d[i + p]) <= 0)
                                        break;
                                ptmp = d[i];
                                d[i] = d[i + p];
                                d[i + p] = ptmp;
                        }
}
/********/
```

Fig. 4-12. The sort function.

cation must be resident in memory. The functions in Fig. 4-13 will build a list of pointers to all filenames matching an ambiguous specification. There are three functions here. opnlist is called first with the maximum number of filenames to allow in the expansion. It acquires enough memory to hold n filenames with the getmem function. This is a Lattice function, but any memory allocation function can be used here. If you change this function, you will need to make a related change in clslist to the proper function for releasing the memory acquired in opnlist. If the needed memory is unavailable, opnlist returns −1. If opnlist has been called previously, without an intervening call to clslist, it will return −2. This means that filelist can still be called with no problems, but the number of files allowed by the original call to opnlist is still in effect.

The clslist function simply frees the memory allocated by an opnlist call. You can call clslist to release the memory taken for the list of filenames when your program has finished with the files, if the space is needed for other processing. It is also necessary to call clslist if you wish to change the maximum number of files allowed in the opnlist call.

```
/**
* NAME
*       opnlist  -- allocate memory for a list of filenames
*       filelist -- get list of filenames
*       clslist  -- free memory allocated by opnlist
*
* SYNOPSIS
*       error = opnlist(n);
*       count = filelist(path, list);
*       clslist();
*
*       int     error;          indicates success/failure of opnlist
*       int     n;              max. number of files to allow
*       int     count;          number of files found, or error
*       char    *path;          pathname to find file list for
*       char    *list[];        array of pointers to files found
*                               list is NULL terminated (must be n+1 in size)
*
* DESCRIPTION
*       opnlist - allocates enough memory to contain "n" filenames.
*
*       filelist - finds all files matching "path", and creates a list of
*               pointers to the filenames in "list". The last pointer is NULL.
*
*       clslist - frees the memory allocated by opnlist. clslist only needs
*               to be called to:
*               1. free the memory allocated by opnlist; or,
*               2. call opnlist again.
*               Otherwise, it is NOT necessary to call clslist and call
*               opnlist again, in order to call filelist again.
*
* RETURNS
*       opnlist - returns zero if OK, -1 if insufficient memory, -2 if
*               already open.
*
*       filelist - returns count of files found, -1 if opnlist was not called
*               or call to opnlist was unsuccessful, -2 if number of matching
*               files exceeded the space allocated by opnlist.
*               NOTE: if -2 is returned, you can still use the list because
*                       it is NULL-terminated.
*
*       clslist - nothing returned.
*
* NOTE:  list[] must contain space for max + 1 files, to allow for a NULL as
*        the last element.
**/

#include <dirsrch.h>

#ifdef  LPTR
#define NULL    0L
#else
#define NULL    0
#endif

#define ERROR   (-1)                    /* fatal error return        */
#define FNSIZE  13                      /* max. filename size        */

/* define variables used by all functions                           */
```

Fig. 4-13. The opnlist, filelist, and cislist functions.

```
static    char      *pbase = NULL, *pnext = NULL, *pend = NULL;
static    int       maxnames = 0;
/******************************************************************/
int       filelist(path, list)
char      *path, *list[];
{
          int       name_cnt, fstat;
          struct    file_dat file;
          char      *strsave();

/* first, check to see that opnlist() has been called              */

          if(pbase == NULL)
                    return(ERROR);

          name_cnt = 0;
          pnext = pbase;                   /* next is at beginning      */

          if((fstat = fff(&file, path)) != 0) {
                    *list = NULL;
                    return(0);
          }

          while(fstat == 0) {
                    if(name_cnt >= maxnames) {
                              *list = NULL;
                              name_cnt = -2;
                              break;
                    }
                    if((*list++ = strsave(file.name)) == NULL) {
                              name_cnt = -2;
                              break;
                    }

                    *list = NULL;
                    name_cnt++;
                    fstat = fnf(&file);
          }

          return(name_cnt);
}
/**********************************************
* opnlist() must be called once, or after any clslist() call, before
* filelist() can be used:
*
* RETURN: -1 if insufficient memory, -2 if already open, else 0.
***/

int       opnlist(n)
int       n;                     /* max. # of filenames to allow in an expansion */
{
          char      *getmem();

          if(pbase != NULL)
                    return(-2);

          if((pbase = getmem(FNSIZE * (n + 1))) == NULL)
                    return(ERROR);
          maxnames = n;
          pnext = pbase;
          pend = pbase + FNSIZE * n;
```

```
                return(0);
}
/*****************************************
* clslist() may be called to release the memory taken by an opnlist() call.
***/

clslist()                    /* returns nothing */
{
        if(pbase)
                rlsmem(pbase);

        maxnames = 0;
        pbase = pnext = pend = NULL;
}
/*****************************************
* strsave() is used only by filelist() to store strings of filenames
*
* RETURN: ptr to saved string, or NULL if no space.
***/

static  char *strsave(s)
char    *s;
{
        int lens;

        lens = strlen(s) + 1;               /* allow for '\0' terminator    */
        if((pnext + lens) >= pend)
                return(NULL);

        strcpy(pnext, s);
        pnext += lens;

        return(pnext - lens);
}
/********/
```

The filelist function is called after opnlist with a pathname argument and an argv type of pointer. filelist returns a count of matching files. The space for the list of pointers is defined by the calling program and should be equal to at least n + 1 elements; that is, if you pass a count of 100 to opnlist, to allow a maximum expansion to 100 filenames, then you should define char *list[101]. This is necessary because filelist will place a NULL pointer in the list element after the last pointer to a filename. It does not matter if the pathname contains an explicit basename rather than an ambiguous one. If filelist finds that file, it will return a pointer to it in the first element of list and a count of one. The count will equal zero if no match was found.

If opnlist has not been called, or clslist has before the call to filelist, it will return −1. If the number of files matched exceeds the capacity of list, that is, if the number of files is greater than the argument passed to opnlist, −2 is returned as the file count. In this case, the list will contain the maximum number of files allowed by the call to opnlist.

Note that it is not necessary to call clslist and then to call opnlist after each call to filelist. filelist can be called over and over again. It will store the new filenames over the old ones in the same memory space allocated by opnlist. Be aware that the list of pointers built by a previous call will no longer be valid, so you might as well pass the

```
#define   MAXLIST 100      /* allow up to 100 files */
char *list[MAXLIST + 1];   /* allow room for NULL pointer */
int   count;
    ...
if(opnlist(MAXLIST) == -1)
    exit(1);               /* not enough memory */
if((count = filelist("\a\b\*.c", list)) > 0)
    sort(list, count);
```

Fig. 4-14. Code that illustrates the use of the filelist and sort functions.

same list to filelist on subsequent calls.

After the call to filelist, the sort function can be called to sort the filenames. The code fragment in Fig. 4-14 illustrates the usage of filelist and sort. You would probably want to provide better error checking with appropriate messages in your own programs. In this example, I have limited the filename expansion to a maximum of MAXLIST. The call to filelist will find all .c files in directory \a\b and return the count of matches. If just *.c had been specified as the pathname, the current directory would be searched. Of course, drive designators are also allowed as part of our definition of a pathname; that is, B:*.c or C:\a\b*.c are OK.

4.7 A TURBO-CHARGED "CAT"

Now that we have all the tools, we can modify the standard cat command to work like it does under Unix: with ambiguous filenames in sorted order. Figure 4-15 shows the new cat program. The usage is:

```
cat [pathname] [pathname] ...
```

The cat command is followed by one or more optional pathnames. If no pathname is specified, input is from the standard input. This allows you to quickly build a simple text file with the following command:

```
cat >textfile
```

This command will accept input from the keyboard until Control-Z is typed as the first character on a line. All input will go into the file named textfile. If an ambiguous filename is specified, all matching files will go to the standard output in sorted order. Note that because this is an ASCII sort, numeric values in a filename will be correctly sorted only if they are decimal-point justified. For example, the following list would NOT be sorted numerically:

    chap.8
    chap.9
    chap.10

These filenames, after sort, would be in the following order:

    chap.10

```
    /* (This program is from p. 154 of the Kernighan and Ritchie text */
    /* modified to use ambiguous filenames                            */

#include <stdio.h>

#define MAXLIST 100      /* max. files in an expansion */

static  char    *name[MAXLIST + 1];

main(argc, argv)         /* cat: concatenate files */
int argc;
char *argv[];
{
    FILE *fp, *fopen();
    char dir[65], pathname[80], **pname;
    int count;

    if (argc == 1) /* no args; copy standard input */
        filecopy(stdin);
    else {
        if(opnlist(MAXLIST) == -1) {
                fprintf(stderr,"cat: not enough memory.\n");
                exit(1);
        }

        while (--argc > 0) {
                if((count = filelist(*++argv, name)) == -2) {
                        fprintf(stderr, "cat: too many files in %s\n",*argv);
                        exit(1);
                } else if(count == -1) {
                        fprintf(stderr, "cat: memory error.\n");
                        exit(1);
                } else if(count == 0) {
                        fprintf(stderr,"cat: no match for %s\n", *argv);
                        continue;
                }
                sort(name, count);
                dirname(*argv, dir);
                pname = name;
                while(count-- > 0) {
                        sprintf(pathname,"%s%s", dir, *pname++);
                        if ((fp = fopen(pathname, "r")) == NULL) {
                                fprintf(stderr,
                                        "cat: can't open %s\n", pathname);
                                exit(1);
                        } else {
                                filecopy(fp);
                                fclose(fp);
                        }
                } /* end of name list */
        } /* end of argv */
    } /* end */
    exit(0);
}
/*********/
filecopy(fp)      /* copy file fp to standard output */
FILE *fp;
{
    int c;
```

Fig. 4-15. The modified cat program.

```
        while ((c = getc(fp)) != EOF)
            putc(c, stdout);
    }
    /*********/
```

chap.8
chap.9

In order to get the proper sorted order, the files must be named so that the numerics are decimal-point aligned:

chap.08
chap.09
chap.10

This naming convention would produce a sorted order the same as shown. Note that the following naming convention will also produce the desired order:

chap08.txt
chap09.txt
chap10.txt

The action of the **sort** function is to do a character-by-character comparison for each column position. It would require a more sophisticated compare function than **strcmp** to give numeric values special consideration.

The **cat** program in Fig. 4-15 illustrates how the **filelist** and **sort** functions can be used to provide a sorted file listing. You will notice that **clslist** is never called in this program. **opnlist** has been called once with a value of MAXLIST. In this case, the MAXLIST definition allows a maximum of 100 filenames in a single ambiguous filename expansion. Additional filenames on the command line are limited to the same maximum. The effect, of course, is not additive. That is, the first command-line filename can expand to the maximum, as can each subsequent command-line filename. In other words, the command:

`cat *.c *.doc`

allows up to MAXLIST .c files and up to MAXLIST .doc files. If an expansion finds more than MAXLIST filenames, **cat** prints a message on the standard error output stating this fact and terminates.

If you think that the limit of 100 files is too few, you can increase the allowance by changing MAXLIST. It is easy to determine the amount of memory needed to store MAXLIST filenames. The **opnlist** function allocates 13 bytes per filename. In this case, space for 100 filenames, or 1300 bytes, has been requested. Given that the amount of static and external memory required by **cat** is quite small, you could easily allocate space for 1000 filenames and still compile this with the small memory model. The space required for the filenames would only be 13000 bytes of the 64K bytes available before stack and other static data is deducted. Of course, the pointer list, which is stored as name[MAXLIST + 1], requires sizeof(char *) times MAXLIST space. In small data models, sizeof(char *) equals two, so the pointer list for a MAXLIST of 1000 is 2000 bytes, which is in addition to the 13000 bytes needed to store 1000 filenames. In other words, we haven't come even close to the 64K limit with a MAXLIST of 1000 filenames.

If you have been perusing the source code for cat, you probably noticed the call to the function dirname following the calls to filelist and sort. dirname is a function that has not been shown yet, but it will be used in most of the programs that call the find-file functions directly or indirectly through the filelist function. dirname.c is shown in Fig. 4-16. Its purpose is to extract the directory name from a pathname. The DOS find-file functions, as you have seen, accept a pathname for the file search and return

```
/**
 * NAME
 *       dirname - extract directory name from pathname
 *
 * SYNOPSIS
 *       ps = dirname(path, dir);
 *
 *       char    *ps;                    points to dir on return
 *       char    *path;                  pathname from which directory is
 *                                           extracted.
 *       char    *dir;                   buffer to place directory name into
 *                                       should be > 64 bytes
 *
 * DESCRIPTION
 *       Extracts just the directory path from a full pathname, assumed to
 * end with a filename.  The last PATH SEPARATOR character is not removed in
 * the directory name; e.g.
 *          "\dir\subdir\file" becomes "\dir\subdir\"
 *          or: "b:filename" becomes "b:".
 * Note that ambiguous filenames are OK; eg, "\a\b\*.c" returns "\a\b\"
 **/

#define PATHSEP '\\'     /* backslash for PC-DOS; slash for Unix        */

char    *dirname(path, dir)
char    *path;
char    *dir;
{
        char    *pend, *dir_sav;

        dir_sav = dir;
        for(pend = path; *pend; pend++);

        while(pend >path && *pend != PATHSEP && *pend != ':')
                pend--;

        if(*pend == PATHSEP || *pend == ':')
                while(path <= pend)
                        *dir++ = *path++;

        *dir = '\0';
        return(dir_sav);
}
/*******************************/
```

Fig. 4-16. The dirname function.

only a filename (basename). If the program needs to open such a file, as **cat** does, the filename alone is not sufficient. It needs the entire pathname. Thus, the directory name must be prepended to the returned basename before the call to open the file.

The **dirname** function was designed primarily for this use. In keeping with our definition of pathname, a drive designator is also considered a directory name. The **dirname** function is called with a pathname and a buffer in which the extracted directory name may be stored. Table 4-1 illustrates how **dirname** works. The pathname passed to **dirname** is a null-terminated string in the usual C convention. The directory name returned is a null-terminated string containing the drive and/or directory name, if any. You will notice that a directory name is returned with the trailing backslash intact. Because the purpose of **dirname** is to return a string that can be prepended to a filename, directory names and drive designators are returned as shown in the table. That way, it does not matter what type of pathname is entered on the command line. As you can see, a simple basename returns a null string, with a first byte of \0. The pathname to a specific file can always be built with a simple call to **sprintf** as shown in the **cat** program, regardless of the pathname construction.

4.8 USING THE ENVIRONMENT

You can add a nice touch to your programs by making use of the DOS *environment*. The environment contains variables that can be set by a user or by a program. The PATH is one of these variables that is often set by a user. As you know, it is used by DOS to find a program that is not in the current directory. Unfortunately, DOS does not consult the PATH (or any other environment variables) when an open-file call is made.

Your programs, however, can consult the environment directly. When is this useful? Any program that accesses or maintains a data file can make productive use of the environment. You are undoubtedly familiar with many programs that keep or refer to data files. You also know that these programs must usually be run in the same directory where the data files exist. In many cases, this is of no concern. There are other times, though, that it would be especially convenient if a program could access its files from some other directory. Just as an example, take the case of a person who often uses a spreadsheet program in conjunction with a word processing program to produce a report. This usually requires that the spreadsheet be created in the directory where the spreadsheet program resides. Then the spreadsheet file must be copied to the word processor directory so that the spreadsheet can be loaded by the word processor. This is not only inconvenient but also wasteful of disk space if you

Table 4-1. How dirname Works.

```
    Pathname                    Directory name returned
    --------                    -----------------------

    "filename.ext"              ""
    "\a\b\*.c"                  "\a\b\"
    "A:filename.ext"            "A:"
    "C:\*.c"                    "C:\"
```

forget to delete the original copy. This example is not necessarily valid anymore, because many word processing programs will accept pathnames to locate files, but I think you get the picture. There are still many programs that do not take advantage of pathnames and even more that do not search the environment.

Environment searches are essential to programs that consult files that are not user specified. For another example, the word processor might be using device driver tables kept for the purpose of determining printer type, display type, and other data. These files are usually created in the current directory when the user specifies his system configuration to the program. If the user then changes to another directory and attempts to execute the program, it will not be able to locate its setup files. The DOS PATH variable allowed DOS to find and execute the program, but now the program cannot find its setup files in the new directory. WordStar users are particularly familiar with this problem, but it is a problem for many other programs, too.

You do not need to let your programs suffer from this deficiency. There are a couple of ways to attack the problem, and they both involve accessing the environment. The first attack is to have your program search the directories indicated by the PATH variable, if a file cannot be found in the current directory. Another possibility is to have the program user set a unique variable into the environment before running your program. This can be a line in an autoexec.bat file, if desired. For example, assume that you are writing a program that keeps a database of real estate listings. You could instruct the program's user to set a line like the following into the environment:

```
set REALDATA=C:\LISTINGS
```

The listings program and data files might both be located in a directory named c:\listings, or just the data might be stored in that directory. If your program searches the environment for the REALDATA entry and finds it, then the program can find its data no matter what the current directory is at run time.

The which Program

Have you ever executed a program and found that it was not the one you had expected? This can happen for a variety of reasons and occurs when you have two or more programs with the same name. These programs would have to be on different drives or in different directories, of course, but the PATH contents might cause DOS to locate a program that was not intended.

You may have two programs with the same name because you have purchased software packages. Two different packages could contain programs with the same name; yet these two programs would probably do entirely different things. For example, you might have the DOS find program in the \DOS directory. You might also have purchased a package of Unix-like utilities that include the find program and have them in the \UTIL directory.

The DOS find program searches a file for a string; the Unix utility searches directories for files based on a variety of options. Obviously, one program will not substitute for the other. If your PATH includes both of the above directories, you know that which find will be executed depends on the order of the directory names in the PATH. You also know that the other find can only be executed, if you change into its directory.

This type of situation can also occur if you create your own programs. When updating a program to a new version, it is common practice to retain the old version until debugging of the new version is completed. This could take days, or even weeks. In the meantime, you will probably have two versions of the same program on your disk with the same name, though in different directories.

While all this program creation and addition of new software packages is going on, which is usually most of the time, you are probably also continuously changing your PATH. Before long, you do not know for sure which program you are executing. (See Fig. 4-17.) When in doubt, just execute which progname, and the path of the program to be executed is displayed. In the case of the two find programs, you can type:

```
which find.exe
```

and the which program will display the pathname to the program that will be executed. Depending on the current directory and the PATH list at the time which is executed, you would see one of the following lines as output from which:

```
\DOS\FIND.EXE
```

or

```
\UTIL\FIND.EXE
```

If you are not sure whether find is an EXE or COM file, the program name could be entered on the which command line as find.*.

The which program does basically the same thing that DOS does when you execute a program: it searches the current directory and then the directories in the PATH, stopping when (and if) it locates the filenames on the command line. More than one filename can be provided, and which will search for each of them. Note that this is a case where "filename" should not include a directory name.

All functions except the main function in which are generalized so that they can be used to search any environment variable that contains a list of directory names. It is the main function in which that specifies that the PATH environment variable is the list to be searched. You can see that the main function for which, in Fig. 4-17, is very simple. If there is not at least one command-line argument, which displays a usage message and exits. Otherwise, it loops through all arguments, calling the srchpath function for each one. If the srchpath function returns TRUE, the pathname is printed on the standard output.

The srchpath function in Fig. 4-18 does all the work. It is aided by two other functions: the getdir function in Fig. 4-19, and the getpaths function in Fig. 4-20. Together these three functions form a unit that can be used to search a list of directory names specified in any environment variable.

The srchpath function is provided a base filename (with no directory name), the name of the environment variable to be used, and a flag to indicate whether or not the current directory is to be searched. There is also a buffer in which srchpath stores the directory name that contains the file. This directory name will have the same format as returned by the dirname function, so that it can easily be prepended to the filename where desired.

```
/**
 * NAME
 *        which -- search PATH for a filename
 *
 * SYNOPSIS
 *        which filename [filename(s)...]
 *
 * DESCRIPTION
 *        Searches paths specified in the PATH environment variable for
 * the first occurrence, if any, of the specified filenames. If a match
 * is found, the path and input filename is printed on the standard output.
 *
 * NOTES
 *        The filename(s) given as argument(s) should not contain a
 * directory name.
 *
 * EXAMPLES
 *        which command.com
 *        ...searches the PATH's for the location of "command.com".
 *
 *        which prog.*
 *        ...searches the PATH's for the first match for "prog.*". Note
 * that "\dirname\prog.*" is the output, not the actual filename found.
 **/

#include <stdio.h>

main(argc, argv)
int     argc;
char    *argv[];
{
        char    path[65];

        if(argc < 2) {
                fprintf(stderr,"Usage: which filename(s)\n");
                exit(1);
        }

        while(--argc > 0)
                if(srchpath(path, *++argv, "PATH", 1))
                        printf("%s%s\n", path, *argv);

        exit(0);
}
/********/
```

Fig. 4-17. The which program.

The which program provides srchpath with a character array called path for the directory name. It should be large enough to accommodate any directory name. Each command-line argument is passed as the filename for the search. The environment variable PATH is supplied and a one is passed to indicate that the current directory is to be included in the search. When the current directory is included in the search, it is the first directory to be searched. To exclude the current directory from the search, a zero should be passed in place of the one.

If srchpath returns TRUE (one), a match was found and is printed on the standard

```
/**
 * NAME
 *       srchpath -- search paths for a filename
 *
 * SYNOPSIS
 *       stat = srchpath(buf, filename, env_var, cur_dir);
 *
 *       int     stat;           return value
 *       char    *buf;           buffer for path returned
 *       char    *filename;      filename to search for
 *       char    *env_var;       environment variable to use for search
 *       int     cur_dir;        = 0 if current directory is to be
 *                               excluded from search; non-zero to include
 *
 * DESCRIPTION
 *       Searches paths specified in "env_var", starting at current directory
 * if "cur_dir" is non-zero, for "filename".  If found, path (eg: "\"
 * or "\dir\subdir\") is placed in "buf". Note: if the file is found in the
 * current directory, the current directory name is returned.
 *
 * RETURNS
 *       1 is returned if a match is found for "filename".
 *       0 is returned if no match is found, or if "env_var" is not in
 * the environment.
 *
 * CAUTIONS
 *       "buf" is altered by this function call. Check the return value
 * before using the contents of "buf".
 *       "buf" should be long enough to hold a pathname. Usually, 65 bytes
 * is sufficient.
 *       "filename" should not include a directory name, though "filename"
 * can include wildcards.
 *
 **/
#include <dirsrch.h>

#define FND     1       /* return val for "match found"                 */
#define NFND    0       /* return val for "no match found"              */

srchpath(buf, filename, env_var, cur_dir)
char    *buf, *filename, *env_var;
{
        char    *path[34], tmpbuf[65];
        struct  file_dat buf2;
        int     i,stat;

/* first search current directory if required                           */
        if(cur_dir) {
                *buf++ = '\\';
                getdir(buf);                    /* get current directory name   */
                if(*buf--)                      /* if not root, add '\'         */
                        strcat(buf,"\\");

                sprintf(tmpbuf, "%s%s", buf, filename);
                if(fff(&buf2, tmpbuf) == 0)
                        return(FND);
        }

/* not in current dir, so search environ. variable                      */
```

Fig. 4-18. The srchpath function.

```
        getpaths(path, env_var);

        stat = NFND;                            /* assume not found          */
        for(i = 0; path[i]; i++) {
                strcpy(buf, path[i]);
                if(buf[strlen(buf) - 1] != '\\')        /* if not root..*/
                        strcat(buf,"\\");               /* add '\'      */

                sprintf(tmpbuf,"%s%s", buf, filename);
                if(fff(&buf2, tmpbuf) == 0) {
                        stat = FND;
                        break;
                }
        }

        return(stat);
}
/*********/
```

output. Otherwise, nothing is printed. Then the next argument on the command-line is searched. This loop continues until all command-line arguments have been exhausted; then which exits.

The srchpath function begins by checking the cur_dir flag to see if the current directory is to be searched. In the case of the which program, the current directory should be searched because DOS would do so. A call to getdir returns the current directory name. Then fff is called to see if there is a match. If there is, srchpath returns to the caller with the current directory name in the caller's buffer.

If the file is not in the current directory (or the current directory was not included in the search), srchpath calls getpaths with a character pointer array and the environment variable. getpaths retrieves the list of paths from the environment variable and builds a list of pointers, one to each directory name, in the array. The array is NULL terminated. This fact is used by the for loop in srchpath to provide a termination of the loop. On each loop iteration, a full pathname is constructed from the directory name and the filename. This pathname is then passed to fff. If fff returns a nonzero value, the match failed and the next directory name in the loop is used to continue the search. Otherwise, if fff returns zero, a match was found and the loop is terminated. srchpath returns to the caller with a TRUE value, and the directory name is in the caller's buffer.

The getdir function in Fig. 4-19 calls DOS function 0x47 to retrieve the name of the current directory. Another technique is used in this function to achieve compatibility with all memory models. Although the makedv function could have been used and would have been efficient in both code size and speed, I have elected to retrieve the current directory in an auto character buffer. This guarantees that the variable is accessible from the stack segment (SS) register. segread is called to obtain the SS contents, and this is transferred to DS as required by the DOS function. After return from the DOS function, the contents of the auto variable are copied to the caller's buffer with strcpy, and a pointer to this buffer is returned to the caller.

The getpaths function in Fig. 4-20 must consult the environment to obtain the list of paths. It retrieves a pointer to the supplied environment variable with a call to the getenv function. If getenv returns NULL, the variable is not in the environment, so getpaths returns immediately. Note that the first element in the supplied character

```
/**
* NAME
*         getdir -- get the current directory via DOS function 0x47.
*
* SYNOPSIS
*         ps = getdir(buf);
*
*         char    *ps;       pointer to "buf"
*         char    *buf;      Buffer to place curr. dir. into (no drive), for
*                            example "" for root, "dir\subdir"; ie, leading '\'
*                            not included for any directory name.
*
* DESCRIPTION
*         Gets the current directory. No leading "\" is provided. The
* directory name is returned exactly as the DOS function provides it.
*
* RETURNS
*         A pointer to "buf" is returned.
*
* NOTES
*         "buf" should be long enough to contain the longest directory name;
* 65 bytes should be sufficient.
*         Uses intdosx(), with provisions to work for all Lattice memory models
* and no special compile parameters needed.
**/

#include <dos.h>

char    *getdir(buf)
char    *buf;
{
        char    *strcpy();
        char    path[FMSIZE + 1];       /* tmp buffer for dir. name      */
        union   REGS inr, outr;
        struct  SREGS segr;

/* get current seg registers so that ss can be assigned to ds            */

        segread(&segr);
        segr.ds = segr.ss;              /* ds = path[] segment for DOS   */
        inr.x.si = (short) path;        /* si = path[] offset for DOS    */

/* set up remaining registers for DOS function call 0x47                 */

        inr.x.dx = 0;                   /* use default drive             */
        inr.x.ax = 0x4700;         /* ah = 0x47, al = don't care         */

        intdosx(&inr, &outr, &segr);

/* path[] contains current dir. on return from above                     */
/* ... copy it to the caller's buffer.                                   */

        return(strcpy(buf, path));      /* return pointer to buf         */
}
/*********/
```

Fig. 4-19. The getdir function.

```
/**
 * NAME
 *       getpaths -- return array of character pointers to paths specified
 *                   in an environment variable.
 *
 * SYNOPSIS
 *       getpaths(pp, env_var);
 *
 *       char *pp[];       array in which pointers to various paths may be
 *                         stored.
 *       char *env_var;    environment variable to use.
 *
 * DESCRIPTION
 *       Searches for "env_var" in the environment. It is assumed that
 * "env_var" is a list of one or more directory names. If "env_var" is
 * found, the directory names line is parsed into individual directory
 * names and a list of pointers to these names is returned in "pp". The
 * last element of "pp" is NULL, to indicate the end of the list.
 *
 * RETURNS
 *       Nothing is returned, but "pp" contains the list of pointers to
 * any directory names found. The last element in "pp" is NULL.
 *       If "env_var" is not in the environment, or is empty, the first
 * element of "pp" is NULL.
 *
 * CAUTION
 *       At least 33 elements should be allowed for in "pp": max = 32 + NULL
 * at end.
 *       The path strings pointed to by "pp" are stored in a static data
 * area. Therefore, this area is destroyed on a subsequent call to this
 * function; the pointers are then invalid.
 **/

/* Lattice defines LPTR if compiling in large data model              */
#ifdef   LPTR
#define NULL    0L       /* NULL is (long) in large data model          */
#else
#define NULL    0        /*...otherwise it is (short)                  */
#endif

/* storage for path strings                                           */
static  char     path[129];       /* max DOS input string length + 1   */

getpaths(pp, env_var)
char    *pp[], *env_var;
{
        int     i;
        char    *getenv(), *penv, *strcpy(), *pe;

        pp[0] = NULL;
        if((pe = getenv(env_var)) == NULL)
                return;

/* must copy contents of "env_var" to static area before altering...   */
        penv = strcpy(path, pe);

        i = 0;
        while(*penv) {
```

Fig. 4-20. The getpaths function.

```
                 pp[i++] = penv;
                 while(*penv) {
                         if(*penv == ';') {
                                 *penv++ = '\0';
                                 break;
                         }
                         penv++;
                 }
         }

         pp[i] = NULL;
}
/*********/
```

pointer array was set to NULL previously, in the event that this happens.

If the pointer returned by **getenv** is not NULL, the contents of the environment variable are copied to a static data area. This is necessary because **getpaths** alters the path list obtained from the environment variable. If we altered the path list itself, it could not be used by any other part of the program. The alteration that is performed is shown below. The string of paths appears similar to the following when it is placed in the environment:

`\;\DOS;\UTIL;\LC;\LC\SOURCE`

There are five directory names separated from each other with a semicolon. The string is null-terminated. The **while** loop in **getpaths** converts each directory name to a null-terminated string by searching the above string from left to right until a semicolon is found. The semicolon is replaced with a NULL byte, and a pointer to the directory name is stored in the character pointer array passed by the caller. Upon return, the character pointer array would contain five pointers, and a sixth pointer that is NULL. This is illustrated in the following table:

```
pa[0] => \
pa[1] => \DOS
pa[2] => \UTIL
pa[3] => \LC
pa[4] => \LC\SOURCE
pa[5] == NULL
```

Remember that each element in the array is a character pointer. The string it points to is terminated with a NULL byte, in the usual convention. Nothing is returned by **getpaths**. The first pointer is NULL if the environment variable does not exist or contains no entries. Because the usual convention for entering a directory name into the environment does not include a terminating backslash, except in the case of the root directory, it should be clearer now what **srchpath** (Fig. 4-18) is doing with each entry in the list. If the last character of the directory name is not a backslash, one is appended before the filename is appended.

The **srchpath** function can make your programs much more convenient to use, whether the program is running from a hard disk or floppies. It frees the program from dependence on the current directory or drive. It also eliminates the need for a *front-end* configuration section in your program in which the user must specify the location of specific files to the program. This configuration stuff not only is less flexible, but also is an inconvenience to both the user and the programmer. It is much easier to change an environment variable to adapt to changing system configurations than it is to change the setup of every program on the system.

Lattice has reacted to the need for this convenience in their new Version 3 of the compiler by adding new file-access functions called **opene** and **fopene**. These functions search the PATH for the specified file. If the file requested for opening is not in the current directory, the PATH will be searched, and if the file is found, it is opened and the directory name returned. Obviously, the new **opene** functions are convenient for accomplishing many of the same purposes for which **srchpath** might be used. They do not, however, allow other environment variables to be searched. In addition, the file is opened for access, which may or may not be desirable depending on the particular program. In the case of **which**, opening the file is unnecessary and would represent an additional overhead in processing time. The **srchpath** and the new **opene** functions together, however, provide an advance in the way that programs have traditionally viewed the system, making life easier for both the programmer and the user.

4.9 FILE MODES

On the PC, file modes are used to provide certain information about a file. Each mode is indicated by a bit in the file mode byte. The file mode byte is stored in the file's directory entry. DOS function 0x43 can be used to read or change any of the file mode bits for a file. Just why one might want to access a file's mode settings will be more apparent when you know what modes DOS provides.

DOS defines six bit flags in the file mode byte. These are shown in Table 4-2. Not all of these modes can be used on a file. In fact, bit three doesn't even concern a file; it's the disk volume label. This mode will be of the least interest of all, in most situations. The rest of the modes are useful for specific situations.

Most PC disk files will have a mode byte (also referred to as an attribute byte in the DOS manual) of zero, or of 0x20 if the file was created or modified after the last BACKUP. These are the two values most likely to be returned by a call to DOS function 0x43 to read the mode byte. Function 0x43 can also be used to set the mode byte to a different value. The read-only, hidden, system, and archive modes are the only ones that can be set with this DOS function. Setting the volume-label and subdirectory modes would find little use in programs, anyway. There are some applications, however, where being able to determine whether or not a file is actually a subdirectory can be useful.

Table 4-2. The Definitions of the Bit Flags in the File Mode.

BIT	MEANING	VALUE
0	read only	1
1	hidden	2
2	system	4
3	volume label	8
4	sub-directory	10 hex
5	archive	20 hex

Bits zero, one, two, and five can be set with a logical OR of their respective values, or by adding the values together. Before getting into the mechanics, let's consider where these modes might be useful. The first mode in the table, bit zero, is the read-only bit. Setting this bit has the effect of refusing write permission to the file. It can be useful in situations where you do not want to be able to accidentally modify a file. If this bit is set, the file also cannot be deleted. If you try to ERASE or DEL a file with this bit set, DOS will respond with the meaningful message "File not found." This can be useful in preventing the accidental loss of files.

Bit one is set to mark the file as hidden. It will not be displayed with the DIR command. It also cannot be opened. This is not very useful as a protection device, because there are many utilities available that will display hidden files and allow the hidden setting to be removed. Of course, it can be somewhat useful for this purpose, because many casual users may not think to look for hidden files. Many DOS copy-protection schemes use hidden files. (They also incorporate some clever programming, because the software developers are aware that the hidden status is easy to change.) Hidden files will be found by the BACKUP program, but not by COPY.

The system mode setting has no use that I have found. The archive setting, bit five, is used by the BACKUP program. It resets this bit when a file is backed up. It will only backup files that have this bit set when the "/m" switch is used with the BACKUP program. DOS sets the archive bit when a file is created or modified.

It can be useful to see what the mode settings for files are on occasion, especially if you think there are some hidden files lurking somewhere on your disk, or if you want to see which files have been modified since the last BACKUP. To do this, we need a C function that calls DOS function 0x43. The chmod function in Fig. 4-21 will do it for us. It can be used to either read or set a file mode. You will notice that it uses strcpy to achieve compatibility with all memory models, just as getdir does in the previous section. If you are using Lattice Version 3, you might want to change the chmod function to use makedv, or use the makedv function presented with the directory search functions in Section 4.5, if you can.

Calling chmod is somewhat clumsy, because a REGS union must be used. That means that dos.h will have to be included, so I added the getmode and putmode functions, which are also in Fig. 4-21. getmode calls chmod to find the mode of a particular file and returns the mode to the caller. putmode calls chmod to set the mode of a file.

The fmodes Program

The fmodes program in Fig. 4-22 will display the mode settings of a file or group of files. A list of filenames can be given on the command line or from the standard input. Wildcard characters are allowed because the directory-search functions are used to locate the files. If you are giving fmodes the filenames from the keyboard, instead of on the command line, type a Control-Z (EOF) to exit the program.

If you are in a subdirectory with only two C source files in it, and type fmodes *.*, you would see the following output from the program:

```
-d----      .
-d----      ..
a-----      prog1.c
a-----      prog2.c
```

```
/**
* NAME
*        chmod, putmode, getmode - set/get file mode
*
* SYNOPSIS
*        err = putmode(newmode, pathname);          set file mode
*        mode = getmode(pathname);                  get current file mode
*        err = chmod(pu, pathname);                 get or set file mode
*
*        int      err;                              error return
*        int      mode;                             file mode return
*        int      newmode;                          file mode to set
*        char     *pathname;                        full pathname of a file
*        union    REGS *pu;                         register setup:
*                 pu->x.ax = 0 or 1                 get or set file mode
*                 if pu->x.ax == 1, then
*                 pu->x.cx = newmode                mode to be set
*
* DESCRIPTION
*        putmode calls chmod to set the file mode of pathname to newmode.
* getmode returns the file mode of pathname by calling chmod.  chmod may
* be called directly to perform getmode or putmode, but the interface is
* less convenient.  Note that chmod requires a pointer to a union that
* contains pre-set values.
*
* RETURN
*        For chmod, putmode and getmode, -1 is returned if error.  If
* successful, chmod and putmode return 0, and getmode returns the current
* file mode.
*        If chmod returns -1, the DOS error code (2, 3, or 5) is in pu->x.ax.
* If chmod is called to get the file mode (pu->x.ax = 0) and err is 0,
* pu->x.cx has the file mode of pathname upon return.
*
* NOTES
*        Unless you need the explicit error code returned by chmod, putmode
* and getmode are usually preferable since the function call is simpler.
* The usual reasons for failure are that the pathname is invalid, or that
* you are trying to to change the mode of a subdirectory.
*        This is DOS function call 0x43.  Refer to the DOS manual, Appendix C,
* for valid file modes.
**/
#include <dos.h>

#define CY        1                   /* carry flag mask                        */

/*********
* set new file mode
*********/

putmode(mode, pathname)
int      mode;
char     *pathname;
{
        union    REGS u;

        u.x.ax = 1;                   /* for set-file-mode                      */
        u.x.cx = mode;
        return(chmod(&u, pathname));
}
/*********
```

Fig. 4-21. The file mode functions.

```
* get current file mode
*********/

getmode(pathname)
char    *pathname;
{
        union   REGS u;

        u.x.ax = 0;                 /* for get-file-mode              */
        return((chmod(&u, pathname) == 0) ? u.x.cx : -1);
}
/*********
* set/get file mode
*********/

chmod(pu, pathname)
union   REGS *pu;
char    *pathname;
{
        char    path[FMSIZE + 1];       /* max pathname size          */
        struct  SREGS s;

/* must allow for large or small data pointers                        */
        strcpy(path, pathname);
        segread(&s);
        s.ds = s.ss;    /* now we know ds points to the pathname       */
        pu->x.dx = (short) path; /* ds:dx point to the pathname for DOS */

        pu->x.ax != 0x4300;     /* DOS function call to ah              */
        return(((intdosx(pu, pu, &s) & CY) ? -1 : 0);
}
/*********/
```

Any mode bits that are set are indicated by an alpha character; otherwise the dash is shown to indicate that the particular bit is clear; that is, that the mode is not set. The modes are in these relative positions: advshr, to indicate archive, directory, volume label, system, hidden, and read-only, respectively. You will never see the "v" setting with fmodes. A separate directory search is required to locate volume labels. I deemed the volume label to be not important enough to include that logic in the program.

The FINDALL definition in fmodes determines which file mode types will be found by the directory search functions. If you recall, an external int named fattrib was defined in the fff function in Section 4.5. It is initialized to zero in that function, meaning that only normal files will be located. Normal files exclude directories and hidden files. By setting fattrib to 0x16 in fmodes, we can include those files in our directory searches. A different setting for fattrib is required to find a volume label, and then only volume labels are located.

As you can see in Fig. 4-22, the logic of fmodes is quite simple. The main function determines whether or not filenames are on the command line. If not, it accepts filenames from the standard input. For each command-line or standard-input filename, the sho_mode function is called to display the mode bits and filename. This function uses dirname to save the directory name, if any, and calls the directory search functions to expand any ambiguous filenames. I elected to call these functions directly, rather than use filelist and sort, because a sorted file display did not seem particularly impor-

```
/**
 * NAME
 *       fmodes - display file modes
 *
 * SYSNOPSIS
 *       fmodes [pathname(s)]
 *
 * DESCRIPTION
 *       Displays file modes for pathnames on command line or from
 * standard input.
 *
 * LINK
 *       fmodes dirsrch filemode dirname
 **/

#include <stdio.h>
#include <dirsrch.h>

#define FINDALL 0x16    /* code for fff & fnf to find all files      */

extern  int     fattrib;                    /* file mode for fff & fnf    */

/* codes stand for archive, directory, volume label, system, hidden, and */
/* read-only                                                             */
static  char    codes[]    = "advshr";
static  char    modeline[] = "------"; /* to display file modes      */

main(argc, argv)
int     argc;
char    *argv[];
{
        int     n;
        char    inbuf[129];

/* the following setting will find all files except volume labels        */
fattrib = FINDALL;
if(argc > 1)
        while(argc-- > 1)
                sho_mode(*++argv);
else
        while((n = scanf("%s", inbuf)) != EOF) {
                if(n < 1)
                        continue;
                sho_mode(inbuf);
        }
}
/*********
 * get and display file modes
 *********/

sho_mode(afn)
char    *afn;
{
        char    dir[65], path[80];
        struct  file_dat file;
        int     more;

        dirname(afn, dir);
        if((more = fff(&file, afn)) != 0) {
```

Fig. 4-22. The fmodes program.

```
                       fprintf(stderr,"Can't find %s\n", afn);
                       return;
               }
          while(more == 0) {
                       sprintf(path, "%s%s", dir, file.name);
                       do_mode(path);
                       more = fnf(&file);
               }
     }
     /*********
     * get file mode and display
     *********/

     do_mode(pathname)
     char     *pathname;
     {
               int        mode, i, j;

     if((mode = getmode(pathname)) == -1) {
               fprintf(stderr, "Can't get mode for %s\n", pathname);
               return;
     }
     strcpy(modeline, "------");
     for(i = 0, j = 32; i < 6; i++, j >>= 1)
               if(mode & j)
                         modeline[i] = codes[i];
     printf("%s\t%s\n", modeline, pathname);
     }
     /*********/
```

tant in the fmodes output. The sho__mode function calls do__mode to actually translate the mode bits into the display form and display the line.

The archive Program

Using the getmode and putmode functions, it is relatively easy to write a program
that manipulates all of the available file modes. I would like to offer a program here
that I have found particularly useful; it uses only the archive bit. The archive program
in Fig. 4-23 originated from the need to simplify the backup process.

Backing up, especially for hard-disk users, is a hassle. Anything that is a hassle
is usually avoided. I found that I was not backing up as often as I should, resulting
in a constant case of anxiety. One of the reasons that backing up is so tedious is that
you often have to wait through a backup of files that you really do not need to back
up. For example, you might be working on a large software project. Even a relatively
simple project might have many source code files. All of these source files have a corresponding object file created by the compiler. In the course of project development
work in just one day, you may modify and recompile several of the source files, and
some unmodified source files have to be recompiled because they depend on a modification in another file. The DOS BACKUP command with the "/m" switch is most
often used to make incremental backups to save time (and diskettes), but all those OBJ
files will be backed up, too.

Usually, the purpose of a back up is to provide insurance against the unspeakable
catastrophe: hard disk failure. This being the purpose, there is little need to keep back

122

```
/**
 * NAME
 *        archive - display/set file archive bit
 *
 * SYNOPSIS
 *        archive [ ! | -n | -y ]
 *
 * DESCRIPTION
 *        archive allows the user to display and optionally set the backup
 * archive bit of PCDOS files. archive takes a list of one or more file/
 * pathnames from the standard input.  The action taken on each of these
 * pathnames depends on the options.
 *
 * Options:
 *      none      - display files that will be backed up by BACKUP with
 *                  the /m switch (archive bit set).
 *      !         - display files that will not (archive bit not set).
 *      -n        - turn the archive bit off on the input files.
 *      -y        - turn the archive bit on.
 **/

#include <stdio.h>
#include <dirsrch.h>

#define TRUE            1
#define FALSE           0
#define ARCH_BIT        0x20

main(argc,argv)
int     argc;
char    *argv[];
{
        int     usage, notback, endf, set_mode(), chk_mode();

        usage = notback = endf = FALSE;
        if(argc == 2)
                if(argv[1][0] == '-')
                        switch(argv[1][1]) {
                        case 'y':
                        case 'Y':
                                get_arch(set_mode, TRUE);
                                endf = TRUE;
                                break;
                        case 'n':
                        case 'N':
                                get_arch(set_mode, FALSE);
                                endf = TRUE;
                                break;
                        default:
                                usage = TRUE;
                                break;
                        }
                else
                        if(argv[1][0] == '!')
                                notback = TRUE;
                        else
                                usage = TRUE;
        else
                if(argc > 2)
                        usage = TRUE;
```

Fig. 4-23. The archive program.

```
        if(usage) {
                fprintf(stderr,"\nusage: archive [ ! | -n | -y ]\n");
                exit(1);
        }

        if(!endf)
                get_arch(chk_mode, notback);

        exit(0);
}
/*********
* read stdin for list of filenames, and get mode of each
*********/

get_arch(action, arg)
int      (*action)(), arg;
{
        char     pathname[128], inbuf[128],dir[128];
        int      fmode, n, more;
        struct   file_dat fil;

        while((n = scanf("%s",inbuf)) != EOF) {
                if(n < 1)
                        continue;
                dirname(inbuf, dir);
                if((more = fff((char *) &fil, inbuf)) != 0) {
                        fprintf(stderr,"Can't find %s\n", inbuf);
                        continue;
                }
                while(more == 0) {
                        sprintf(pathname,"%.115s%s",dir, fil.name);
                        if((fmode = getmode(pathname)) != -1)
                                (*action)(pathname, fmode, arg);
                        else
                                fprintf(stderr,"Can't get file mode for %s\n",
                                        pathname);
                        more = fnf((char *) &fil);
                }
        }
}
/*********
* check file mode and determine whether to display or not
*********/

chk_mode(fname, curmode, notback)
char     *fname;
int      curmode, notback;
{
        if(((curmode & ARCH_BIT) != 0) != notback)
                printf("%s\n", fname);
}
/*********
* set archive bit on or off
*********/

set_mode(fname, curmode, arch)
char     *fname;
int      curmode, arch;
{
        if(((curmode & ARCH_BIT) != 0) != arch)
                if(putmode(fname, curmode ^ ARCH_BIT) == -1)
                        fprintf(stderr,"Can't set mode in %s\n", fname);
}
/***********************************************/
```

up copies of the OBJ files; they can be recreated by the compiler. Yet the OBJ files can be eliminated from the backup process in only a couple of ways, neither of which is very convenient. One way to avoid backing them up is to delete them all before backing up. It is easy to delete them, but it may take the compiler an hour to compile all the source code to replace them. This can be quite a pain on a daily basis. Another way to avoid backing up the OBJ files is to use filenames in the BACKUP command. That will usually require at least two backup commands: one to save all the .c files and another to save all the .h files. In practice, there are usually other files you will want to save, such as documentation files, temporary data files that took hours to build, and so on.

The whole process would be much easier if you could tell BACKUP which files NOT to back up. That is why I wrote **archive**. It can be used in several ways, including giving the effect of telling BACKUP which files not to back up. Since I created **archive**, I have been backing up much more often and feeling better for it. To solve the problem in the situation just described, **archive** is used first to set the archive bit for all files in the directory (or directories) that are to be backed up. It is then used to reset the archive bit on all OBJ files. Then the BACKUP command (with /m) will back up all files except OBJ files.

The **archive** program is also useful for getting a status check on the need for a back up. It will display all files that have the archive bit set, meaning those files that were created or modified since your last backup. In addition, **archive** will display all files that do NOT have the archive bit set. This way you can be certain that no important files are excluded from back up.

The **archive** program works by taking a list of pathnames from the standard input. That way, a file of pathnames can be built for recurring use. I built a file containing all the directory names on my hard disk. It is easy to do by piping the output of the TREE command through the FIND filter and redirecting output to a file. Each line in the file will look something like the following:

```
Path: \a\b
```

A text editor can be used to modify each line to the format needed by **archive**:

```
\a\b\*.*
```

It usually only takes a few keystrokes to do a global find-and-replace to make these changes to the entire file. If this file containing the pathnames is called **dirfile**, the following command will tell **archive** to search all pathnames in the file and display those files that need to be backed up.

```
archive <dirfile
```

If you see nothing, then there are no files that need to be backed up. If, instead, you wish to see all files that will not be backed up (when the /m switch is used with BACKUP), just add the exclamation point option to the command line:

```
archive ! <dirfile
```

There are two other options that may be used on the **archive** command line: **−n** and **−y**. Use these with caution because they modify the archive bit. The command:

```
archive -n <dirfile
```

will clear the archive bit ("no backup") for all pathnames in the file **dirfile**. The **−y** option sets the archive bits. All three options, !, -n, and −y, are mutually exclusive; only one of them can be used on a command line. Only the last two change anything, and neither of these result in a display of anything from **archive** if all goes well. It does its work silently, unless an error is encountered.

Because **archive** takes the list of pathnames from the standard input, there are other ways it can be used besides redirecting input from a file. It can be used interactively by simply typing the command, with any of its options. You will not be prompted for anything; **archive** will just sit there and wait for you to enter a pathname. Press Control-Z when you are ready to exit. Another possibility is to pipe the pathnames to **archive**:

```
echo *.obj *.exe | archive -n
```

This command will clear the archive bit on all OBJ and EXE files in the current directory. Note that archive exits automatically when input is redirected or piped. It is necessary to type Control-Z only when using **archive** interactively.

Lattice Version 3 contains three functions to access file attribute (or mode) settings. **getfa** returns a file attribute; **chgfa** sets a new attribute; and **chmod** is similar to **chgfa**. The **chmod** is similar to the Unix **chmod** function in name, but the arguments are different. The main reason for this is that Unix provides a different and more extensive set of permission bits.

In closing this chapter, I would like to mention again that the new Lattice Version 3 C compiler includes many functions similar to those presented in this chapter. Other compiler libraries contain some of them, too. In most cases, you will want to use the library version of a function, if it exists. One case in which you might prefer the version in this chapter is when you wish to modify the function. The source code for the Lattice library functions is quite expensive, though some other compilers include the source with the compiler purchase. Another benefit of the functions in this chapter is that they can serve as guidelines for developing your own functions.

Chapter 5

PC Asynchronous Communications

This chapter is an introduction to programming the PC's communication ports. By the time you have finished the chapter, you will have a program that can be used to dial up a host computer and carry on a session with that computer, or to communicate with another PC. If you have never done any asynchronous programming, I think you will find that it is not too difficult—at least not when using the polling method in this chapter. If you have used the polling method in your own programming of asynchronous ports on the PC, you can skim quickly through this chapter and get on to the meaty stuff in Chapter 6.

5.1 A LITTLE BACKGROUND

The general purpose of asynchronous programming is to communicate with another device. In other words, it is to make your PC communicate with such things as printers, modems, and other computers. These days, there are a wide variety of devices that can be operated over an asynchronous port: digitizers, plotters, and even lighting and burglar alarms can be controlled this way. The programming in this chapter provides the foundation you need to communicate with any of these devices.

Why use asynchronous communications? Are there other ways? The two basic ways that a computer communicates with other devices are through serial and parallel ports. As you might think, each way has its advantages and disadvantages. But what is a port? On any computer, it is a doorway in and out of the processor, or CPU. On the PC, it is basically an 8-bit doorway. On other computers, it may be 16 bits, or something else. The ports allow the CPU to transfer data to and from other devices.

The CPU ports are all parallel ports; that is, they can transfer an entire byte at once. A serial port can transfer only one bit at a time. That means that it takes eight transfer operations to transfer one byte. Thus, parallel transfers are much quicker than serial transfers. So why use serial transfers? And how can this be done if all the CPU ports are parallel ports? I bet you thought I was going to be giving you answers, not questions.

Serial transfers are used where parallel transfers are difficult to manage. As you might imagine, a parallel transfer to another device requires a separate wire to carry each bit, so at least an 8-wire cable is needed. In practice, the cable will have additional wires to carry other signals, too. Just look at your parallel printer cable (if you can). On the outside, it may look just like your modem cable, which is a serial cable. But you can bet that the printer cable has many more wires. The point is that parallel cables are more expensive than serial cables, especially the longer the cables become. Over long distances, there is also a problem of line noise, or *crosstalk* between all these data wires. I suppose you have noticed that the phone company does not use ribbon cable between its poles.

To communicate over very long distances, serial cables are the answer. The phone line allows us only a single wire for the transmission of data, so only serial transfers can take place over phone lines. In our PCs, we need a way to convert our parallel data to serial data, before we can use the phone lines to communicate with a distant computer. There are two ways this can be done: write a program that takes each byte and spools the bits out over a single bit of the port, one at a time, or use a serial interface. Bit spooling requires a very precise timing scheme on both the transmit and receive ends, and a half-crazed programmer to write the programs. Obviously, the serial interface is the solution.

The PC uses a more or less standard RS-232 serial interface for serial data transfers. If you have a modem, either external or internal, then you also have an RS-232 serial interface. External modems require an asynchronous card in your PC. It is the RS-232 interface, and it is what the cable from your modem is attached to. If you have an internal modem card, the serial interface is integrated into the modem card. That is one of the disadvantages of internal modems. You cannot use the serial interface for a printer or any other serial device; it is dedicated to the modem.

It is the serial interface circuit that does the bit spooling for you. The PC sends a byte to a CPU port connected to the serial interface (which is why it might be called a serial port), and the interface spools the bits over the modem cable to the modem. The modem converts each bit into a sound frequency on the phone line. That's why you hear that high-pitched squeal. Receiving data is just this process in reverse. Using a serial interface standardizes communications and simplifies the programming.

Equipment You Will Need

You probably understand now that you will need an asynchronous (serial) card or integrated serial port and modem to use asynchronous programs. If you have been using a communications program to dial up other computers, you have everything you need. A modem is optional and is necessary only if you wish to communicate over phone lines. Without a modem, two computers or other devices can communicate over a direct cable connection. This is a connection between the serial ports of each device.

A *null modem* cable can be used to connect the serial ports of two PCs that are near to each other. The cable is so-called because no modem is involved in the connection. Building modem and null modem cables is not particularly difficult, but you need the proper tools, supplies, and information. The information is widely available, as are the tools and supplies, but if you have not built cables before, it is probably just as easy and economical for you to acquire the proper cable from your local computer vendor or through mail order. If you do wish to build your own cable to connect two PCs together, Fig. 5-3 in Section 5.3 shows the connections to make a null modem cable.

5.2 PROGRAMMING THE ASYNCHRONOUS PORTS

Obtaining the proper hardware is only half the job. You also need software to perform the actual data transfers. In this chapter, I am going to present a terminal program that can be used with a modem or with a direct cable connection to communicate with another computer.

There are two methods of serial port input/output available on the PC. One is the polling method, and the other uses system interrupts. The terminal program in this chapter will use the polling method. The next chapter presents the interrupt-driven method. The functions developed in this chapter will be applicable to the terminal program in the next chapter. For a terminal program, the interrupt-driven method is preferable, but the basics used in developing the polled method are essential to the understanding of communications, and there are situations in which the polled method, the simpler one, is quite adequate.

Before we can have a terminal program, we need some basic functions for port input and output. These are similar to the functions we use from the standard library for console input and output. We need a function to get a character from the port and a function to send a character to the port. There are a couple of other functions we will need, too, for housework. These functions are shown in Fig. 5-1.

The two functions in Fig. 5-1 that will be used the most are **comin** and **comout**. They are used for port input and output, respectively. The **cominit** function is used to set up the port for use, and **comoff** disables the port. **p_base** is provided to allow the terminal program to use either of the PC's two communication ports, which are called COM1 and COM2.

Don't let all the #**define** statements in Fig. 5-1 intimidate you. I will not be using all of them. They are there to ease the modification process, should you wish to add your own flavors later. COM1BASE and COM2BASE are used only one at a time, depending on whether you wish to use COM1 or COM2 as the communication port. The terminal program will allow you to use either port.

5.3 DETAILS OF PORT USAGE

So far, I have been talking about the serial port as if it were a single entity. For communications purposes, it is, but one communications port actually requires seven CPU ports for complete operation on the PC. For COM1, these seven ports are consecutively numbered starting at COM1BASE. That is, COM1 uses ports 0x3f8 through 0x3fe. Each of these ports is used for a different purpose; thus, the definitions that follow are used to access the appropriate port when it is needed.

```
/**
* MODULE
*       portio.c -- asynchronous i/o functions
*
* NAME
*       cominit -- prepare com. port for i/o
*       comoff  -- disable com. port
*       comin   -- receive data
*       comout  -- transmit data
*       p_base  -- change port number
*
* SYNOPSIS
*       error = cominit();
*       comoff();
*       cin = comin();
*       error = comout(cout);
*       base = p_base(portnum);
*       int portbase;
*
*       int error;              error return
*       int cin;                input value
*       char cout;              output value
*       int base;               port base
*       portnum;                port number, 1 or 2
*       int portbase;           contains base port for COM1 or COM2; set by
*                               "p_base", defaults to COM1.
*
* DESCRIPTION
* cominit -- prepares port for input/output; uses port assigned to "portbase".
*            Sets DTR and RTS for corresponding port.
*
* comoff  -- disables com port according to "portbase"; resets DTR and RTS.
*
* comin   -- scans input port designated by "portbase". If data available,
*            it is returned, else -1 is returned.
*
* comout  -- outputs character to "portbase" port. Returns zero if successful,
*            else -1 is returned.
*
* p_base  -- sets "portbase" for COM1 or COM2, according to "portnum", which
*            is either 1 or 2. Returns "portbase" for "portnum".
*
* RETURNS
*       cominit Always returns zero.
*       comoff  Returns nothing.
*       comin   Returns the character if available, else -1 to indicate no
*               character is in the RX register.
*       comout  Returns zero if character is successfully transmitted, else
*               -1 is returned to indicate time-out error, TX register not
*               ready.
*       p_base  Returns "portbase" of port number 1 or 2.
**/
/* define port base address, and offsets from base */

#define COM1BASE        0x3F8   /* base port for com1                        */
#define COM2BASE        0x2F8   /* base port for com2                        */


/* port offsets from base */
```

Fig. 5-1. The portio functions.

```
#define TX        0                    /* transmit data                    */
#define RX        0                    /* receive data                     */
#define IER       1                    /* interrupt-enable register        */
#define IIR       2                    /* interrupt identification register */
#define LCR       3                    /* line control register            */
#define MCR       4                    /* modem control register           */
#define LSR       5                    /* line status register             */
#define MSR       6                    /* modem status register            */

/* line status values */

#define RCVRDY   1                     /* char available in RX register    */
#define OVRERR   2                     /* overrun error                    */
#define PRTYERR  4                     /* parity error                     */
#define FRMERR   8                     /* framing error                    */
#define BRKINT   0x10                  /* break signal                     */
#define XMTRDY   0x20                  /* transmit register ready          */

/* modem status values */

#define CTS      0x10                  /* clear to send                    */
#define DSR      0x20                  /* data set ready                   */
#define RI       0x40                  /* ring indicator                   */
#define CD       0x80                  /* carrier detect                   */

/* modem control bits */

#define DTR      1                     /* data terminal ready              */
#define RTS      2                     /* request to send                  */


int     portbase = COM1BASE;    /* default to COM1:                        */

/*********************************************************************/
/** initialization function; called once at beginning of program    */

cominit()
{

/* disable interrupts, set dtr and rts */

        outp(portbase + IER, 0);
        outp(portbase + MCR, DTR | RTS);

        return(0);       /* no-error return                         */
}

/* disable DTR and RTS ********************************************/

comoff()
{
        outp(portbase + MCR, 0);
}
/* communications subroutines ********************************/
/* byte-input    */
/* Returns: -1 if no byte available, else byte (0 - 0xff)       */

comin()
{
        return((inp(portbase + LSR) & RCVRDY) ? inp(portbase + RX) : -1);
}
/*********************************/
```

```
/* byte-output; will time-out if xmtrdy doesn't become true.    */
/* Returns: -1 if timeout, else NULL                            */

static  long      xwttime = 24000; /* 4-sec. wait for time-out   */

comout(c)
char    c;
{
        long      timout;

/* set time-out in case xmt buffer never empty */

        timout = xwttime;

        while((inp(portbase + LSR) & XMTRDY) == 0)
                if(--timout < 0L)
                        return(-1);        /* time-out error       */

        outp(portbase + TX, c);
        return(0);
}

/*********************************
# set portbase
*/

p_base(portnum)
int     portnum;
{
        if(portnum == 1 || portnum == 2)
                portbase = portnum == 1 ? COM1BASE : COM2BASE;
        return(portbase);
}
/********/
```

Before going on, I would like to point out that the BIOS provides calls for port input and output. If I used the BIOS calls, there would be no concern with port addresses. There are, however, some problems with the BIOS routines—primarily that they reset the request-to-send signal inappropriately. By accessing the ports directly, I will also have better control.

Getting back to the port #define statements, I will mention that I will be using only some of these in this terminal program. TX and RX refer to the port that is used for transmitting and receiving one byte. All of these definitions are considered to be an offset from either COM1BASE or COM2BASE; that is, the offset from the base port is the same whether we are using COM1 or COM2 for communications. TX and RX are both defined as zero. Thus, data is transmitted and received from the same port, which is equal to the port base address plus zero, or 0x3f8 for COM1.

Ports IER and IIR are used for interrupt control, which will not be used in this terminal program. I also will not need the LCR port, because DOS will take care of that for me. It is used for setting the baud rate and other communications parameters. The DOS mode command will set those parameters for me. The MSR port is used for checking the modem status. Most commercially available communications software uses the modem status signals, but it is not necessary. The simple terminal program in this chapter will not use the modem status, or MSR, port, either. By the way, the

"R" in MSR means register. On the CPU, it is a port. On the interface chip, it is called a register.

RS-232 Line Status

The next section of definitions, which are line status values, are used to check the RS-232 status (was that obvious?). The LSR contains bit flags that can be checked with these definitions. The RCVRDY definition is used to determine when the serial interface has received a byte from the modem (or over the cable in a direct connection). If this bit is set, a byte is waiting to be read at the RX port. Conversely, if this bit is clear (zero), there is no data available yet. As you can see, the RCVRDY bit must be checked before reading the RX port. That is what the **comin** function does. It scans the serial port for input, much like the **bscanc** function in Chapter 3 scans the keyboard for input. **comin** reads the LSR and masks out all bits except RCVRDY. If the bit is set, the expression evaluates to TRUE, and the RX port is read. This is the value that is returned by the function. On the other hand, the expression evaluates to FALSE (zero) if the bit is clear, and a −1 is returned. To duplicate the effect of the **bgetc** function, which loops through **bscanc** until a character is typed on the keyboard, with the **comin** function, you could use the following code:

```
while((c = comin()) == -1) ;
```

When this loop terminates, **c** will contain the character received from the serial port. In practice, though, you are not likely to see this code quite this way. The primary reason is that this loop allows no way out if a character is never received from the serial port. Therefore, you will see a very different coding scheme in the terminal program.

The next three definitions for line status values are OVRERR, PRTYERR, and FRMERR. These bits, if set, indicate that an error has occurred in receiving the last byte. OVRERR means that an overrun error has occurred. This error occurs if the program fails to read a byte from RX before the next one is received. The previous byte is overwritten and lost forever when this byte is received. This can happen if the program is so busy that it does not get back to the input request before the next character is received. Why would the program be so busy? It depends on what the program is doing with each byte when it is received, and at what baud rate the serial port is set. If the serial port is set to transfer data at 9600 bits per second (or baud, as it is sometimes called), there is precious little time for the computer to do anything with the current character before the next is received. The characters might be coming in at about 960 per second. There is certainly not enough time to display the character, because it takes too long to scroll the display up one line. That is why polling of the input is not used by commercial terminal software. Only interrupt-driven input can keep up at high speeds when each character that is received must be displayed. There is time, however, when receiving at 300 bps. Experimentation with the terminal program in this chapter will be limited to this speed. The interrupt-driven terminal program in Chapter 6 will keep up with any speed.

The PRTYERR bit is set if a parity error occurs. Parity is simply a bit sent along with the data byte that indicates whether the number of one bits in the data is even or odd. The transmitting system sets the parity bit to indicate which is the case. The receiving interface checks the parity bit received against its view of what the parity should be. If they do not match, the parity-error bit is set. Parity checking can be enabled as even or odd, or disabled. This is done through the LCR, which is what the mode command in DOS does. This type of error simply means that one or more bits were garbled during transmission.

The FRMERR bit flags a framing error. This bit is set if the serial interface thinks that one or more bits were lost before the byte was received. These error flags are not particularly useful. What do you do if an error is detected? Obviously, the byte received is in error, or a byte was missed. But it is possible to receive incorrect data without it being detected by the serial interface circuit. For example, two bits in a byte could be reversed by line noise during transmission. That error would not be detected by the parity check or the frame check. Most terminal programs ignore these error bits. Because line noise usually affects several consecutive characters in the transmission, it is obvious that garbage is appearing on the display screen.

Communications programs that offer "error free" file transfers employ their own methods of checking for transmission errors. That is why you must have the same file transfer scheme at each end. They each need to agree on how the transfer is to be done and what to do if an error occurs. XMODEM is one of the better-known file transfer methods, but many communications programs have a proprietary method. Regardless of the transfer scheme used, they all employ basically the same method. A handshaking scheme occurs where a block of data is passed along with some kind of checksum. One popular checksum type is called a CRC checksum, which stands for cyclical redundancy check. Because of the way it is calculated, it is usually 99 percent accurate or better. If the transmitted CRC is not equal to the calculated CRC at the receiving end, the receiver signals the transmitter to retransmit the last block.

If you are interested in seeing what happens when one of the LSR errors occurs, you can change comin to return a certain character when such errors are detected. As it is now written, the errors are ignored, but let's say that we want to return a question mark whenever any LSR error is indicated. comin would be changed to the code shown in Fig. 5-2. This version of comin will return a question mark rather than the input character if an error is reported by the LSR. The fact that an error has occurred can be represented more graphically by using a character that is impossible to receive. One of the characters above ASCII 128 could be used, because these characters are peculiar to the PC and not likely to be received from a host computer. Of course, you will not know which error occurred, because the question mark is returned if any one of the three error bits is set. You can go a step further by defining inpstat as an integer outside of the function, rather than as an auto variable, as it is here. The calling program can then check the contents of inpstat when the question mark (or other character defined as an error return) is received, by declaring inpstat as extern. If you do use the question mark as an error return, you should definitely use this method before assuming that an error has occurred, because the question mark is a common character to receive from any source. Only if you are going to display all characters as received, without taking any other action, is the question mark acceptable as an error indicator. Then it is up to the program user to determine by visual inspection whether or not errors are occurring.

```
comin()
{
    int  c, inpstat;

    inpstat = inp(portbase + LSR);     /* get input status    */
    if(inpstat & RCVRDY) {             /* if byte ready...     */
        c = inp(portbase + RX);        /* get it, and chk for  */
        if(inpstat & (OVRERR : PRTYERR : FRMERR)) /* error     */
            c = '?';                   /* replace if error     */
    } else
        c = -1;                        /* no byte available    */
    return(c);
}
```

Fig. 5-2. The revised comin function.

The XMTRDY flag is the last bit we are concerned with in the LSR. This bit will be set when the serial port is ready to accept the next byte for transmission. The **comout** function waits for this bit to be set before the byte is output to TX. You will notice that **comout** sets a counter before it begins waiting for XMTRDY. This counter is decremented on each scan of the LSR. If it goes to zero, it is assumed that the port is never going to be ready to transmit another character, so the attempt is terminated and a −1 is returned to indicate this condition. The count is set to wait for about four seconds on a 4.77 MHZ PC. This should be more than long enough for any clock speed, though. Usually, the longest the program might have to wait for XMTRDY is about one-thirtieth of a second. If the time-out does occur, it is probably because there is no serial port in the system or because you are trying to output to COM2 when only a COM1 port has been installed. Time-out can also occur if there is a hardware failure.

Modem Status and Control

The next two sets of definitions in Fig. 5-1 are for modem status and modem control. It is easier to understand these if they are considered together, because they are closely related. They are used for handshaking between the computer and the modem. Note the comments next to each definition. For example, CTS is the clear-to-send signal. It is an input to the computer from the modem, as are all modem status bits. The modem control bits, conversely, are outputs from the computer to the modem. The handshaking occurs this way. The computer sets the DTR (data-terminal-ready) bit in the MCR (modem-control register or port). The modem responds by setting the DSR (data-set-ready) bit in the MSR. The terminal program can then check to see if this bit is set. If it is not, there may be something wrong with the modem. Most modems will ignore the computer until DTR is set.

Some modems have a switch that can be set to make the modem "think" that it is seeing DTR at all times. The Hayes Smartmodems have such a switch. If this switch is activated, it does not matter whether or not the computer sets the DTR bit in the MCR. I prefer to leave this switch off and to let the communications program control DTR. Unfortunately, some programs will not work this way. Others will not work properly the other way. Most programs will tell you which way to set the switch. The advantage of allowing the program to control DTR (if it will) is that the program can make the modem "drop the line" (hang up the phone) by clearing the DTR bit.

The program then sets the RTS (request-to-send) bit in the MCR. The modem responds to this by setting CTS (clear-to-send) in the MSR. This is just another modem check available to the communications program to make sure that everything is going well. In practice, both DTR and RTS are usually set at the same time. The basic handshaking is now complete. If you examine the cominit function in Fig. 5-1, you will see that it sets DTR and RTS. It also outputs zero to the interrupt enable register, IER. This ensures that all communications interrupts are disabled. The comoff function simply clears DTR and RTS. cominit is called before communications begin, and comoff is called before the program exits to DOS.

Two other modem status bits are available. These are the RI (ring-indicator) and CD (carrier-detect) bits. The RI bit is set when the modem senses that the phone is ringing. Not all modems support this signal, but the Hayes modems do. It can be monitored by a communications program so that the modem can be commanded to answer the phone when it rings. There is usually also a switch in the modem that will command the modem to answer the phone. That is why some modems are referred to as *auto-answer*.

The CD bit is set when the modem senses that another modem is at the other end of the phone line. It will remain set as long as a communications session is in progress. If the connection is broken for any reason, the CD bit will be cleared by the local modem. Communications programs can monitor the CD bit to make sure that a connection to another modem exists.

Communications Summary

It might be useful to summarize the roles of the various ports for asynchronous communication on the PC at this point. Most of the information has been covered now, but it might not be clear how it fits together. There are two ports used for data input and output, called RX and TX in the portio.c definitions. As we have seen, these are physically the same port. The line-status register (LSR) and the modem-status register (MSR) are used to monitor the progress of the communication. The line-control register (LCR) and the modem-control register (MCR) are used to setup the communications session. The LCR is used to initialize the serial port, and the MCR initializes the modem. Finally, the interrupt-enable register (IER) and the interrupt-identification register (IIR) are used for interrupt-driven port input and output, which is demonstrated in Chapter 6.

The technical reference manual is an invaluable resource for the study of asynchronous communications on the PC. It will not tell you how to program, but it is full of useful information about port status and control. The best way to gain understanding about asynchronous programming is to study other programs and to experiment on your own.

A Little More on Cables

It is the MSR that determines how many wires must exist in the modem cable. There must be one for DTR, unless a modem switch is set to force DTR. There must be a wire for RTS, and there must be two return wires for DSR and CTS. There must also be return wires for CD and RI. Then two more wires are required for data transfer, one for RX and one for TX. That all adds up to eight wires needed in a modem cable, plus one or two for ground connections. In practice, some of these connections may be left out. Without concerning ourselves with communications software at the moment, there are a minimum of three connections needed: RX, TX, and signal ground. Only three wires in a cable are needed to connect two PCs together for communication.

When a modem and communications software are added, more connections may be necessary. As explained earlier, the modem will not respond to the DSR and CTS signals unless it receives the DTR and RTS signals from the computer. The communications program you are using may refuse to work if it does not find the DSR and CTS signals set. Both the modem and the program can be "fooled," however, into thinking these connections exist. This can be handy if the cable you are using does not have enough wires to make all the connections. Beware, though, that by deceiving the modem and the program, they will not be able to inform you when (or if) something in the communications goes awry. Most of the time, this is not a serious loss of functionality. It is usually quite apparent to the operator when something is not working right, without the program telling him so.

How do you fake the connection? Again, the modem responds with certain signals when a connection has been established. A communications program that expects to see these responses will see them if the DTR pin at the serial interface is shorted to the DSR and CD pins. CAUTION: do the shorting on the cable, not on the interface. Refer to the PC technical reference manual for the pin numbers of these signals. If you do not set a switch in the modem to force DTR, you will need to pass that connection through, in addition to the shorts. You might also need to short the RTS pin to CTS. This sort of experimentation is more easily done with a device known as a *break-out* box than with a soldering iron. The disadvantage of the breakout box is that two cables may be required, because the box is inserted between the connections. Many of these boxes are provided with a cable, so shop around.

Note that when making a direct cable connection from PC to PC, the RX and TX pins are crossed in the cable. This is not done when you are connecting to a modem. Figure 5-3 illustrates a null modem cable that can be used to connect two PCs together. This will work with most communications programs.

Fig. 5-3. A null-modem cable.

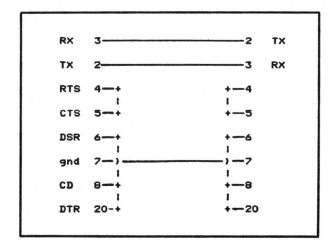

5.4 A TERMINAL PROGRAM

Now that we have functions for port control, a simple terminal program can be developed. As you can see in Fig. 5-4, the **term1** program is small. It is designed to communicate with a host computer, like the ones the information services use. **term1** should work with any computer that supports dial-up ASCII terminals. It may be necessary to make some minor modifications to the program for it to work properly with some computers. This will be explained shortly. It will also be necessary to make a couple of minor changes to use **term1** for PC to PC communication.

I would like to emphasize that **term1** does not configure the communications ports. This was left out for simplicity. Therefore, before running **term1**, the DOS **mode** command must be used to configure the ports. Use one of the **mode** commands shown in Fig. 5-4. Once the **mode** command has been given, it is usually not necessary to repeat it. If you run another communications program or reboot the computer, you will need to give the **mode** command again before running **term1**. If you are not sure that the port is properly configured, you can give the **mode** command anyway. It does not hurt to repeat it as often as you wish.

The **mode** commands in Fig. 5-4 set either communication port one or two to a speed of 300 bits per second, no parity (parity checking is disabled), eight-bit word length, and one stop bit. This setting will work with most dial-up computers. If you know, for instance, that the computer to which you will be connecting wants even parity and a seven-bit word length, adjust the **mode** command accordingly:

```
MODE COM1:300,E,7,1
```

Even if your modem is capable of speeds higher than 300 bps or you have a direct cable connection, I recommend that you do your initial experimentation with **term1** at 300 bps. Later, I will explain more about this.

The **term1** program is very simple; it does none of the fancy things that most commercial products do. For example, you will need to know your modem's dialing command to instruct it to dial the phone. When you execute **term1**, you will see a sign-on message that tells you to press the escape key to exit, which returns you to DOS. Until you press escape, all keys typed will be output to the communications port. If you have a modem attached, you should see your key strokes displayed on the screen. If you do not, check to see that your modem power is on, that the modem cable is connected, and that you did not forget to run the **mode** command. Also, if your modem is connected to the COM2 port, you need to execute the **term1** command with the number two on the command line:

```
term1 2
```

This tells **term1** to use the COM2 port for communications.

Some modems do not display characters as you type them; others have an internal switch setting to enable and disable the display. You will need to check your modem documentation for this, if you see nothing when you type. If you are using a Hayes compatible modem, you can run a test by typing:

```
ATZ
```

```
/**
 * NAME
 *      term1 -- dumb terminal program using port polling
 *
 * SYNOPSIS
 *      term1 [2]
 *
 * DESCRIPTION
 *      Optional command-line parameter of 2 may be entered to use COM port
 * number 2, otherwise COM port number 1 is used.
 *      This terminal program uses port polling; therefore, it is limited
 * to a maximum speed of 300 bps.
 *
 * CAUTION
 *      Term1 does not set the baud rate of the com port. Use the DOS MODE
 * command to setup the port BEFORE running "term1":
 *
 *      MODE COM1:300,N,8,1
 *      MODE COM2:300,N,8,1
 *
 *      Use one of the above MODE commands before running "term1". If you
 * use COM2 in the MODE command, run "term1 2".
 **/

#include <stdio.h>
#include <extkeys.h>

#define ESCAPE  27      /* Esc key for exit                             */

main(argc, argv)
int     argc;
char    *argv[];
{
        int     c, port;

/* see if port number specified on command line                        */

        if(argc == 2) {
                if((port = (*++argv)[0] - '0') != 2 && port != 1) {
                        fprintf(stderr,"usage: term1 [2]");
                        exit(1);
                }
                p_base(port);
        }

/* set DTR and RTS                                                      */

        cominit();

/* sign on                                                             */

        printf("[ Terminal Mode: Press Escape to exit ]\n\n");

/* begin terminal polling                                              */

        while(1) {

/* if char ready, display it and repeat; else go on...                 */
```

Fig. 5-4. The term1 program.

```
                    if((c = comin()) != -1) {
                            bputcr(c & 0x7f);          /* mask parity bit     */
                            continue;
                    }

/* if char from keyboard, check for exit request, else transmit           */

                    if((c = bscancr()) != -1 && c < K_BASE) {
                            if(c == ESCAPE)
                                    break;
                            if(comout(c) == -1) {
                                    fprintf(stderr,"term1: Time-out error.\n");
                                    break;
                            }
                    }
            }
        .} /* end of while loop                                           */
        comoff();          /* disable com port                           */
        exit(0);
}
/********/
```

Note that Hayes modem commands must be in uppercase. The ATZ command tells the modem to reset itself. To dial the phone, the Hayes command is:

`ATD5551234`

The ATD is the dialing command, and the digits are the phone number to dial. You must press Return after each command before the modem will execute it.

You can use the ATH command to tell the modem to hang up the phone, or you can press escape to exit term1. This will also cause the modem to hang up the phone, unless you have the modem switch set that forces DTR true, as explained in the previous section.

If you have two PCs cabled together and are running term1 on each PC, you probably noticed that neither PC displays what is being typed on it, but it does display what is being typed on the other PC. The next section explains why this occurs and how to alter term1 to display the typed characters.

5.5 HOW REMOTE COMMUNICATION WORKS

Connecting with a remote computer for the first time is always a trial-and-error experience, as you know if you have done much of this. Why this is so will be easier to understand if you understand how term1 works. Then you will also understand why commercial communications programs seem to offer so many setup options.

By examining the term1 program in Fig. 5-4, you will see that the main function first examines the command line to see if the user has requested the program to use COM2. If he has, the p_base function in Fig. 5-1 is called to set the port base for COM2. Otherwise, the startup default port COM1 is used. You will notice that COM1 is also accepted as a command-line option, but it is not necessary to specify COM1, as it is the default. Then the cominit function is called to set DTR and RTS (data-terminal-ready and request-to-send). If you have an external modem attached, you should see the DTR light come on when term1 loads. On the Hayes modem, this light is labeled TR. This light will go out when you exit **term1**, if the force-DTR switch in the modem is off. The **comoff** function clears DTR and RTS.

After calling **cominit**, the sign-on message is displayed by **term1**. It then enters the **while** loop, which executes continuously until the Escape key is pressed. This loop performs all port input/output and console input/output; that is, this loop controls the entire communications process. The logic within the loop goes like this:

Step 1.   Call **comin** to see if an input byte has arrived at the port.

Step 2.   If a byte is available, display it with a call to the BIOS display function from Chapter 2, **bputcr**. Then return to Step 1. If no byte was available in Step 1, continue to Step 3.

Step 3.   Call the BIOS keyboard scan function from Chapter 3, **bscancr**, to see if a key has been pressed.

Step 4.   If a key is available and it is the Escape key, break out of the loop. If a key is available, and is not the Escape key, call **comout** to output the byte to the serial port. Then go to Step 1. If no key is available, go to Step 1.

This is the entire logic for polled communications. The input port and the keyboard are continuously scanned for data. Data coming in on the port is displayed; keyboard data is output to the serial port. As you can see, keyboard data is not being displayed. How is it that you see what you are typing? Most host, or dial-up, computers *echo* the data they receive. In other words, when you press a key, the character is transmitted to the host computer. The host computer then transmits that character back. **term1** receives the character as incoming data and displays it. If **term1** was to display each character typed from the keyboard in addition to the incoming data, you would see two characters displayed for every one you typed. This echo process is referred to as *echoplex*, though it is often inaccurately called *full duplex*. There are some host computers that do not echoplex, but it is rare these days. If you communicate with such a computer, you will need to add a line to **term1** that displays characters as you type them.

Also note the use of the raw display function, **bputcr**, for port input data. This is one part of the program that may need modification, depending on the remote computer. Many host computers will add a linefeed character following the echo of a carriage return. That is, two characters are returned for one received, in this case. If you find that pressing the carriage return is not giving you a linefeed when using **term1**, you will need to add code following the call to **bputcr** to check the incoming character. If it is a carriage return, add your own linefeed with another call to **bputcr**. When checking input characters, be sure you mask the character with 0x7f first, as is done on the call to **bputcr**. This is necessary because the eighth bit of the received character may be a parity bit, if the transmitting computer is using parity checking and you are not.

I also use the raw keyboard scan function in **term1**. Most host computers expect a carriage return, not the linefeed you would get with the translated keyboard scan function. There is also the possibility that the Escape key is needed in your communications with a remote computer. In that case, you should define some other key as the **term1** exit key. Because **extkeys.h** has been included, it would be easy to use F1, for example, as the exit key:

```
#define ESCAPE K_F1
```

Then you will need to eliminate the c < K_BASE test and add a line like:

```
if(c > K_BASE)
    if(c == ESCAPE)
        break;
else
        continue;
```

If you want to use **term1** on two PCs that are to communicate with each other, you only need to make a couple of changes. You simply need to display your own keyboard strokes and to add linefeeds to carriage returns. Adding linefeeds can be done easily by using the translated versions of the keyboard and display functions. Change **bputcr** to **bputc**, and **bscancr** to **bscanc**. To display your own typing, add a call to **bputc** to display the keyboard character after it is output to the port with **comout**. Both PCs should be using this modified version of **term1**.

I think that it is apparent now that there are many variables involved in communicating with a remote computer. That is why so many commercial communications programs allow you to configure such things as whether to add linefeeds to carriage returns and which key to use for an exit key. They also often allow you to choose whether to mask the eighth bit on input characters, for the reason given above.

You are probably thinking that these options could also be programmed into **term1**. Then the user could specify which ones to use, perhaps through command-line arguments. In theory, you would be correct, but there is a problem in doing this with **term1**.

The reason I suggested that you experiment with **term1** at a speed of 300 bps is that the polling method is not fast enough to keep up with 1200 bps communications. Adding options to **term1** would slow the polling even more. To see what I mean, try using **term1** at 1200 bps. It will seem to do fine until the display screen has to scroll. The first few characters of the next line will be missing. It takes longer to scroll the PC display than it does to receive characters at 1200 bps.

To give you an idea of how long this scrolling takes, compared to the port input speed, consider this. I wrote an XMODEM type of file-transfer program using the polling method that works at 9600 bps, eight times faster than 1200 bps. In this program, the input data is not displayed. Because the data is received in 128-byte blocks, plus a few characters more for control data, I only needed to place each incoming character into memory storage. Then the file transfer program can take all the time it needs to validate the data and write it to disk, because the next block is not transmitted until the program signals for it. So you see, there are circumstances where the polling method is fast enough.

Chapter 6

Advanced PC Communications

This chapter presents an interrupt-driven terminal program. This program can operate at speeds up to 9600 bps, where as the polled terminal program in Chapter 5 was unable to operate at a speed faster than 300 bps. If you have a 1200 or 2400 bps modem, you will be able to use its full capacity, and if you have a direct cable connection to another computer or a 9600 bps modem, you will be able to run this terminal program at that speed.

There are other advantages besides speed. Because the data input is buffered, there is time for the terminal program to perform other chores in addition to simply displaying the incoming data. For example, terminal emulation code could be added to the program to make the PC act like a DEC or Televideo terminal. A printer toggle could be added to make a hardcopy of a communications session in progress. To make the program more flexible, a capture buffer as well as any of the options discussed in Chapter 5 could be implemented.

The functions in this chapter form a communications library that can be linked with any communications program you might wish to develop. A simple terminal program much like the one in Chapter 5 is presented to illustrate the use of these functions. Many of the functions from Chapter 5, some with modifications, are used here.

6.1 THE LOGIC OF INTERRUPT-DRIVEN COMMUNICATIONS

You will recall that the terminal program in Chapter 5 continuously polled the RS-232 input port to see if any data had arrived. The primary problem with that method is that data might come in before the program can poll the port again. The result is lost data. You saw that happen if you tried to use the **term1** program at any speed faster than 300 bps.

A communications interrupt is the answer to the lost-data problem. In interrupt-driven communications, a byte of data arriving at the communications port interrupts the CPU so that it can retrieve the byte before another one overwrites it. That way, it does not matter what the computer is doing at the moment a byte becomes available. Whatever the computer is doing is halted momentarily so that the input is retrieved. After the input is tucked safely away, the computer resumes whatever it was doing when it was interrupted. Then the next incoming byte interrupts the computer again, and so on.

The heart of the communications interrupt mechanism is buried deeply in the hardware design of the PC. To access and use it, a chip in the PC and the circuitry on the RS-232 card must be properly programmed; and an *interrupt-service* routine must be provided. The PC technical reference documentation is an invaluable aid in these matters. You will need it if you want to modify the functions in this chapter. You do not need it to use them in your own communications programs.

This is the only chapter of the book in which I must resort to some assembly-language programming. The interrupt-service routine mentioned above must be written in assembly language. I know of no C compilers for the PC that provide a method for writing an interrupt-service routine in C. So that the interrupt routine can be linked with C programs, it is very closely tied with the Lattice C compiler. If you are using another compiler, you will need some understanding of assembly language in order to make modifications to the interrupt module. The modifications needed are those that make an assembly language module compatible with your compiler. I have tried to explain where modifications might be necessary as I present the modules.

The remaining functions are written in C. A circular buffer will be needed. Each port interrupt will store the incoming byte in this buffer. The terminal program can retrieve characters from the buffer at its leisure. The rest of the functions are for control of the interrupt mechanism. Some are to initialize the PC to accept the interrupt, and the rest are to restore the interrupt mechanism to its original state when the terminal program is finished with it.

6.2 THE CIRCULAR BUFFER

The circular buffer functions are shown in Fig. 6-1. There are three functions in this module: one to add a character to the buffer, one to retrieve the next character from the buffer, and one that resets the buffer to empty. Why use a circular buffer? Because the data is coming into the buffer at a different rate than it is going out. The logic keeps track of two positions in the buffer: the head and the tail. The head points to the next character to be retrieved from the buffer, and the tail keeps track of the next position available to contain an incoming character. When the head and tail are equal, the buffer is empty. The buffer is full if the addition of another character to the buffer would make the head and tail equal.

The buffer size is defined to be BSIZE characters. You will also notice the definition of the labels XOFF and XON. XOFF/XON control is used to keep the buffer from filling to capacity. Most host computers respond to an XOFF character, which is a Control-S key combination, by suspending transmission. The transmission is resumed

```
/**
 * MODULE
 *       circbuff.c
 *
 * NAME
 *       putccb -- add a character to the circular buffer
 *       getccb -- get a character from the circular buffer
 *       flushcb -- reset buffer to empty
 *
 * SYNOPSIS
 *       stat = putccb(c);
 *       c = getccb();
 *       flushcb();
 *
 *       int     stat;             equals c; or -1 if buffer full
 *       char    c;                char stored / retrieved
 *
 * DESCRIPTION
 *       putccb - adds a character to the buffer. If the buffer is "nearful"
 *                XOFF is output to the port via "comout" in "iportio.c".
 *       getccb - gets a character from the buffer. Outputs XON if necessary.
 *       flushcb -resets buffer to empty.
 *
 * RETURN
 *       putccb returns the character if successful; if buffer is full, -1 is
 * returned.
 *       getccb returns the next character from the buffer; if buffer is
 * empty, -1 is returned.
 *       flushcb returns nothing.
 *
 * CAUTIONS
 *       These functions are for use with interrupt-driven port i/o.
 *
 **/

#define TRUE     1
#define FALSE    0
#define XOFF     19              /* ^S                    */
#define XON      17              /* ^Q                    */
#define BSIZE    2000            /* buffer size           */

static  char    buf[BSIZE];      /* buffer storage area                      */
static  int     is_on = TRUE;    /* flag for getccb                          */

/* buffer info                                                               */
struct  circbuff {
        int     head;    /* next char avail to getccb                        */
        int     tail;    /* next position for putccb                         */
        int     cnt;     /* # of char's currently in buffer                  */
        int     nearful;/* # of char's when near full                        */
        int     size;    /* size of buffer, in bytes                         */
        char    *data;   /* ptr to buffer                                    */
        };
/* data avail. to other functions                                            */

struct  circbuff cb = { 0, 0, 0, BSIZE/5*4, BSIZE, buf};

/***********************
 * put a char into buffer - return -1 if buffer full; else return char
 ********************/
```

Fig. 6-1. The circbuff functions.

```
putccb(c)
char    c;
{
        int     curr;

        curr = cb.tail;              /* save current pos. temporarily     */
        if(++cb.tail >= BSIZE)
                cb.tail = 0;

        if(cb.tail == cb.head) {
                cb.tail = curr;
                return(-1);
        }

        if(++cb.cnt == cb.nearful)
                is_on = comout(XOFF);

        cb.data[curr] = c;
        return(c & 0xff);
}
/***********************
# return a char from buffer; -1 if buffer empty
***********************/

getccb()
{
        int     curr;

        if((!is_on) && (cb.cnt < 500))
                is_on = (comout(XON) == 0);
        if(cb.tail == cb.head)
                return(-1);          /* empty */

        curr = cb.head;
        if(++cb.head >= BSIZE)
                cb.head = 0;

        cb.cnt--;
        return(cb.data[curr] & 0xff);
}
/************************
# flush (empty) buffer - returns nothing
***********************/
flushcb()
{
        cb.cnt = 0;
        cb.tail = cb.head;
}
/********/
```

upon receipt by the host of an XON, or Control-Q, character. The struct circbuff is defined to contain information about the buffer. The head and tail are indexes into the buf array. The cnt is the current number of characters in the buffer, and nearful is defined to be some percentage of the buffer capacity. There is also a variable to contain the size of the buffer, and a pointer to the first byte of the buffer. The size value is not used in the circular buffer logic, but it is defined because it might be of use in some applications.

I have set the **nearful** value to 80 percent of the buffer size in the initialization of the structure. If and when the buffer count reaches this value, the **putccb** (for put character in circular buffer) function will transmit an XOFF character. Note that the **putccb** function is called only by the interrupt-service routine, not by the communications program. As such, **putccb** is a part of the interrupt routine.

The **getccb** function is called by the communications program to fetch a byte from the buffer. If **putccb** had to transmit an XOFF, then **getccb** will transmit an XON when the buffer empties to a certain point.

At 9600 bps, the buffer would eventually fill if a lot of data is being displayed, because the data can not be displayed fast enough. The XOFF/XON toggles will stop and start the host transmission smoothly so that the program user will never notice. It will appear as though the data is continuously displayed.

If the applications program should decide at any time that it would like to ignore any characters remaining in the buffer, it can call **flushcb** to reset the buffer to empty. Any data in the buffer is "lost." This can be useful in file transfer programs or as a user-designated command to abort the current transmission.

6.3 INTERRUPT-VECTOR CONTROL

The control of the interrupt mechanism begins with the functions in Fig. 6-2. The PC interrupt table in low memory contains two interrupt vectors for communications, one for the COM1 port and one for the COM2 port. INT 12 (decimal) is the COM1 interrupt, and INT 11 is the COM2 interrupt. Don't ask me why COM1 uses the higher interrupt number; I'm just a programmer.

Whenever a program must change the system configuration, it should restore the system to its original state when finished. That is the purpose of the **save_vec** and **rstr_vec** functions in Fig. 6-2. **save_vec** simply saves the contents of the communications interrupt vectors in a static data area. **rstr_vec** is called to restore the vectors to their original contents.

The functions in Fig. 6-2 call those in Figure 6-3. This module contains a function called **getintv** that retrieves the contents of an interrupt vector. It does this by "peeking" the data from the vector table. Because an interrupt vector is a four-byte memory address, two short integers are used to store it. The first short contains the offset; the second contains the segment. If you are using Lattice Version 3, you can replace the **peek** with a call to DOS function 0×35, using an **intdoss** structure. This change isn't necessary, however.

The **putintv** function calls DOS function 0×25 to set an interrupt vector. **putintv** expects the vector argument to be in the form returned by the **getintv** call. The **putintv** function is used in two places in the communications program. You have seen the first use in Fig. 6-2. It will also be called to insert the vector to the interrupt-service routine into either the INT 11 or INT 12 table position.

6.4 ENABLING THE INTERRUPTS

Once the vector to the interrupt routine has been placed into the interrupt table position, the interrupts can be enabled. The functions in Fig. 6-4 will enable and disable the interrupts. The interrupt mechanism must be enabled before port input can

```
/**
* MODULE
*        commvec.c
*
* NAME
*        save_vec -- save communications interrupt vectors
*        rstr_vec -- restore communications interrupt vectors
*
* SYNOPSIS
*        save_vec();
*        rstr_vec();
*
* DESCRIPTION
*        save_vec retrieves the current contents of interrupt 11 and
* 12 vectors and stores them in a static data area.
*        rstr_vec restores the interrupt vectors saved by save_vec.
*        These functions are designed for use with the interrupt-driven
* communications program.
**/
/*****************************
* save intr vectors for com1 & com2 @ int 12 & int 11
*****************************/

static   short    ivecs[2][2];     /* 2 4-byte buffers for 2 int vectors    */

save_vec()
{
        getintv(11, ivecs[0]);
        getintv(12, ivecs[1]);
}


/*****************************
* restore int vectors saved above
*****************************/
rstr_vec()
{
        putintv(11, ivecs[0]);
        putintv(12, ivecs[1]);
}
/********/
```

Fig. 6-2. The commvec functions.

```
/**
* MODULE
*        intvec.c
*
* NAME
*        getintv -- get an interrupt vector
*        putintv -- set an interrupt vector
*
* SYNOPSIS
*        getintv(inum, ibuff);
```

Fig. 6-3. The intvec functions.

```
*       putintv(inum, ibuff);
*
*       int     inum;               interrupt number
*       short   *ibuff;             pointer to array of two short integers
*
* DESCRIPTION
*       getintv - retrieves the current interrupt vector for interrupt
* number "inum". Offset, segment are placed in ibuff[0], ibuff[1].
*
*       putintv - sets the interrupt vector for "inum". ibuff assumed
* to contain the offset, segment as for "getintv".
*
* RETURNS
*       Neither function returns a value. "getintv" returns with the vector
* of "inum" in "ibuff".
*
* NOTES
*       "ibuff" is an array of two short integers. The calling program
* should define:
*
* short ivector[2];
*
* and call these functions this way:
*
* getintv(inum, ivector);         to get current vector for "inum"
* putintv(inum, ivector);         to restore vector for "inum"
**/

#include <dos.h>

/*********
* get an interrupt vector
*********/

getintv(inum, ibuff)
int     inum;
short   *ibuff;                        /* must be at least 2 shorts           */
{
        peek(0, inum * 4, (char *) ibuff, 4);
}
/*********
* set an interrupt vector
*********/

putintv(inum, ibuff)
int     inum;
short   *ibuff;
{
        union REGS u;
        struct SREGS seg;

        u.h.ah = 0x25;              /* DOS set-intr call                   */
        u.h.al = inum;
        u.x.dx = ibuff[0];          /* offset and...                       */
        seg.ds = ibuff[1];          /* segment of intr vector              */
        intdosx(&u, &u, &seg);
}
/*********/
```

```
/**
* name:   intctl.c
*
*        2 functions:
* 1.     i_enable(portnum);        enable interrupt mechanism for portnum 1 or 2
* 2.     i_disable();              disable for COM1 and COM2
**/

/* need "portbase" in iportio.c                                              */

extern    int       portbase;

/** defines for intr control **/
#define IMR      0x21              /* port addr of intr mask reg            */
#define IRQ3     0xf7              /* AND mask to turn on com2 intr         */
#define IRQ4     0xef              /* ditto for com1                        */
#define MCR      4                 /* modem control register offset         */
#define IER      1                 /* intr-enable register offset           */

/** switches/masks for MCR, IER, and IIR                                    */
#define MC_INT   8                 /* OR switch to turn on MCR intr, b3=1   */
#define RX_INT   1                 /* OR to turn on RCV-data intr in IER,   */
                                   /* b0=1                                  */
#define RX_MASK  7                 /* AND input from IIR with this before... */
#define RX_ID    4                 /* value if RCV-data intr;               */
                                   /* eg: AND rx_mask, CMP rx_id            */


/***********************
* enable intr mechanism for com1 or com2.
* CAUTION: intr vectors and the intr-service routine must be in place
* before calling this function.
***********************/

i_enable(pnum)
int       pnum;             /* 1 or 2 for com1: or com2:                     */
{
          int     c;

/*** set MCR to allow interrupts from asynch card ***/
          c = inp(portbase + MCR) | MC_INT;
          outp(portbase + MCR, c);

/*** set RCV-data intr in IER ***/
/*** note that this also disables the other interrupt types allowed by IER ***/
          outp(portbase + IER, RX_INT);

/*** mask out appropriate bit in 8259 reg to allow int at IRQ3 or IRQ4 ***/
          c = inp(IMR) & (pnum == 2 ? IRQ3 : IRQ4);
          outp(IMR, c);
}
/***********************************
* disable both comm interrupts
***********************************/

i_disable()
{
          int     c;
```

Fig. 6-4. The intctl functions.

```
/*** set bits to disable both IRQ3 and IRQ4 in 8259 ***/
        c = inp(IMR) | ~IRQ3 | ~IRQ4;
        outp(IMR, c);

/*** reset all bits in IER, disabling all types of interrupt ***/
        outp(portbase + IER, 0);

/*** reset MCR bit to disable interrupts allowed from asynch card ***/
        c = inp(portbase + MCR) & ~MC_INT;
        outp(portbase + MCR, c);
}
/*********/
```

be received by the PC. It must be disabled before the original interrupt vectors are restored, when the communications program is finished.

The i__enable function expects a port number of either one or two as an argument. The argument is not checked for validity, but if the number is not two, then one is assumed by the function. This function will enable interrupts for only one port at a time. The i__disable function, however, partially disables the interrupts for both COM1 and COM2 simultaneously, but only completely disables the interrupts for the current portbase. I tell you this in case you want to change ports on the fly. If you do, you should call i__disable for the current port before changing portbase. You will recall that portbase is set with the p__base(portnum) function. Before calling i__enable with the port number, p__base should be called with that port number. In other words, the steps are as follows: (1) call p__base; (2) place the interrupt vector; (3) call i__enable. To change ports on the fly, call i__disable; then repeat the above three steps. A single function has been written to take care of the order. It appears later.

The i__enable function programs the RS-232 card and the 8259 interrupt controller chip in the PC to enable the interrupt mechanism. Bit three in the modem-control register (MCR) must be set to allow the RS-232 circuitry to generate an interrupt. Note that the MCR is read, and bit three is set with a logical OR. The result is then output to the port. This is the normal way to set a bit flag without disturbing the others. Then the interrupt enable register (IER) must have bit zero set to tell the card to allow an interrupt on received data. Other bits in the IER enable other types of interrupt. We do not want any other types, so those bits are simultaneously cleared with this output, disabling any other interrupt type. The RS-232 card is now capable of generating an interrupt on received data, but the PC will not accept the interrupt.

To get the PC to accept the interrupt, the 8259 chip must be told to do so. This is done by clearing either bit three for COM2 or bit four for COM1 in the interrupt mask register (IMR). Note that this port number is a long way from the asynch port numbers. That's because it is not an asynch circuit. It controls all of the PC interrupts, including the clock, the keyboard, and the disk drives. Thus, we must be careful programming this device. The current value of the IMR is read, the proper bit for either COM1 or COM2 is cleared with a logical AND, and the result is written back to the port. The i__disable function reverses most of the setup done by the enable function. Be especially cautious when keying these two functions into the PC. For example, note that the disable function sets the interrupt-request bits (to disable the interrupts) in the IMR with a logical OR of NOT IRQ3, and then an OR of NOT IRQ4. A logical

AND of NOT MC__INT is used to reset the MC__INT bit in the MCR. All bits in the IER are cleared to zero to disable all types of interrupt.

Now we are ready to communicate. That's all there is to it. We just need some functions for port input/output similar to those in **portio.c** from Chapter 5, and a terminal program to bring it all together—and one more thing: the interrupt service routine.

6.5 PORT I/O AND INITIALIZATION

The **portio.c** functions from Fig. 5-1 have been modified for use with interrupt-driven port i/o and presented in **iportio.c** in Fig. 6-5. These functions have the same name and calling procedure, so do not include them in the same library with the **portio.c** (Fig. 5-1) functions. You will probably want to keep the polled communications functions from Chapter 5 in a separate library from the interrupt communications functions in this chapter.

The **cominit, comoff,** and **comin** functions have been modified. **cominit** now places the interrupt vector in the interrupt table and calls **i__enable**, in addition to setting DTR and RTS. You will notice that the call to **putintv**, which places the vector to the interrupt-service routine in the vector table, calls a function named **cintaddr**. The **cintaddr** function returns the address of the interrupt routine. It is an integral part of the interrupt routine, presented later.

The presence of the **cominit** function makes it unnecessary to concern yourself with the order in which the various functions to enable interrupts are called. Whenever the communications port is set to COM1 or COM2, or changed, it is only necessary to call **i__disable** to disable interrupts on the current port, **p__base** to set the **portbase**, and **cominit**. Note that **cominit** can be called more than once without adverse effect. That means that your program logic can be written to call **cominit**, for instance, whenever terminal mode is entered. That way, you can include a menu option that allows the user to change ports and then re-enter terminal mode. As far as **cominit** is concerned, it will not matter whether the user actually changed ports or not. Note that you should disable interrupts before calling **cominit**. Because **cominit** places the interrupt vector in the vector table, it is possible for an interrupt to occur while the placement is in progress. If that happened while the vector placement was incomplete, the processor might be directed to an unknown place, causing a system crash. It is sufficient to simply execute **outp(IER, 0)** before calling **cominit**, or you could call **i__disable** instead. Setting the IER to zero prevents the port interrupts, while **i__disable** resets all ports related to the interrupt mechanism.

The only difference in **comoff** from the Chapter 5 version, is that it calls **i__disable** to disable the interrupt mechanism. The **i__disable** function can be called directly to disable interrupts without breaking the phone connection.

The **comin** function no longer requests input directly from the input port, because input is accepted by the interrupt routine and placed into the circular buffer. Therefore, **comin** calls **getccb** to retrieve a character from the buffer. The return is a -1 if there are no characters in the buffer; otherwise the character is returned.

The port output function **comout** is unchanged from the Chapter 5 version, as is **p__base**. Now we are ready for the interrupt-service routine.

```
/**
 * MODULE
 *        iportio.c -- asynchronous i/o functions
 *
 * NAME
 *        cominit -- prepare com. port for i/o
 *        comoff  -- disable com. port
 *        comin   -- receive data - extract from circ. buffer
 *        comout  -- transmit data
 *        p_base  -- change port number
 *
 * SYNOPSIS
 *        error = cominit();
 *        comoff();
 *        cin = comin();
 *        error = comout(cout);
 *        base = p_base(portnum);
 *        int portbase;
 *
 *        int error;                error return
 *        int cin;                  input value
 *        char cout;                output value
 *        int base;                 port base
 *        portnum;                  port number, 1 or 2
 *        int portbase;             contains base port for COM1 or COM2; set by
 *                                  "p_base", defaults to COM1.
 *
 * DESCRIPTION
 * cominit -- prepares port for input/output; uses port assigned to "portbase".
 *            Sets DTR and RTS for corresponding port.
 *
 * comoff  -- disables com port according to "portbase"; resets DTR and RTS.
 *
 * comin   -- scans circular buffer for input data. If data available,
 *            it is returned, else -1 is returned.
 *
 * comout  -- outputs character to "portbase" port. Returns zero if successful,
 *            else -1 is returned.
 *
 * p_base  -- sets "portbase" for COM1 or COM2, according to "portnum", which
 *            is either 1 or 2. Returns "portbase" for "portnum".
 *
 * RETURNS
 *        cominit Always returns zero.
 *        comoff  Returns nothing.
 *        comin   Returns the character if available, else -1 to indicate no
 *                character is in the circular buffer.
 *        comout  Returns zero if character is successfully transmitted, else
 *                -1 is returned to indicate time-out error, TX register not
 *                ready.
 *        p_base  Returns "portbase" of port number 1 or 2.
 **/

/* define port base address, and offsets from base */

#define COM1BASE        0x3F8   /* base port for com1                   */
#define COM2BASE        0x2F8   /* base port for com2                   */
```

Fig. 6-5. The iportio functions.

```
/* port offsets from base */

#define TX        0               /* transmit data                        */
#define RX        0               /* receive data                         */
#define IER       1               /* interrupt-enable register            */
#define IIR       2               /* interrupt identification register    */
#define LCR       3               /* line control register                */
#define MCR       4               /* modem control register               */
#define LSR       5               /* line status register                 */
#define MSR       6               /* modem status register                */

/* line status values */

#define RCVRDY    1               /* char available in RX register        */
#define OVRERR    2               /* overrun error                        */
#define PRTYERR   4               /* parity error                         */
#define FRMERR    8               /* framing error                        */
#define BRKINT    0x10            /* break signal                         */
#define XMTRDY    0x20            /* transmit register ready              */

/* modem status values */

#define CTS       0x10            /* clear to send                        */
#define DSR       0x20            /* data set ready                       */
#define RI        0x40            /* ring indicator                       */
#define CD        0x80            /* carrier detect                       */

/* modem control bits */

#define DTR       1               /* data terminal ready                  */
#define RTS       2               /* request to send                      */


int     portbase = COM1BASE;     /* default to COM1:                      */

/*******************************************************************************/
/** initialization function; called once at beginning of program            */

cominit()
{
        int     c, pnum;
        short   buff[2];
        char    *cintaddr();

        pnum = portbase == COM1BASE ? 1 : 2;     /* get port #            */
/*** enable intr processing... ***/
/* get addr of intr routine and install                                   */
        putintv(pnum == 2 ? 11 : 12, cintaddr(buff));
        i_enable(pnum);                          /* enable comm intr's    */
        c = inp(portbase + MCR) | DTR | RTS;     /* set dtr & rts         */
        outp(portbase + MCR, c);
        return(0);      /* no-error return                                */
}

/* disable DTR and RTS ********************************************************/

comoff()
{

        i_disable();
        outp(portbase + MCR, 0);
}
```

154

```
/* communications subroutines ***********************************/
/* byte-input                                                   */
/* Returns: -1 if no byte available, else byte (0 - 0xff)       */
/* Gets input from circular buffer                              */

comin()
{
        return(getccb());
}
/*********************************/
/* byte-output; will time-out if xmtrdy doesn't become true.    */
/* Returns: -1 if timeout, else NULL                            */

static  long    xwttime = 24000; /* 4-sec. wait for time-out    */

comout(c)
char    c;
{
        long    timout;

/* set time-out in case xmt buffer never empty */

        timout = xwttime;

        while((inp(portbase + LSR) & XMTRDY) == 0)
                if(--timout < 0L)
                        return(-1);     /* time-out error        */

        outp(portbase + TX, c);
        return(0);
}


/********************************
* set portbase
*/

p_base(portnum)
int     portnum;
{
        if(portnum == 1 || portnum == 2)
                portbase = portnum == 1 ? COM1BASE : COM2BASE;
        return(portbase);
}
/********/
```

6.6 THE INTERRUPT SERVICE ROUTINE

The interrupt-service routine that accepts the communications port input and places it into a circular buffer is called intserv.asm, as shown in Fig. 6-6. Three separate routines are included in this module. Two are to be called from a C program, and the third is the interrupt routine. The two C functions are cintaddr, which was mentioned in the previous section, and intinit. The intinit function must be called once when the terminal program, or any program using the interrupt routine, starts up.

The intserv.asm module must be assembled with the Microsoft or IBM Macroassembler. You will notice that there is an INCLUDE file called dos.mac at the beginning of the listing. If you have the Lattice compiler, then you have dos.mac. It may

```
INCLUDE DOS.MAC
;**********************************************************************
; module:
;       intserv.asm
;
; name:
;       com_int -- interrupt service routine; not available to C call.
;       intinit -- saves DS for use by "com_int".
;       cintaddr --returns interrupt vector of "com_int".
;
; synopsis:
;       intinit();
;       ps = cintaddr(buff);
;
;       char    *ps;             pointer to buff
;       char    *buff;           four-byte buffer for interrupt vector
;
; description:
;       com_int -
;       Contains interrupt service routine for com-port interrupt 'on data
; available'.
;
;       cintaddr -
;       A function callable from C that will return the full
; segment:offset address of the interrupt-service-routine entry point.
;
;       intinit -
;       A routine that saves the current data segment (ds) for use
; by the intr-serv routine.
;
;       CAUTION:
;       The int-serv-routine depends on an external variable in the data
; segment called 'int portbase'.  It MUST contain the base port address
; of the appropriate com port; e.g. portbase = 0x3f8 for com1:, or 0x2f8 for
; com2:, BEFORE enabling the interrupt service routine.
;
;       ALSO:   intinit() must be called once before intr's are enabled.
;**********************************************************************
;port values and data
;********************

;8259 command port and end-of-interrupt cmd data
ICR             equ     20h             ;command port addr
EOI             equ     20h             ;command data signaling end-of-intr

;selected port addresses
RX              equ     0               ;offset from 'portbase'; rcv reg.
IIR             equ     2               ;ditto; for intr. id. reg.

RX_MASK         equ     7               ;AND mask, before using...
RX_ID           equ     4               ;value of IIR if RCV intr pending
                                        ;eg: AND rx_mask; CMP rx_id


;**************************
; declare data variable needed by intr routine
;**************************
DSEG
                extrn   portbase:word   ;must be assigned before enabling
ENDDS                                   ;this intr routine!
```

Fig. 6-6. The intserv functions.

156

```
;define structure for stack access by routine that returns intr entry point.
        dyns    struc
old_bp          dw      ?
retn            db      CPSIZE dup(?)   ;4 if lprog, else 2
buff            db      DPSIZE dup(?)   ;4 if ldata, else 2
        dyns    ends


;*******************************
;the interrupt service routine, not accessible from C
;*******************************

if      lprog
                extrn   putccb:far      ;m/b declared before segment if far
endif

                PSEG
if      lprog eq 0
                extrn   putccb:near     ;m/b declared after segment if near
endif

com_int         proc    far             ;always far for intr routine

                push    bp              ;must save all registers, since a C
                push    ax              ;routine will be called.
                push    bx
                push    cx
                push    dx
                push    si
                push    di
                push    ds
                push    es

                mov     bp,sp           ;save sp in bp
                mov     ax,cs:dssave    ;get prog's data segment
                mov     ds,ax           ;to make sure ds & es are correct
                mov     es,ax
                mov     si,portbase     ;get port base address into si
                mov     dx,si           ;and into dx
                add     dx,IIR          ;pt to intr id reg.
                in      al,dx           ;get intr id's
                and     al,RX_MASK      ;mask off unwanted bits
                cmp     al,RX_ID        ;is it a RCV'd data intr?
                jnz     ignore          ;no, go

                mov     dx,si           ;yes, base back to dx
                add     dx,RX           ;pt to RCV data port
                in      al,dx           ;get input-data
                xor     ah,ah           ;ensure high byte is zero
                push    ax              ;pass to putccb
                call    putccb          ;attempt to add char to circ buffer
                                        ;and ignore return value
                mov     sp,bp           ;remove arg from stack
ignore:         mov     al,EOI          ;signal 8259: end-of-interrupt
                out     ICR,al

                pop     es              ;restore reg's & return
                pop     ds
                pop     di
                pop     si
                pop     dx
                pop     cx
                pop     bx
```

```
                pop     ax
                pop     bp
                iret
com_int         endp
;***********************************
; Routine to return the entry address of the interrupt service routine,
; callable from C.
;       char    *cintaddr(buff);          char buff[4];
;***********************************
                public  cintaddr
        if LPROG
cintaddr        proc    far
        else
cintaddr        proc    near
        endif
                push    bp
                mov     bp,sp

; get pointer to buff according to small/large data model
if LDATA
                les     di, dword ptr [bp].buff
else
                mov     di, word ptr [bp].buff
endif

;*** only 1 of the ff. 3 'ifs' can be true! ***
if LPROG
                mov     ax,offset com_int
endif
if S8086
                mov     ax,offset pgroup:com_int
endif
if D8086
                mov     ax,offset cgroup:com_int
endif
                cld                     ;to incr di
                stosw                   ;store offset into buffer
                mov     ax,cs           ;get segment of intr serv routine
                stosw                   ;store segment into buffer

;return ptr to 'buff'(same value as received)
if LDATA                                ; ax:bx = seg:offset
                les     bx,dword ptr [bp].buff
                mov     ax,es
else                                    ; ax = offset
                mov     ax,word ptr [bp].buff
endif
                pop     bp
                ret
cintaddr        endp
;***********************************************************
; MUST be called once prior to enabling comm interrupts
;***********************************************************

dssave          dw      0               ; ds saved here by ff.& used by int
                                        ; routine
                public  intinit
        if LPROG
intinit         proc    far
        else
intinit         proc    near
        endif
```

```
            mov      cs:dssave,ds      ;save prog data segment for intr rout.
            ret
intinit     endp
            ENDPS
            end
;**********************************
```

be on your disk under a different name, like sm8086.mac. This file determines the Lattice memory model. To assemble intserv.asm for linking with C programs compiled with the small memory model, you need to rename sm8086.mac to dos.mac and have it in the same directory as intserv.asm.

If you are using a different compiler, you can consult the dos.mac file that has been reprinted in Appendix A. If you have enough information about your compiler and a little assembly language knowledge, you should be able to modify dos.mac to work with your compiler. The appendix explains the information you will need.

The code for the interrupt-service routine in Fig. 6-6 is in a procedure labeled com_int, which is the first of three procedures in the module. This procedure has not been defined as public because it is not to be called from a C program. You will note that the portbase variable defined in the iportio.c module is declared as an extrn. The interrupt routine needs the portbase in order to retrieve the input from the proper port.

The portbase variable is assumed to be in the data segment, which is addressable from the DS register. The Lattice compiler guarantees that all externally defined data is in the data segment. In its start-up module, c.obj, the compiler sets up the DS register to access external data; however, the DS register contents are unknown when the interrupt routine is executed. A communications interrupt can occur while the computer is processing some other interrupt, such as a keyboard or clock interrupt. The other interrupt routine may have set DS to something else.

Because the contents of DS is unknown when control passes to com_int, the intinit function has been included in the module. It is to be called from C before interrupts are enabled. All it does is save the current contents of the DS register in a memory area where com_int can retrieve it. Thus, com_int can be sure that it is addressing portbase properly.

The Interrupt Code

The interrupt code is relatively simple. Just before the com_int procedure begins, you see a conditional assembly directive. It declares the putccb function that stores a character in the circular buffer. This must be done to access a C function from assembly language. The C function must be declared as either near or far, depending on the memory model designated in dos.mac. PSEG is a macro in dos.mac that expands to a segment name and also a class name for some memory models.

The rest of the code in com_int is explained in the comments. The interrupt routine must save any registers used. Then it retrieves the value saved by the intinit call as the contents of the DS register and sets both DS and ES to this value. The value of portbase is used for all port accesses. The first thing that must be done is to check the interrupt identification register (IIR). The interrupt routine must make certain that the interrupt was caused by received data. If it was not, the interrupt is reset and exits.

If this is a received-data interrupt, then the routine retrieves the byte from the port and stores it in the circular buffer by calling **putccb**. Then the 8259 chip is reset, and the routine exits.

Now you can see why the interrupt routine could not be written entirely in C. There is no way in C to save and restore registers or to execute the IRET (return from interrupt) instruction.

The Interrupt-Routine Vector

The **cintaddr** procedure follows the interrupt routine. As I mentioned earlier, it is called from C to get the interrupt routine vector. This function was included in the interrupt module to guarantee that it would return the correct segment:offset of the interrupt routine for all memory models. It is also necessary to include **cintaddr** in this module because **com_int** is not a public entry point. Note that **cintaddr** must be declared **char *** by the calling program, if the return value is to be used as it is in **cominit**.

Modifying intserv.asm

If you need to modify any of the procedures in Fig. 6-6 for another compiler, there are only a few things you will need to consider. First, you must make sure that the assembly is for the proper memory model. You can probably use **dos.mac** to accomplish this. Just assign the proper values to the memory-model equates in **dos.mac** for program and data size, as explained in Appendix A. You will probably need to change the segment and class names, and possibly also the group names to conform with those used by your compiler.

Second, you will need to make sure that arguments accessed on the stack and the return values are handled correctly for your compiler. Most compilers pass arguments on the stack, so you will probably not need to make any changes for the single argument passed to **putccb**. You will, however, need to make sure that **cintaddr** is correctly obtaining the buffer pointer and that it is returning the pointer properly.

Third, Lattice requires that only the BP register be saved in an assembly function. If your compiler requires that other registers be saved, you will need to add code to save and restore those registers. Finally, you will want to make sure that the **portbase** variable is accessible in the data segment; that is, that the DS register is setup by the program startup module to access **portbase**.

A Word of Caution

If you find that you must make any modifications, I would like to suggest that you experiment with scratch diskettes in the drives. A wild interrupt can be troublesome. It is likely that an out-of-control interrupt would only necessitate a reboot or that the system be shut down and restarted, but you will want to play it safe and not endanger any valuable data. If you are using a hard disk, you will not be able to use a scratch diskette, so you should make sure that any precious data is backed up before playing with hardware interrupts.

You must also be absolutely certain that you disable the interrupts before your communications program exits to DOS. If you don't, an interrupt could still occur. This would certainly cause a system crash, because the interrupt routine is no longer in place.

6.7 AN INTERRUPT-DRIVEN TERMINAL PROGRAM

The **term2.c** module in Fig. 6-7 is designed to work with the interrupt functions in this chapter. It is very similar to the **term1.c** program in Chapter 5. It still depends on the DOS **mode** command to set up the communications parameters. Now, however, you can use any baud rate that your equipment will support. If you have a direct cable connection to another computer that supports 9600 BPS communications, you can use the **mode** command to set the port to that speed. Any slower speed will also work, of course.

The **term2** program demonstrates how easy it is to use the interrupt functions. Also notice that the termination key has been changed to the PC End key. This change requires a little different logic in the terminal-mode code. That code has been isolated into its own function called **term**.

You will notice that the first function called, after the command line is examined for a COM2 request, is **intinit**. After this call, the interrupt-service routine has the current data segment for access to the **portbase** variable defined in **iportio.c**. The C functions defined in the interrupt-service routine serve another purpose that I did not mention before. They allow the interrupt-service routine to be stored in a library and pulled into the program at link time, by making a call to one of the functions in **intserv.asm**. The call to **intinit** serves this purpose.

Next, the current contents of the communications interrupt vectors are saved with the call to **save__vec**. Then the **brk__off** function from Chapter 2 is called to disable the Control-Break keys. This is done to prevent the user from terminating the program before it has a chance to disable interrupts and restore the vectors. With the Break key disabled, it is safe to call **cominit**, to enable the communications interrupts, and enter the terminal function, **term**.

The **term** function terminates and returns to the **main** function when the End key is pressed. At this point, the interrupts are disabled by **comoff** and the original interrupt vectors are restored by **rstr__vec**. The exit to DOS automatically re-enables the Control-Break keys.

Dumb Versus Smart Terminals

Programs like **term2** are called dumb terminal programs because they do not process display control codes. A dumb terminal can only scroll information as it is received. Thus, you might think of a dumb terminal as nothing more than a video printer. Many dial-up computer services assume that they are communicating with a dumb terminal, unless the caller advises the system otherwise. There might be some method available to "tell" the host computer that it is communicating with a smart terminal.

A smart terminal and smart terminal programs allow the host computer more control over the display format. PC users are accustomed to programs that completely control the display. The screen is cleared, and information is displayed at fixed locations on the display. Smart terminals provide cursor location capabilities via control codes, sometimes referred to as escape sequences. An escape sequence is simply a string of one or more characters following an ASCII escape character (for ASCII terminals).

A program running on the host computer system creates a screen display by sending the appropriate escape sequences and display characters to the terminal. The ter-

```
/**
 * NAME
 *      term2 -- dumb terminal program using interrupt-driven port input
 *
 * SYNOPSIS
 *      term2 [2]
 *
 * DESCRIPTION
 *      Optional command-line parameter of 2 may be entered to use COM port
 * number 2, otherwise COM port number 1 is used.
 *
 * CAUTION
 *      Term2 does not set the baud rate of the com port. Use the DOS MODE
 * command to setup the port BEFORE running "term2":
 *
 *      MODE COM1:1200,N,8,1
 *      MODE COM2:1200,N,8,1
 *
 *      Use one of the above MODE commands before running "term2". If you
 * use COM2 in the MODE command, run "term2 2".
 **/

#include <stdio.h>
#include <extkeys.h>

#define ESCAPE  K_END    /* Esc key for exit is the End key                  */

main(argc, argv)
int     argc;
char    *argv[];
{
        int     port;

/* see if port number specified on command line

        if(argc == 2) {
                if((port = (*++argv)[0] - '0') != 2 && port != 1) {
                        fprintf(stderr,"usage: term2 [2]");
                        exit(1);
                }
                p_base(port);
        }

        intinit();       /* save DS in intr service routine                  */
        save_vec();      /* save interrupt vectors                           */

/* disable ctrl-break                                                        */
        brk_off();

/* initialize port                                                           */

        cominit();

/* sign on                                                                   */

        printf("[ Terminal Mode: Press \"End\" key to exit ]\n\n");

/* begin terminal polling                                                    */

        term();
```

Fig. 6-7. The term2 module.

162

```
        comoff();          /* disable com port                        */
        rstr_vec();         /* restore orig. interrupt vectors         */
        exit(0);
}
/********/
/* terminal function                                                   */

term()
{
        int    c;

        while(1) {

/* if char ready, display it and repeat; else go on...                 */

                if((c = comin()) != -1) {
                        bputcr(c & 0x7f);              /* mask parity bit         */
                        continue;
                }

/* if char from keyboard, check for exit request, else transmit        */

                if((c = bscancr()) != -1) {
                        if(c == ESCAPE)
                                break;
                        if(c >= K_BASE)
                                continue;
                        if(comout(c) == -1) {
                                fprintf(stderr, "term2: Time-out error.\n");
                                break;
                        }
                }
        } /* end of while loop                                         */
}
/********/
```

minal knows which characters are a command to do something, such as position the cursor to row seven, column one, and which characters are to be displayed. It knows this because of the escape character, which alerts the terminal that the next character or characters will be a command. Smart terminals usually have many other capabilities, such as clearing the display from the cursor position to the end of the line or the end of the screen. They can use video attributes like reverse video, bold characters, underlining, and even double-wide or double-high characters. The DOS keyboard and display device driver, ansi.sys, makes the PC *emulate* some terminal control codes.

Most smart terminals have other capabilities too. Some are specially designed to perform a specific function, like graphics or color display. The programs on the host computer are written to assume some particular terminal type, though many programs will work with several types. Many commercial communications programs for the PC have one or more emulation modes. That just means that they will act like a particular manufacturer's smart terminal.

Unfortunately, there has been little standardization of the control codes used by various terminal brands. The escape sequence to clear the screen on a DEC VT-100 terminal is completely different from the sequence on a Televideo 925, for example. Even different models from the same manufacturer will often vary in the use of control codes. In recent years, there has been a move toward more standardization. The ANSI Committee has provided a set of standard control codes for common terminal operations on ASCII terminals, and many terminals now support this standard.

You can add terminal emulation routines to **term2**, if you find that you need it. To do that, you first need to determine which terminal type you want to emulate. Then obtain the terminal reference documentation from the manufacturer or vendor. Two parts of the **term** function will need to provide the emulation: the display function and the keyboard-input function. Those functions used in the **term** function will be replaced by your emulation routines.

The function in **term** that is called to display characters will be responsible for sensing the escape sequences and performing the appropriate action. For example, the display function will monitor characters for an escape character. When one is received, a flag is set to indicate that the next character or characters will be a command. After all command characters have been received, they are interpreted and translated into the action required on the PC. Characters that are not part of a command are simply displayed as usual.

The keyboard-input function might also require emulation. The PC arrow keys and perhaps the function keys must be translated to the codes the terminal would transmit for those keys. As you might imagine, all this processing of input/output characters takes some time. Only the interrupt-driven **term2** can be used to provide emulation. The polling method of **term1** in Chapter 5 is too slow, but the buffering of input characters by **term2** gives the program plenty of time to process incoming characters for emulation activity. The interrupt functions for communications provide the backbone for any communications task you might have.

6.8 SETTING THE COMMUNICATIONS PARAMETERS

We have been using the **mode** command to initialize the communication port parameters: the baud rate, parity, word length, and the number of stop bits. It is convenient and sometimes necessary to set the parameters from within the communications program. To do that, a function is needed to perform the required initialization of the baud-rate generator and the line-control register (LCR).

We could use the BIOS INT 0×14 to perform the setup, but I have elected to program the LCR and baud rate generator directly. The BIOS routine actually saves little if any programming work. Instead, by programming the port directly, we will have more options available. The **setcomm** function in Fig. 6-8 takes advantage of the **portbase** definition in **iportio.c** to program the appropriate port, COM1 or COM2.

The initial call to **setcomm** should come before interrupts are enabled—that is, before i__enable is called. This could be done in the **cominit** function in **iportio.c** or in the main function before **cominit** is called. After the initial call, **setcomm** can be called again whenever necessary to change any port parameters, such as the baud rate. This function is a necessity if your program allows the user to change the port number within the program. **setcomm** must be called whenever the port number is changed, to be certain that the parameters are set correctly. For example, assume that your program allows the user to change the port number through a command or menu selection. After the program accepts the port number, but before calling **p__base** with the new port number, a call is made to **comoff**. Then **p__base** is called to set the new **portbase**. Now

```
/**
 * NAME
 *       setcomm -- set communications parameters
 *
 * SYNOPSIS
 *       setcomm(baud, parity, word, stop);
 *
 *       int      baud;           desired baud rate
 *       char     parity;         (N)one, (E)ven, or (O)dd
 *       int      word;           5, 6, 7, or 8 bit word length
 *       int      stop;           1 or 2 stop bits
 *
 * DESCRIPTION
 *       setcomm programs the RS-232 baud rate generator and line control
 * register for the desired communications parameters.
 *
 * RETURNS
 *       Nothing is returned.
 *
 * CAUTIONS
 *       setcomm depends on "portbase" in "iportio.c" to obtain the correct
 * port to be set (either COM1 or COM2).
 *       No validity checking is done on the parameters.
 *
 * EXAMPLE
 *       setcomm(1200, 'n', 8, 1);
 *
 *       Set the current "portbase" to 1200 baud, no parity, eight-bit word
 * length, and one stop bit.
 **/

#define LCR     3               /* line control register                  */
#define DLLSB   0               /* divisor latch port for LSB             */
#define DLMSB   1               /* and MSB of baud rate divisor           */

extern  int     portbase;       /* need correct port to program           */

setcomm(baud, parity, word, stop)
int     baud, word, stop;
char    parity;
{
        short   divisor, parm;

/* do not attempt to set params if portbase is zero                       */

        if(!portbase)
                return;

/* set baud rate generator                                                */
/* divisor = 1.8432 Mhz clock frequency / (baud * 16)                     */

        if(baud)
                divisor = 115200L/baud;
        else
                divisor = 96;    /* use 1200 baud if zero baud arg         */

        outp(portbase + LCR, 0x80);             /* set DLAB               */
        outp(portbase + DLMSB, divisor >> 8);   /* output MSB of divisor*/
        outp(portbase + DLLSB, divisor & 0xff); /* and LSB of divisor    */
```

Fig. 6-8. The setcomm function.

```
/* construct byte for LCR parameters: parity, stop bits, word length    */

        if((parity &= Ox5f) == 'O')
                parm = 1 << 3;
        else if(parity == 'E')
                parm = 3 << 3;
        else
                parm = 0;                       /* assume N, if not E or O    */

        parm |= (((stop - 1) & 1) << 2) | ((word - 5) & 3);

/* simultaneously set LCR params and reset DLAB                              */

        outp(portbase + LCR, parm & Ox1f);
}
/********/
```

setcomm and cominit can be called, in that order. This logic is fine even if the port number was not actually changed.

If your program allows a change in the port number, it might be more convenient to place the above logic within the **term** function (Fig. 6-7). Then, whenever the **term** function is called, you will be sure that the setup is correct for the current port:

```
extern    portnum;

static    oldport = -1;  /* any invalid value */

term()
{
    int  c;

    if(portnum != oldport) {
        comoff();
        oldport = portnum;
    } else
        i_disable();
    p_base(portnum);
    setcomm(baud, parity, word, stop);
    cominit();
    ...rest of function...
}
```

This code fragment shows the changes to make to the **term** function. It assumes that the current port number is in the external variable **portnum**. It also assumes that **portbase** already contains a valid value, which it will if it has been initialized by the compiler as done in **iportio.c**. You can remove the call to **cominit** in the **main** function of **term2** if you are using this procedure. You should make sure that the **main** function defines **portnum** with a valid port number.

The **oldport** variable is used to test for an actual port number change. The first time **term** is called, it will appear to be a port number change because **oldport** is set to an impossible port number. This will cause **oldport** to be set to the current port number. It is not necessary that **comoff** be called on the first entry, but it doesn't hurt anything. On all subsequent entries into **term**, **comoff** will be called if **portnum** is changed.

Otherwise, i_disable is called. This allows you to write a program in which the user can exit the **term** function and re-enter it without breaking the phone connection. If no connection exists, it doesn't matter, but if the port number is changed between calls to **term**, the interrupts will be properly disabled and re-enabled, and the parameters will be set. The test is necessary because **comoff** resets DTR, which would break an existing phone connection.

I would like to repeat that the above **term** logic requires that both **portbase** and **portnum** contain valid values before **term** is called the first time. Do not overlook this important matter. Also, this variation is meant only to provide an example. Other possible placements of the setup functions in the program are where the actual change to the port number or port parameters are made. I would like to suggest that you get the original version of **term2** in Fig. 6-7 working before you begin experimenting with variations. Then it will be easier to diagnose any problems that might occur.

The setcomm Particulars

It will be easier to understand what **setcomm** in Fig. 6-8 is doing if you can refer to the technical reference manual section on the LCR. The baud rate generator, a circuit on the 8250 chip supporting serial data transfers, must have a "divisor" corresponding to the baud rate desired. This divisor is calculated from the baud rate passed as one of the arguments to **setcomm**. Once the divisor is determined, it is passed as two eight-bit values to the baud rate generator. Figure 6-8 shows the exact method for doing this. Note that **setcomm** will accept any baud rate as an argument. That means that the port could be programmed for a baud rate of 477—not a very useful number. The technical reference manual includes a table of commonly used baud rates, if you are not familiar with them. A Hayes Smartmodem 1200, for example, would expect the port to be programmed at 1200 baud in most cases. It will also allow a baud rate of 300.

After the baud rate is programmed, the parity, word length, and number of stop bits must be programmed into the LCR. These are programmed by setting the appropriate bits in an eight-bit value. When the bits have been set as needed, the value is output to the LCR. It is a matter of turning on the right switches, so to speak.

You now have all the tools you need to write your own self-contained communications package. You can even add file transfer functions. For example, you could add an XMODEM file transfer or one of the other public domain transfer methods like Kermit. You might even want to design your own file-transfer protocol. Because you have the means available to receive and transmit data, you can concentrate on the other aspects of writing a communications package, those aspects that are not directly related to port and interrupt control. After all, any communications package is going to have to control the ports and interrupts. The extra features are what distinguish the most useful programs.

Appendix A

An Include File
for Assembly Language

The information in this appendix is intended as an aid to programmers using a C compiler other than the Lattice C compiler.

Lattice provides an include file with its compiler for use when creating assembly-language functions to be called from C programs. This file, called DOS.MAC, is reproduced in Fig. A-1. Including this file in an assembly language source file allows the programmer to use assembler conditionals to write a function that will work for any memory model. The programmer must set the LPROG and LDATA equates to conform with the particular memory model desired. As in C programs, zero means false and non-zero means true. In Fig. A-1, these are set to zero for the small memory model.

The DOS.MAC include file must be included in the interrupt service routine assembly in Chapter 6. If you are using the Lattice compiler, you already have DOS.MAC. It must also be included in the assembly of the functions in Appendix C and Appendix F, if you are using those functions. Lattice users will not need those functions because they are provided in the library, but users of other compilers might need them. Owners of other compilers might have operationally equivalent functions. Check your compiler's library documentation before attempting to use these. It could save you a lot of work.

The interrupt-service routine will not be available in your standard library. If you are not using the Lattice compiler, you must adapt DOS.MAC to work with your compiler. I will attempt to explain the important points in this module, but you will need a good understanding of your compiler's code-generation technique to adapt DOS.MAC to its needs.

The LPROG equate is set to zero to indicate that a small program model is desired. If LPROG is one, a large program model is desired. The LDATA equate is used the

```
        .XLIST
        PAGE    58,132
;*******************************************************************************
;name: dos.mac -- renamed from sm8086.mac, for small memory model
;
;*******************************************************************************
;       This module is reprinted with permission.
;*******************************************************************************

;*******************************************************************************
; INCLUDE file for Lattice assembly language C modules - small memory model
; This module is included with the Lattice C Compilers, and is the property
; of Lattice, Inc.
;
; Lattice is a registered trademark of Lattice, Inc.
;*******************************************************************************

;**
;
; This macro library defines the operating environment for the 8086 S
; memory model, which allows 64Kbytes of data and 64Kbytes of program.
;
;**
MSDOS   EQU     2

;**
;
; The following symbols define the 8086 memory mode being used.  Set LPROG
; to 1 for a large program segment (greater than 64K-bytes), and set LDATA
; to 1 for a large data segment.  Set COM to 1 to generate .COM files
; instead of .EXE files.  Note that if COM is not zero, then LPROG and
; LDATA must be 0.
;
;**
COM     EQU     0
LPROG   EQU     0
LDATA   EQU     0

;**
;
; The following symbols are established via LPROG and LDATA as follows:
;
;       S8086   set for small model (small prog, small data)
;       D8086   set for model with large data, small prog
;       P8086   set for model with large prog, small data
;       L8086   set for large model
;
;**
        IF      (LPROG EQ 0) AND (LDATA EQ 0)
S8086   EQU     1
D8086   EQU     0
P8086   EQU     0
L8086   EQU     0
        ENDIF

        IF      (LPROG EQ 0) AND (LDATA NE 0)
S8086   EQU     0
D8086   EQU     1
P8086   EQU     0
```

Fig. A-1. The DOS.MAC file.

169

```
L8086     EQU       O
          ENDIF

          IF        (LPROG NE O) AND (LDATA EQ O)
S8086     EQU       O
D8086     EQU       O
P8086     EQU       1
L8086     EQU       O
          ENDIF

          IF        (LPROG NE O) AND (LDATA NE O)
S8086     EQU       O
D8086     EQU       O
P8086     EQU       O
L8086     EQU       1
          ENDIF
;**
;
; The DSEG and PSEG macros are defined to generate the appropriate GROUP
; and SEGMENT statements for the memory model being used.  The ENDDS and
; ENDPS macros are then used to end the segments.
;
;**
DSEG      MACRO
DGROUP    GROUP     DATA
DATA      SEGMENT WORD PUBLIC 'DATA'
          ASSUME  DS:DGROUP
          ENDM
ENDDS     MACRO
DATA      ENDS
          ENDM

          IF        S8086
PSEG      MACRO
PGROUP    GROUP     PROG
PROG      SEGMENT BYTE PUBLIC 'PROG'
          ASSUME  CS:PGROUP
          ENDM
ENDPS     MACRO
PROG      ENDS
          ENDM
          ENDIF

          IF        D8086
PSEG      MACRO
CGROUP    GROUP     CODE
CODE      SEGMENT BYTE PUBLIC 'CODE'
          ASSUME  CS:CGROUP
          ENDM
ENDPS     MACRO
CODE      ENDS
          ENDM
          ENDIF

          IF        P8086
PSEG      MACRO
_CODE     SEGMENT BYTE
          ASSUME  CS:_CODE
          ENDM
ENDPS     MACRO
_CODE     ENDS
```

```
              ENDM
              ENDIF

              IF        L8086
PSEG          MACRO
_PROG         SEGMENT BYTE
              ASSUME    CS:_PROG
              ENDM
ENDPS         MACRO
_PROG         ENDS
              ENDM
              ENDIF
;**
;
; The BEGIN and ENTRY macros establish appropriate function entry points
; depending on whether NEAR or FAR program addressing is being used.  The
; only difference between the two is that BEGIN generates a PROC operation
; to start a segment.
;
BEGIN         MACRO     NAME                        ; begin a function
              PUBLIC    NAME
              IF        LPROG
NAME          PROC      FAR
              ELSE
NAME          PROC      NEAR
              ENDIF
              ENDM

ENTRY         MACRO     NAME
              PUBLIC    NAME
              IF        LPROG
NAME          LABEL     FAR
              ELSE
NAME          LABEL     NEAR
              ENDIF
              ENDM

;**
;
; The following symbols are defined to help set up a STRUC defining the
; stack frame:
;
;       CPSIZE -> code pointer size (2 or 4)
;       DPSIZE -> data pointer size (2 or 4)
;
; These wouldn't be necessary if it were possible to use macros or even
; conditionals within a STRUC.
;
              IF        LPROG
CPSIZE        EQU       4
              ELSE
CPSIZE        EQU       2
              ENDIF
              IF        LDATA
DPSIZE        EQU       4
              ELSE
DPSIZE        EQU       2
              ENDIF

;********
; The following equates have been added to the Lattice module.
; They are used in the INT86X.ASM and SEGREAD.ASM functions in the appendices.
```

```
;********
;        Define an offset for use when accessing stack arguments.
;
;        The return address (2 or 4 bytes) and the BP register are on the
;stack below the arguments.  Thus, the first argument is SP + FILLER.
;********
        if      LPROG
FILLER  equ     6
        else
FILLER  equ     4
        endif

        .LIST
```

same way to indicate whether a small or large data section is desired. The major difference between small and large, for both the program and data sections, is the size of
a pointer. In addition, different segment and class names are used for the program segments in each of the four possible memory models. The program model also determines the access to the function arguments that are on the stack. Large program models
have a four-byte return address on the stack, while the small program models have
a two-byte return address. An assembly-language function needs this information, because the arguments are above the return address. You will need to know the method
used to return a value to the calling program. For example, Lattice returns a one- or
two-byte value in register AX. Finally, the BP register must be saved and restored
in a Lattice function. This is the only register, besides the segment registers, that must
be preserved. As far as the data section goes, you can see in the DSEG macro in Fig.
A-1 that all external and static data resides in the DATA segment. Only dynamically
allocated data can reside outside this segment, and this can occur only in a large (LDATA
not equal to zero) data model.

If you understood the previous paragraph and the code in the assembly language
functions like the interrupt routine, you should have no trouble adapting DOS.MAC
and the assembly functions to your compiler's requirements. I am sorry that I cannot
give you more help in this area. I honestly wish that I could, but the two primary ingre-
dients in writing assembly functions are beyond the scope of this book. The first ingre-
dient needed is a working knowledge of PC assembly language. The other is good
documentation on your C compiler's code-generation techniques. If you have both of
these, you are well on your way.

The DOS.H Header File

Part of the DOS.H header file supplied with the Lattice compiler is reproduced in Fig. B-1. This file provides the union and structure declarations that are used to define the arguments supplied to the **intdos** and **int86** functions.

```
/**
 * Reprinted with permission.
 *
 * NAME
 *       dos.h -- header file for use with interrupt and DOS functions
 *
 * DESCRIPTION
 *       This module is a partial reproduction. It contains the structure
 * and union definitions needed to interface with the "int86" and "intdos"
 * functions.
 ***********************************************************************************
 * Lattice header file.
 * Lattice is a registered trademark of Lattice, Inc.
 **/

/* filename and pathname size for MSDOS/PCDOS            */

#define FNSIZE 16        /* file name node size for MSDOS */
#define FMSIZE 64        /* maximum file name size        */

/**
```

Fig. B-1. The DOS.H header file.

```
*
* The following structures define the 8086 registers that are passed to
* various low-level operating system service functions.
*
**/

typedef char    byte;

struct XREG
        {
        short ax,bx,cx,dx,si,di;
        };

struct HREG
        {
        byte al,ah,bl,bh,cl,ch,dl,dh;
        };

union REGS
        {
        struct XREG x;
        struct HREG h;
        };

struct SREGS
        {
        short es,cs,ss,ds;
        };
/********/
```

BIOS Interface Functions

The int86x and int86 functions are provided here. Lattice users have these functions in the Lattice library. The int86 function, shown in Fig. C-1, is in assembly language and depends on DOS.MAC in Appendix A. The int86 function is in C, and it calls int86x. The two DOS interface functions in Appendix D, intdos and intdosx, also call int86x. Thus, int86x forms the foundation for all of the BIOS and DOS interface functions that I have provided. This keeps the assembly language confined to a single module.

I wrote INT86X.ASM to provide programmers using other compilers with functions that are equivalent to the Lattice interface functions. Your compiler might have equivalent functions, in which case, you will not need this one.

You should be aware that there is one operational difference between INT86X.ASM and the int86x function supplied with the Lattice compiler. The functions in the book do not rely on this difference; therefore, either this function or the Lattice function may be used. The difference is this: upon return from this version of int86x, the SREGS data structure passed as an argument to this function contains the contents of the segment registers returned by the INT called. Thus, the SREGS data might be altered.

I returned the segment registers so that this version of int86x could be used in BIOS or DOS calls that return data in a segment register. The Lattice int86x function cannot be used for such calls. This means that you must be sure to reload the SREGS structure before each call to this int86x version.

THE int86 FUNCTION

The int86 function in Fig. C-2 calls the int86x function. int86 can be used for BIOS

```
INCLUDE DOS.MAC

;*********
; NAME
;       int86x - call a software interrupt
;
; SYNOPSIS
;       flags = int86x(intno, inregs, outregs, segregs);
;
;       int     flags;           processor status flags after interrupt
;       int     intno;           interrupt number to be called
;       union   REGS *inregs;    input registers
;       union   REGS *outregs;   output registers
;       struct  SREGS *segregs;  segment registers
;
; DESCRIPTION
;       This function performs a software interrupt.  It may be used to
; call a DOS or BIOS function.  Consult the DOS manual and/or the Technical
; Reference Manual for the appropriate interrupt number.  'inregs' must
; contain the register values required by the interrupt to be called;
; 'outregs' will contain the returned register values.  'segregs' must contain
; the values with which the segment registers are to be loaded.  Note that
; only the 'DS' and 'ES' registers are actually loaded, even though the
; 'SREGS' structure contains values for all the segment registers. The 'REGS'
; union and 'SREGS' structure are defined in 'DOS.H'.
;
; RETURNS
;       'flags' = the processor status flags after the interrupt call.  Also,
; the returned values of 'DS' and 'ES' are placed in 'segregs'.
;
; NOTES
;       Before this function is called, the 'segregs' structure is usually
; loaded with a 'segread' function call, which provides the current segment
; register values.
;
;       Note that 'inregs', 'outregs', and 'segregs' are pointers passed to
; the 'int86x' function.
;
;*********

; define structure to access arguments on stack

TMPSIZE equ     4                       ;stack space for temporaries

s_86x   struc
ds_save dw      ?                       ;temp. storage for caller's ds, es registers
es_save dw      ?
        db      FILLER dup(?)
intno   dw      ?
inregs  dw      DPSIZE/2 dup(?)
outregs dw      DPSIZE/2 dup(?)
segregs dw      DPSIZE/2 dup(?)
s_86x   ends

; structure for inregs and outregs

reg_s   struc
axreg   dw      ?
bxreg   dw      ?
```

Fig. C-1. The int86x function.

176

```
cxreg    dw      ?
dxreg    dw      ?
sireg    dw      ?
direg    dw      ?
reg_s    ends

; structure for segregs

seg_s    struc
esreg    dw      ?
csreg    dw      ?
ssreg    dw      ?
dsreg    dw      ?
seg_s    ends
         PSEG
         public  int86x
         if      LPROG
int86x   proc    far
         else
int86x   proc    near
         endif
         push    bp              ;also save bp
         sub     sp,TMPSIZE
         mov     bp,sp           ;will use bp to access stack arguments
         mov     [bp.es_save],es ;save caller's es & ds registers
         mov     [bp.ds_save],ds
         mov     ax,[bp.intno]   ;get interrupt number
         mov     cs:intcode+1,al ;and insert into code
         mov     si,[bp.inregs]  ;get input register ptr offset
         if      LDATA
         mov     ds,[bp.inregs+2] ;and segment if necessary
         endif
         mov     ax,[si.axreg]
         mov     bx,[si.bxreg]   ;get caller's registers
         mov     cx,[si.cxreg]
         mov     dx,[si.dxreg]
         mov     di,[si.direg]
         push    [si.sireg]      ;save si temporarily
         mov     si,[bp.segregs] ;get offset of ptr to segment reg values
         if      LDATA
         mov     ds,[bp.segregs+2] ;and segment if necessary
         endif
         mov     es,[si.esreg]   ;only ds and es are loaded
         mov     ds,[si.dsreg]
         pop     si              ;retrieve si from stack
         push    bp              ;save in case altered by interrupt

intcode  label   byte
         int     0               ;dummy interrupt number

         pop     bp              ;get bp back in case it was lost
         pushf                   ;save flags for return
         push    si              ;save reg's needed
         push    ds
         mov     si,[bp.segregs]
         if      LDATA           ;must set ds
         mov     ds,[bp.segregs+2]
         else
         mov     ds,[bp.ds_save]
         endif
         mov     [si.esreg],es
         pop     [si.dsreg]      ;return ds after interrupt
```

177

```
        mov     si,[bp.outregs]
        if      LDATA
        mov     ds,[bp.outregs+2]
        endif
        pop     [si.sireg]      ;restore si value for caller
        mov     [si.direg],di   ;and remaining registers
        mov     [si.axreg],ax
        mov     [si.bxreg],bx
        mov     [si.cxreg],cx
        mov     [si.dxreg],dx
        pop     ax              ;FLAGS into ax for return
        mov     ds,[bp.ds_save] ;restore caller's ds,es
        mov     es,[bp.es_save]
        add     sp,TMPSIZE
        pop     bp
        ret
int86x  endp
        ENDPS
        end
;****************************************************************
```

calls that do not require segment register parameters. Note that **int86** must provide an SREGS pointer anyway, because **int86x** expects it. The data, however, is unknown; that is, it's garbage. This will not matter if the BIOS call does not expect any data in the segment registers, but if the call does expect data in the segment registers, you'd better be wearing your seat belt. Because **int86x** is also called by **intdos** in Appendix D, the same caution applies to its use. Make sure the segment registers are not needed by the BIOS or DOS function before calling either **int86** or **intdos**.

```
/**
* NAME
*       int86 -- execute 8086 INT (software interrupt) instruction
*
* SYNOPSIS
*       #include <dos.h>
*
*       flags = int86(intno, inregs, outregs);
*
*       int     flags;          processor status flags
*       int     intno;          interrupt number to execute
*       union   REGS *inregs;   pointer to input registers
*       union   REGS *outregs;  pointer to output registers
*
* DESCRIPTION
*       This function executes the 8086 interrupt specified by "intno".
* "inregs" contains the input registers to be passed to the interrupt.
* "outregs" contains the contents of the registers returned by the interrupt.
* "dos.h" contains the REGS declaration for registers.
*
* RETURNS
*       The processor status flags returned by the interrupt call are
* returned in "flags".
*
* CAUTIONS
```

Fig. C-2. The int86 function.

```
*       This function calls "int86x", and is meant to be used by interrupt
* routines that do not require segment registers.
*       Note that the REGS arguments are passed as pointers.
**/

#include <dos.h>

int86(intno, inregs, outregs)
int     intno;
union   REGS *inregs, *outregs;
{
        struct  SREGS seg;      /* dummy seg argument for int86x call   */

        return(int86x(intno, inregs, outregs, &seg));
}
/*******/
```

Appendix D

DOS Interface Functions

Figure D-1 contains the intdosx and intdos functions. If your compiler does not have equivalent functions, you might be able to use these. They depend on INT86X.ASM in Appendix C. Whether you can use the intdos functions depends on your success in adapting INT86X.ASM to your compiler.

All DOS functions are called with an INT 0x21 interrupt call. Thus intdosx can call int86x with 0x21 as the interrupt number. The specific DOS function is requested by loading the appropriate function code into register AH. The intdosx call is generally used when segment registers must be passed to a DOS function. See Appendix E for the segread function, which is used to obtain the current contents of the segment registers.

The intdos function can be used to make DOS calls that do not require parameters in the segment registers. intdos calls intdosx with a dummy argument for the segment registers, so the same caution applies here as with int86 in Appendix C.

```
/**
* NAME
*         intdosx -- call DOS with general registers and segment registers
*         intdos  -- call DOS with general registers only
*
* SYNOPSIS
*         #include <dos.h>
*
```

Fig. D-1. The intdosx and intdos functions.

```
*          flags = intdosx(inregs, outregs, segregs);
*          flags = intdos(inregs, outregs);
*
*          int     flags;             processor status flags
*          union   REGS *inregs;      pointer to input registers
*          union   REGS *outregs;     pointer to output registers
*          struct  SREGS *segregs;    pointer to input segment registers
*
* DESCRIPTION
* intdosx --      DOS function call. "inregs" and "segregs" contain the input
*                 registers for the DOS function. The "segread" function
*                 can be used to get the segment registers. "intdosx" will
*                 actually load only the DS and ES registers for the DOS call.
*
* intdos  --      DOS function call without segment register input. This
*                 function can be used to call DOS functions that do not
*                 require any segment register setup.
*
*
* Note that these functions are passed pointers to the REGS unions and the
* SREGS structure, defined in "dos.h".
*
* RETURNS
*        Both functions return the processor status flags as returned by
* the DOS function call.
**/

#include <dos.h>

intdosx(inregs, outregs, segregs)
union REGS *inregs, *outregs;
struct SREGS *segregs;
{
        return(int86x(0x21, inregs, outregs, segregs));
}
/********/

intdos(inregs, outregs)
union REGS *inregs, *outregs;
{
        struct  SREGS seg;        /* dummy arg */

        return(intdosx(inregs, outregs, &seg));
}
/*******/
```

Appendix E

The Segment
Register Function

Figure E-1 contains a **segread** function that is equivalent to the Lattice function. It returns the current contents of the 8086 segment registers. It is usually used in conjunction with the **int86x** and **intdosx** functions to obtain the segment registers when needed for the BIOS or DOS call.

SEGREAD.ASM requires the DOS.MAC **include** file from Appendix A. This function is much simpler than INT86X.ASM; if you were able to adapt INT86X.ASM for your compiler, you will have no trouble with this one. Like the BIOS and DOS interface functions, **segread** is passed a pointer to a data structure. DOS.H contains the declaration for the SREGS structure.

```
INCLUDE DOS.MAC

;*********
;
;  NAME
;          segread - return current value of segment registers.
;
;  SYNOPSIS
;          segread(segregs);
;
;          struct  SREGS *segregs;          segment registers
;
;  DESCRIPTION
```

Fig. E-1. The segread function.

```
;       Places the current value of the segment registers into 'segregs'.
; The 'SREGS' structure is defined in 'DOS.H'.  This function is usually
; called before calling 'int86x' or 'intdosx'.
;
;*********

; structure for segregs

seg_s     struc
esreg     dw        ?
csreg     dw        ?
ssreg     dw        ?
dsreg     dw        ?
seg_s     ends

; define offset to stack argument

arg       equ       FILLER

          PSEG
          public    segread
          if        LPROG
segread   proc      far
          else
segread   proc      near
          endif
          push      bp
          mov       bp,sp
          mov       bx,[bp.arg]        ;get pointer to segregs
          push      ds                 ;save register used for segregs, and
          push      ds                 ;to restore to original
          if        LDATA
          mov       ds,[bp.arg+2]      ;and segment if large data model
          endif
          mov       [bx.esreg],es      ;store segment registers in segregs
          mov       [bx.csreg],cs
          mov       [bx.ssreg],ss
          pop       [bx.dsreg]
          pop       ds
          pop       bp
          ret
segread   endp
          ENDPS
          end
```

Appendix F

Port Input and

Output Functions

Most C compilers provide port input and output functions. If yours does not, you might be able to adapt the Lattice functions for your use. They are reproduced in Fig. F-1. As with the other assembly language functions, this one depends on the DOS.MAC include file in Appendix A.

```
;*******************************************************************************
; Lattice is a registered trademark of Lattice, Inc.
; Reprinted with permission
;*******************************************************************************

        TITLE   PORT I/O FUNCTIONS
        SUBTTL  Copyright 1982 by Lattice, Inc.
        NAME    PORTIO
        INCLUDE DOS.MAC

        IF      LPROG
X       EQU     6                       ;OFFSET OF ARGUMENTS
        ELSE
X       EQU     4                       ;OFFSET OF ARGUMENTS
        ENDIF

        PSEG
;**
;
; name            inp -- input byte from port
;
```

Fig. F-1. The port i/o functions.

```
; synopsis        c = inp(port);
;                 int c;            returned byte
;                 int port;         port address
;
; description     This function inputs a byte from the specified port
;                 address and returns it as the function value.
;
;**
        PUBLIC  INP
        IF      LPROG
INP     PROC    FAR
        ELSE
INP     PROC    NEAR
        ENDIF
        PUSH    BP                ;SAVE BP
        MOV     BP,SP
        MOV     DX,[BP+X]         ;GET PORT ADDRESS
        IN      AL,DX             ;GET INPUT BYTE
        XOR     AH,AH             ;CLEAR HIGH BYTE
        POP     BP
        RET
INP     ENDP
        PAGE
;**
;
; name            outp -- output byte to port
;
; synopsis        outp(port,c);
;                 int port;         port address
;                 int c;            byte to send
;
; description     This function sends the specified character to
;                 the specified port.
;
;**
        PUBLIC  OUTP
        IF      LPROG    ,
OUTP    PROC    FAR
        ELSE
OUTP    PROC    NEAR
        ENDIF
        PUSH    BP                ;SAVE BP
        MOV     BP,SP
        MOV     DX,[BP+X]         ;GET PORT ADDRESS
        MOV     AX,[BP+X+2]       ;GET OUTPUT BYTE
        OUT     DX,AL
        POP     BP
        RET
OUTP    ENDP
        ENDPS
        END
```

Appendix G

Function Index

Index

Edited by Marilyn L. Johnson

C Programmer's Utility Library

If you are intrigued with the possibilities of the programs included in *C Programmer's Utility Library* (TAB Book No. 2855), you should definitely consider having the ready-to-run disk containing the software applications. This software is guaranteed free of manufacturer's defects. (If you have any problems, return the disk within 30 days, and we'll send you a new one.) Not only will you save the time and effort of typing the programs, the disk eliminates the possibility of errors that can prevent the programs from functioning. Interested?

Available on disk for IBM PCs with 128K at $24.95 for each disk plus $1.00 each shipping and handling.